WITHDRAWN

Compromised Data

Library & Media Ctr.
Carroll Community College
1601 Washington Road
Westminster, MD 21157

Compromised Data

From Social Media to Big Data

Edited by
Ganaele Langlois, Joanna Redden
and Greg Elmer

Bloomsbury Academic
An imprint of Bloomsbury Publishing Inc

B L O O M S B U R Y
NEW YORK · LONDON · NEW DELHI · SYDNEY

Bloomsbury Academic

An imprint of Bloomsbury Publishing Inc

1385 Broadway	50 Bedford Square
New York	London
NY 10018	WC1B 3DP
USA	UK

www.bloomsbury.com

BLOOMSBURY and the Diana logo are trademarks of Bloomsbury Publishing Plc

First published 2015

© Ganaele Langlois, Joanna Redden, Greg Elmer and Contributors, 2015

All rights reserved. No part of this publication may be reproduced or transmitted in any form or by any means, electronic or mechanical, including photocopying, recording, or any information storage or retrieval system, without prior permission in writing from the publishers.

No responsibility for loss caused to any individual or organization acting on or refraining from action as a result of the material in this publication can be accepted by Bloomsbury or the author.

Library of Congress Cataloging-in-Publication Data

Compromised data: from social media to big data/edited by Ganaele Langlois, Joanna Redden and Greg Elmer.
pages cm
Includes bibliographical references and index.
ISBN 978-1-5013-0650-1 (hardback: alk. paper) – ISBN 978-1-5013-0651-8 (pbk. : alk. paper) – ISBN 978-1-5013-0653-2 (ePub) – ISBN 978-1-5013-0652-5 (ePDF) 1. Data mining–Social aspects. 2. Social media. 3. Online social networks.
4. Big data I. Langlois, Ganaele. II. Redden, Joanna, 1975- III. Elmer, Greg, 1967-
QA76.9.D343C4785 2015
006.3'12–dc23
2015005746

ISBN: HB: 978-1-5013-0650-1
PB: 978-1-5013-0651-8
ePub: 978-1-5013-0653-2
ePDF: 978-1-5013-0652-5

Typeset by Deanta Global Publishing Services, Chennai, India
Printed and bound in the United States of America

Contents

Contents

Notes on Contributors

Lisa Blackman is professor of media and communications at Goldsmiths, University of London, UK. She is the editor of *Body & Society* and coeditor of *Subjectivity*. She has published four books: *Immaterial Bodies: Affect, Embodiment, Mediation* (Sage/TCS, 2012); *The Body: The Key Concepts* (Berg, 2008); *Hearing Voices: Embodiment and Experience* (Free Association Books, 2001); *Mass Hysteria: Critical Psychology and Media Studies* (Palgrave Macmillan, 2001). Her new project is *Haunted Data: Social Media, Queer Science and Archives of the Future*.

Axel Bruns is an ARC Future Fellow and professor in the Creative Industries Faculty at Queensland University of Technology in Brisbane, Australia, where he leads the QUT Social Media Research Group. He is the author of *Gatewatching: Collaborative Online News Production* and *Blogs, Wikipedia, Second Life, and Beyond*, and the editor of *Uses of Blogs*, *A Companion to New Media Dynamics*, and *Twitter and Society*. http://snurb.info/, @snurb_dot_info.

Jean Burgess (@jeanburgess) is associate professor of digital media at Queensland University of Technology, Australia. Her research focuses on the cultures and politics of social and mobile media platforms, and new methods for studying them. Her coauthored and coedited books include *YouTube: Online Video and Participatory Culture* (Polity Press, 2009), *Studying Mobile Media: Cultural Technologies, Mobile Communication, and the iPhone* (Routledge, 2012), *A Companion to New Media Dynamics* (Wiley-Blackwell, 2013), and *Twitter and Society* (Peter Lang, 2014).

Sky Croeser is a lecturer and researcher with the Department of Net Studies, Curtin University, Western Australia. Her research focuses on the ways in which activists not only use, but also shape, technology. Her book, *Global Justice and the Politics of Information: The Struggle Over Knowledge,* was published in 2015 with Routledge. You can find out more about her work at http://scroeser.net.

Greg Elmer is professor of media at Ryerson University, Toronto. He is an award-winning media producer and director. Greg's books on surveillance, politics, and new media have been published by MIT Press, Peter Lang, and Arbeiter Ring Press.

Robert W. Gehl is an associate professor in the Department of Communication at the University of Utah. His book, *Reverse Engineering Social Media* (Temple, 2014), offers a critical exploration of sites such as Facebook, Twitter, Wikipedia, and alternative social media. He has published in *New Media and Society*, *Social Text*, *Communication Theory*,*First Monday*, and *Communication and Critical/ Cultural Studies*.

Tim Highfield is Vice-Chancellor's Research Fellow in Digital Media at Queensland University of Technology, Brisbane, Australia. His fellowship project is "Visual Cultures of Social Media," building on his prior research into social media, politics, popular culture, and playful practices. His first book, *Social Media and Everyday Politics*, is due for publication in late 2015. For more details, see http://timhighfield.net or @timhighfield on Twitter.

Ingrid M. Hoofd is an assistant professor in the Department of Communications and New Media at the National University of Singapore (NUS). Her research interests are philosophy of technology and theories of representation. Her work addresses the ways in which alter-globalist activists, as well as left-wing academics, mobilize discourses and divisions in an attempt to overcome gendered, raced, and classed oppressions worldwide, and the ways in which such mobilizations are implicated in what she calls "speed-elitism."

Yuk Hui studied computer science and philosophy in Hong Kong and London. He is currently a postdoctoral researcher at the Centre for Digital Cultures in Leuphana University Lüneburg, and before that, was a postdoctoral researcher at the Institut de Recherche et d'Innovation of Centre Pompidou. He is the editor (with Andreas Broeckmann) of *30 Years after Les Immatériaux: Art, Science and Theory* (Meson Press, forthcoming) and the author of *On the Existence of Digital Objects* (University of Minnesota Press, forthcoming).

David Karpf is an assistant professor in the George Washington University School of Media and Public Affairs. He is the author of *The MoveOn Effect: The Unexpected Transformation of American Political Advocacy* (Oxford University

Press, 2012), and is currently completing a second book on analytics and activism. He blogs at shoutingloudly.com and tweets as @davekarpf.

Ganaele Langlois is an assistant professor in the Department of Communication Studies at York University. Her research focuses on social media, critical theory, and software studies. She is the author of *Meaning in the Age of Social Media* (Palgrave, 2014) and co-author of *The Permanent Campaign: New Media, New Politics* (Peter Lang, 2012).

Fenwick McKelvey is an assistant professor in information and communication technology policy in Canada at the Department of Communication Studies at Concordia University. He researches algorithmic media—the intensification of software within communication infrastructure. His research has appeared in *Fibreculture*, the *Canadian Journal of Communication*, *Television and New Media* and *First Monday*.

Joanna Redden is an assistant professor in the Department of Communication, Media and Film at the University of Calgary. Her research focuses on big data and governance, and how digital technologies are changing news, activism, and politics. She is the author of *The Mediation of Poverty: The News, New Media and Politics*.

Alessandra Renzi is an assistant professor in Emergent Media at Northeastern University where she explores the relays between media, art, and activism through ethnographies and media production. Her current research focuses on the impact of platform design on participation and social engagement. She coauthored with Greg Elmer *Infrastructure Critical: Sacrifice at Toronto's G8/G20 Summit*, a book on the criminalization of social movements.

1

Introduction: Compromised Data—From Social Media to Big Data

Ganaele Langlois, Joanna Redden, and Greg Elmer

We are surrounded by what appear to be, on the surface, contradictions: governments promote openness, open-access, and open data (Goldstein and Dyson 2013) while engaging in secretive and widespread surveillance (Greenwald 2014), persecution of whistleblowers, and preemption of protests (Elmer and Opel 2008). Similarly, the "social"—as in social media and social marketing—is the latest buzzword in the high-tech world these days while social services and provisions designed to generate greater equality are systematically cut under the guise of austerity or efficiency. We are living through an information and social revolution: it has never been easier to share information, and yet access to information about the social—particularly social data—is often denied, as such data is privately owned, incomprehensible to the nonspecialist, silenced, or eliminated. As this book demonstrates, data is being employed to accelerate prevalent neoliberal redefinitions of the role of the state and the transformation of citizenship into consumer practices. In this context, discussions of data are instrumentalized or limited to how data can be used to generate wealth, improve efficiencies, and encourage entrepreneurialism. Decisions made about data generation, collection, and aggregation privilege and facilitate further marketization, management, and control, while limiting opportunities for democratic engagement, participation, and contestation. This new paradigm—wherein the social is already compromised—relies heavily on automated software to collect, store, correlate, and analyze data. The name and contour of this new paradigm remains nebulous: "big data" would be the most recent expression, although it could be called "big social data"[1] to differentiate it from the kind of data analytics employed in the hard sciences.

[1] See, for instance, the following team of researchers at King's College London: http://big-social-data. net/.

The mineable social

We are concerned about the transformation of the social. The social is indeed a loose term to refer to modes and practices of being together. And yet the social is also a political and ethical project, in that a critical reflection about the social requires unveiling and questioning the power relations that lead to systematic inequalities, victimization, and marginalization of groups and individuals. Current attempts to limit and prevent this particular kind of social project—one that is not attached to market and IT principles—should come as no surprise. Indeed, Margaret Thatcher's pronouncement that "there is no such thing as society" continues to inspire a set of policies that not only seek to undermine, but altogether remove social imperatives (Hall, Massey, and Ruskin 2013). More recently, Prime Minister Stephen Harper warned citizens and the media that it was no time to "commit sociology"[2] as a response to calls for an investigation into the shockingly high rate of murder among aboriginal women in Canada. Foucault (2010) offers a compelling rationale for this sort of claim in his thoughts on American neoliberalism. The doctrine of American neoliberalism encompasses four basic tenets: first, a ferocious defense of free-market competition and its freedom from government intervention and regulation; second, the claim that all aspects of life can be folded within economic principles, that is, that all aspects of life should be managed according to their market value; third, a focus on individuals as independent economic agents concerned primarily with their own happiness, comfort, and wealth; and finally, fourth, the transformation of all that does not fit in to economic principles into a question of crime and punishment. Hence, for the Canadian prime minister, there is no *social* grouping of aboriginal women, only individual victims and criminal perpetrators. Further, there is no incentive for a costly federal inquest into this issue, as such an inquest does not fit in to market principles.

To most readers, such a picture is but a brief summary of some thirty years of lament in the social sciences. Yet the social has returned; the same people who refuse and denounce sociology now embrace a new form of the social, one that is technologically mediated and more apt to fit within market principles.

---

[2]   See Julie Kaye and Daniel Béland, 2014, "Stephen Harper's Dangerous Refusal to 'Commit Sociology,'" *The Toronto Star*, August 22. Accessed September 4, 2014. http://www.thestar.com/opinion/commentary/2014/08/22/stephen_harpers_dangerous_refusal_tocommit_sociology.html.

This version of the social is new and radically different from its previous unmarketable version. This new version of the social was not born in the mind of social scientists, but rather of technology entrepreneurs supported by advances in computer science (Mayer-Schönberger and Cukier 2013). This new version is inseparable from data collection and management. Simply put, a piece of data is a piece of factual information: date of birth, age, gender, geographic coordinates, a time stamp, what was said at one time, and so on. The big data paradigm is not simply about collecting all kinds of facts about everything from human beings to commodities, from weather patterns to traffic patterns. Rather, it is about establishing relations between all these different facts and moments. In other words, it is about managing data and transforming it into usable and sellable knowledge. The data paradigm thus requires systems for data collection, data storage, data retrieval, data processing, and finally the transformation of correlated data into usable information. So, for instance, age and shopping habits might not mean much by themselves, but correlated with other people's age and shopping habits, will help establish a specific consumer profile that is valuable for marketing companies.

Automated large-scale corporate mining of social data has been around for at least a decade, if not longer (see Elmer 2004). One could think of Amazon— founded in 1994—as the first Web-based corporation to track and correlate users' behaviors on their website in order to produce book recommendations. Fast-forward ten years to 2004 and we have the launch of Google's Gmail system. Google's worldwide introduction of Gmail touted the possibility of having a free, large storage space and never having to erase emails again. Users could use the service for free, as long as they agreed to have their incoming and outgoing emails scanned by a piece of software to produce targeted advertising. In so doing, Google's marketing approach already introduced three key pillars of current forms of social data analysis: the transformation of all aspects of social life into a searchable, minable, and ultimately profitable database; the reliance on automated software-based processes of analysis as more trustworthy and accurate than human ones; and faith in corporations to find solutions to social complexity. We could thus say that the recent turn toward big social data is the latest expansion of a process that started with the rise of social media corporations. This turn is, of course, also facilitated by our acceptance of government and business use of our data. This acceptance, as argued by van Dijck (2014), can in part be explained by the gradual normalization of "datafication" in our daily lives, as our social exchanges and relations increasingly became encoded, quantified, and commodified and used to track, target, and predict individual and social behaviors.

The rise of social media corporations was a pivotal moment in the transformation of the social into data-minable business ventures. From the outside, social media platforms are services that allow people to connect online in real time. Social media are both communication platforms and platforms for connectivity: users can exchange all kinds of information in an environment designed to facilitate social connection and presence. Each social media platform offers different modes of connectivity, from friendship networks (Facebook) to short burst of texts (Twitter) and instant pictures (Instagram). In a fairly short order, social media platforms have become repositories of social life in all its aspects, from intimate pictures of families and important events in one's life to participation in global social movements. Social media corporations were the first to find a way to mine social life in order to open new markets. While we tend to think of social media corporations as free services to facilitate social connectivity among users, these corporations should be understood as platforms to deploy strategies to get users to produce data. For instance, Facebook invites users to connect with members of their social networks and encourages them to keep in touch through constant updates about their lives. Such data is then collected and data analytics allows for the extraction of all kinds of social knowledge that can then be sold for a profit to advertisers and marketers. Social media corporations, then, were the first to systematically make a profit (or at least high corporate valuations) out of users' mundane social life. Furthermore, social media corporations do not only sell social knowledge—they also provide the means through which such knowledge can direct action, for instance, increasing the probability of a user clicking on a link. Social media corporations are not simply in the business of reflecting on and facilitating the social: they make it possible to orient social processes and feelings, and to modulate responses to social stimuli.

Big social data and governance

Social data analytics is now being promoted as a means to solve a host of real-world problems. Big data solutionism, it has been argued, has reached a level of mythic proportions (Morozov 2014; Crawford, Milner, and Gray 2014). According to its proponents, data analytics helps understand complexity by discerning patterns and highlighting correlations among diverse and large pools of information (Mayer-Schönberger and Cukier 2013). Data analytics also makes it possible to move from the broad to the specific, and thus to see where individuals are located within their complex environment, fueling a whole range of privacy concerns. Data analytics offers ways to visualize future scenarios and thus to foresee problems likely to arise. When focused on social issues, data analytics seems to offer nothing short of a complete understanding of the social, along with a promise to make the social manageable. The use of data to track and control populations, particularly those deemed problematic, has a long and extensive history. However, the scope, ubiquity, and opacity of contemporary data collection and processing present new challenges to those fighting discriminatory practices (Eubanks 2014; boyd, Levy, and Marwick 2014; Andrews 2013). Managing the social, here, has different connotations, from political control to the opening of new markets. Indeed, it comes as no surprise that governments and industry have been funding the development of different forms of social data collection and analysis. From big data grants and publicly funded pilot projects to new business ventures, social data has quickly become a hotbed of innovation.

The translation of the social into mineable and searchable data has opened up new entrepreneurial venues and collaborations among IT businesses, government, and computer scientists. Such translation is seen, from a neoliberal standpoint, as a happy resolution of social woes through the production of targeted and informed solutions. An example of such approach to the social is the Chicago Police Department's use of data analytics in crime prevention (Pickels 2014). Using a sophisticated and secret algorithm that correlates crime rates, poverty rates, and past criminal convictions, the Chicago Police Department was able to target a group of four hundred people likely to commit a crime in the future. These people were then notified that they were being carefully monitored, so that if they ever attempted to commit a crime, they would likely be caught. In the minds of the Chicago police, such measures prevent crime at the same time as they make the best use of available resources. This kind of data-driven policing is not, however, without obvious limitations. For one, the targeting of specific groups overlaps, particularly in Chicago, with racial profiling and further intensifies it. Indeed, the data for crime statistics is often biased: crimes committed by white people tend to be underreported compared to crimes committed by people of color. Second, the guilty until proven innocent stance is legally corrupt and deterministic in that it denies the possibility of change through social rehabilitation. Third, the capacity for an organization to easily access and use all kinds of personal data raises questions over privacy and personal integrity. Finally, such attempts to preempt crime do nothing to resolve the social causes of criminality, namely poverty, lack of education opportunities and training, and systematic social and race inequalities.

It is important to understand that data management embeds specific kinds of economic and governmental logics within social processes (Vis 2013; Baym 2013). Data correlation often ties commercial and free-market logics to what constitutes, in the case of personalized advertising, for instance, social happiness and status. The current push toward big data expands the scope of data management to all aspects of governance. Big data currently takes the form of both public and private initiatives to develop new ways of gathering, managing, and generating knowledge out of large-scale and disparate data sets (Weiss and Zgorski 2012). All kinds of scientific, social, and geographical data, for instance, are being put together in order to create new knowledge and to develop different kinds of scenarios. For instance, big data is used to understand the potential impact of climate change on resource economies,[3] human migration, and political instabilities. Big data is thus about the connectivity of different types of information in order to understand complexity and aid with decision-making. With this new paradigm, we are seeing a complete reorganization of the governance of the social. In North America and Western Europe, big data cannot be separated from neoliberal approaches to governance, where the capacity to model the future cannot be dissociated from capitalist interests and from attempts at managing growing social inequalities rather than solving them (Gangadharan and Woolley 2014). Big data in that sense is approached as a way of controlling and reacting to the negative effects of capitalism rather than completely transforming economic, political, and social relationships. The National Security Agency scandal and the subsequent revelations that government agencies around the world routinely collect vast amounts of social data in collaboration with social media corporations is another indicator of the shift from research that seeks to understand and address the causes of social problems to research that helps to manage and control the consequences of these problems.

Thus, data is not only about producing valuable and marketable information and knowledge; it is also about increasing the automation of many forms of decision-making—from credit rating to the flagging of persons of interest—through the correlation of large data sets. Data is furthermore about the

---

[3] http://www.unglobalpulse.org/big-data-climate.

increasing opacity of large-scale decision making as it becomes hidden or proprietary, along with the enabling software. As such, we are currently witnessing broad changes to the ways in which data is located at the center of decision-making processes that reach all aspects and levels of social life, from large-scale social knowledge to the intimate knowledge of private psychic processes. Indeed, data serves to produce social realities (Kitchin 2014): it identifies economic opportunities as well as threats; it serves to control large populations as well as all aspects of one's life, from access to health care to one's desires and modes of connecting with others. At the same time, it is important to note that data management is as much about processing data sets according to free-market principles as it is about forgetting other kinds of data that could serve to create more nuanced or alternative ways of understanding current and past social dynamics. Example of this can be seen in Canada, where there is active governmental prevention of research or research presentation that would contradict the political agenda of the federal government, especially with regard to climate change and nonrenewable resource extraction (Klinkenborg 2013).

Compromised data

The question that spurred the making of this book is: What happens when the social is transformed into data? Data is not a mirror of the social; it implies the abstraction of everything from thoughts, emotions, and facts into sets of computable symbols. What is being compromised through such a translation? What is lost when the richness and complexity of the social is abstracted into data? Further, the choice of data—what gets collected—also raises the question of what is being compromised: What kind of social information is being collected, and what kind of information is ignored? Here, we enter into the question of the design of data projects—the choices that are made as to what kind of data should be collected, how it should be processed, and what kind of interpretation, or knowledge, can be derived from it. Indeed, while data analytics evokes images of computer-assisted scientific objectivity, the actual projects that employ social data are designed in response to or in alliance with political and economic concerns. Research design, in short, is muddled and bears the risks of further compromising the kind of social picture that emerges out of social data analysis (Helles and Jensen 2013). In short, compromises are introduced and follow data from its generation to its collection and selection, and to its analysis. The collection and analysis of big social data comprises a new information system informed by its own obscure sets of values, subjective practices (boyd and Crawford 2012) and rationalities.

This book considers how the new data paradigm compromises our understanding of the social and of ourselves and considers the social and political implications of these compromises. Overall, the book asks what happens when the analysis of the social that informs business and government practices is hidden in either proprietary or secretive data processing systems, such as corporate-owned algorithms. From state surveillance to the commodification of all aspects of social life, it appears that it is not simply data that is compromised, but all of us as social beings as well. Increasingly, concerns are being raised about the lack of transparency and oversight of data collection and data brokerage industries as more information comes to light about their ability to create extremely detailed profiles, the lack of public awareness of how their data is being commodified, and the discriminatory and predatory practices, privacy infringements, and "consent engineering" to which they are subject (Tufekci 2014; US Federal Trade Commission 2014; Office of the Privacy Commissioner 2014).

The aim of this volume is to further analyze this new transformation of the social as a data-minable field. It operates at the crossroads of the following theoretical traditions: social studies of science and technology (Latour 1988), critical theory of technology and subjectivity (e.g. Stiegler 2011, 2013), and software studies (Fuller 2008). This book first asks about the political and economic context within which social data processes are designed, funded, and developed in order to find out which interests are being served through the development of current forms of big social data and its analysis. As such, it complements contemporary research on big data industries (Mosco 2014) by asking how the social that emerges out of social data might be compromised by political and economic pressures and concerns. In different ways, the chapters in this book demonstrate that we are witnessing the rise of new forms of alienation, where individuals and collectivities are deprived of the means to be able to understand and take charge of social issues and their solutions. That is, this book shows that social data tend to operate through opacity and secrecy: information is taken from individuals, processed through black-boxed algorithms that produce a certain kind of knowledge, and then some kind of solution is given back to individuals as the only possible answer to the given social problem. This structure of social circulation and decision making is profoundly nondemocratic, yet it is being touted as the only possible road to take. Pushing against this latter conclusion, here we collectively explore the stakes of a reappropriation of social data analytics. How, we ask, can we avoid being compromised by data? At present, data is compromised, and we are compromised by data. Yet—and here is the final question this book addresses—is it still possible to use social data to think about new designs and new ethics of understanding and (en-)acting in the social? A large portion of *Compromised Data* is devoted to exploring what kinds of research, collaboration, and reenvisioning of data itself could be done in order to transform data analytics from a control mechanism to a critical process of social transformation.

Rebuilding the social

The emerging picture of big social data shows that critical forms of accountability are being pushed to the margins of both social science and public research. Doing social research, more and more, means doing the kind of research that fits into the existing big social data paradigm. The collection and analysis of social data limits and constrains what can be known and what can be done in very particular ways. Several authors in this collection examine the repercussions of such dynamics. David Karpf's analysis of petition platforms reveals how organizational logics and data analytics lead to organizational compromises that limit and shape the kinds of civic participation possible on these sites. While data-driven activism often appears and is discussed as spontaneous and viral, Karpf details the political and organizational work done to nudge and craft political action and engagement. Joanna Redden considers how big data influences government decision making and raises concerns about how the computationalization and datafication of policymaking may limit how we understand social problems and thereby impoverish our responses to those problems. Ingrid Hoofd calls for more critical reflection of how new media technologies are altering research in the social sciences and humanities. In particular, she uses the concept of "speed-elitism" to critique contemporary algorithmic and object-oriented knowledge generation and practices. Fenwick McKelvey, Greg Elmer, and Axel Bruns and Jean Burgess question our very ability to conduct research into social media, examining in particular the ways in which social media corporations have managed to enclose and regulate access to data. McKelvey demonstrates that while social media corporations thrive on "open," participatory communication, they have at the same time structured their platforms in ways that deprive the general public of access to the data they produce and the ability to conduct their own research and analysis. Indeed, social media platforms operate at two levels: the level of open communication, where users post and share information, and the level of data management, extraction, and analysis, which is only accessible to specific partners. As a result, research that fits within the for-profit motive of social media corporations is heavily favored. Research for the public interest, on the other hand, is being further marginalized, as access to data is made difficult, if not downright impossible (Burgess and Bruns). Lastly, Elmer revisits the history of data scraper technology as a parallel history of data personalization. He argues that research methods or scraper "analytics" must recognize and address the various processes through which social media data is always and already personalized at the expense of the social.

Robert Gehl, responding in part to McKelvey, Burgess and Bruns, and Elmer advocates a reverse engineering approach: in short, a deconstruction and disarticulation of data processes in order to reveal biases, interests, and compromises. Addressing the challenges of big social data does not simply require new methods, but an entirely new research politics—researchers should take a more active and invested stand in their field of research. As opposed to a big data paradigm that advocates for and reinforces the separation between researchers and their objects of study, several authors in this collection advocate for a new research paradigm, one that pays attention to and respects the demands of research participants. Common to these authors is a keen awareness of the limitations of big data as a research method. The first step to this new research paradigm is the acknowledgment that big data cannot provide a comprehensive understanding of the social, or even a complete understanding of a social event. Indeed, data analytics is only one step in the research process, and should be complemented with more qualitative approaches, such as participant observation and interviews (Sky Croeser and Tim Highfield). Data analytics, in this new research context, becomes a means to question assumptions about the constitutions of social groups and individuals. As data analyses are done and shared with research participants, data analytics ceases to impose an abstracted picture of the social and becomes a means for collaborative reflection. That is, data becomes a way of pushing boundaries and fostering more experimental and creative forms of social involvement and transformation (Alessandra Renzi and Ganaele Langlois). Such propositions for research highlight the need to pay attention to the fluidity of social life and offer ways of thinking about data analytics as a way to uncover collective potentials. In so doing, a new politics of research that comes into focus, one that pays careful attention to biases inherent to the big data paradigm and that uses collaborative practices to deconstruct such biases and enable true critical reflection on the social.

Last but not least, contributors to this volume advocate not only for new research paradigms and methods, but also for a redefinition of the concept of data itself. Data is abstraction; it evokes and invokes a scientific mode of inquiry, one based on measurements and correlations. But what would it mean to define social data not simply as an abstract information set, but rather as a set of indicators of social life in its fluidity, its divergent temporalities, its many modes and forms of circulation? Lisa Blackman and Yuk Hui explore this question in depth by using a genealogical approach that links the question of social data with other forms of mediation of the social. Both chapters remind us that social data is not only a product of computer science; it is also linked to processes of archiving, of remembering and forgetting. From this perspective, social data becomes thick and multidimensional. It does not simply exist to be classified, measured, and correlated, but as a trace of practices that establish cultural and social continuities and discontinuities. In the words of Lisa Blackman, social data becomes literally haunted—it leaves trails and associations that can be followed and untangled. Social data does not need to serve neoliberal logics; it can be used to follow the unraveling of social lives and to bring to life new ways of being together, of building and practicing the social.

References

Andrews, Lori. 2013. *I Know Who You Are and I Saw What You Did: Social Networks and the Death of Privacy*. New York: Free Press.

Baym, Nancy K. 2013. "Data Not Seen: The Uses and Shortcomings of Social Media Metrics." *First Monday* 18(10). doi:10.5210/fm.v18i10.4873.

boyd, d. and K. Crawford. 2012. "Critical Questions for Big Data." *Information, Communication & Society* 15(5): 662–79.

boyd, danah, Karen Levy, and Alice Marwick. 2014. "The Networked Nature of Algorithmic Discrimination." In Seeta Peña Gangadharan, Virginia Eubanks, and Solon Barocas, eds. *Data and Discrimination: Collected Essays*. New America: Open Technology Institute. Accessed November 5, 2014. http://newamerica.org/downloads/OTI-Data-an-Discrimination-FINAL-small.pdf.

Crawford, Kate, Kate Milner, and Mary L. Gray. 2014. Special Section Introduction: "Critiquing Big Data: Politics, Ethics, Epistemology." *International Journal of Communication* 8: 1663–72.

Elmer, Greg. 2004. *Profiling Machines: Mapping the Personal Information Economy*. Cambridge, MA: The MIT Press.

Elmer, Greg and Andy Opel. 2008. *Preempting Dissent: The Politics of an Inevitable Future*. Winnipeg: Arbeiter Ring Publishing.

Eubanks, Virginia. 2014. "Big Data and Human Rights." In Seeta Peña Gangadharan, Virginia Eubanks, and Solon Barocas, eds. *Data and Discrimination: Collected Essays*. New America: Open Technology Institute. Accessed November 5, 2014. http://newamerica.org/downloads/OTI-Data-an-Discrimination-FINAL-small.pdf.

Foucault, Michel. 2010. *The Birth of Biopolitics: Lectures at the Collège de France, 1978–1979*. Trans. Graham Burchell. New York: Picador.

Fuller, Matthew, ed. 2008. *Software Studies: A Lexicon*. Cambridge, MA: The MIT Press.

Gangadharan, Seeta Peña and Samuel Woolley. 2014. "Data-Driven Discrimination." *Slate*, June 6. http://www.slate.com/articles/technology/future_tense/2014/06/big_data_can_perpetuate_poverty_and_inequality.html.

Goldstein, Brett and Lauren Dyson. 2013. *Beyond Transparency: Open Data and the Future of Civic Innovation*. San Francisco: Code for America Press.

Greenwald, Glenn. 2014. *No Place to Hide: Edward Snowden, the NSA, and the U.S. Surveillance State*. New York: Metropolitan.

Hall, Stuart, Doreen Massey, and Micheal Ruskin. 2013. "After Neoliberalism: The Kilburn Manifesto." *Soundings*. Accessed June 10, 2014. http://www.lwbooks.co.uk/journals/soundings/manifesto.html.

Helles, Rasmus and Klaus Bruhn Jensen. 2013. Introduction to the special issue: "Making data – Big Data and Beyond." *First Monday* 18(10). Accessed June 10, 2014. http://firstmonday.org/article/view/4860/3748.

Kitchin, Rob. 2014. *The Data Revolution: Big Data, Open Data, Data Infrastructures and Their Consequences*. New York: Sage.

Klinkenborg, Verlyn. 2013. "Silencing Scientists." *The New York Times*, September 21. http://www.nytimes.com/2013/09/22/opinion/sunday/silencing-scientists.html.

Latour, Bruno. 1988. *Science in Action: How to Follow Scientists and Engineers through Society*. Cambridge, MA: Harvard University Press.

Mayer-Schönberger, Viktor and Kenneth Cukier. 2013. *Big Data: A Revolution That Will Transform How We Live, Work, and Think*. Boston: Eamon Dolan/Houghton Mifflin Harcourt.

Morozov, Evgeny. 2014. "The Rise of Data and the Death of Politics." *The Guardian*. July 20. http://www.theguardian.com/technology/2014/jul/20/rise-of-data-death-of-politics-evgeny-morozov-algorithmic-regulation.

Mosco, Vincent. 2014. *To the Cloud: Big Data in a Turbulent World*. Boulder: Paradigm Publishers.

Office of the Privacy Commissioner. 2014. *Data Brokers: A Look at the Canadian and American Landscape*. OPC Privacy Research Papers. Accessed October 31, 2014. https://www.priv.gc.ca/information/research-recherche/2014/db_201409_e.asp.

Pickels, Whitney. 2014. "Unleashing the Power of Data for the City of Chicago." *Chicago Policy Review*. Accessed November 11, 2014. http://chicagopolicyreview. org/2013/10/14/unleashing-the-power-of-data-for-the-city-of-chicago/.

Stiegler, Bernard. 2011. *Decadence of Industrial Democracies*. Trans. Daniel Ross. Cambridge, UK: Polity Press.

Stiegler, Bernard. 2013. *What Makes Life Worth Living: On Pharmacology*. Trans. Daniel Ross. Cambridge, UK: Polity Press.

Tufekci, Zeynep. 2014. "Engineering the Public: Big Data, Surveillance and Computational Politics." *First Monday* 19(7).

US Federal Trade Commission. 2014. *Data Brokers: A Call for Transparency and Accountability*. Washington, DC: US Federal Trade Commission. Accessed October 31, 2014. http://permanent.access.gpo.gov/gpo49532/140527 databrokerreport.pdf.

van Dijck, José. 2014. "Datafication, Dataism and Dataveillance: Big Data Between Scientific Paradigm and Ideology." *Surveillance & Society* 21(2): 197–208.

Vis, Farida. 2013. "A Critical Reflection on Big Data: Considering APIs, Researchers and Tools as Data Makers." *First Monday* 18(10). doi:10.5210/fm.v18i10.4878.

Weiss, Rick and Lisa-Joy Zgorski. 2012. "Obama Administration Unveils 'Big Data' Initiative: Announces $200 Million in New R&D Investments." Office of Science and Technology Policy. http://www.whitehouse.gov/sites/default/files/microsites/ostp/big_data_press_release.pdf.

Part One

Data, Power, and Politics

2

Big Data as System of Knowledge: Investigating Canadian Governance

Joanna Redden

Introduction

We are said to be entering a new era of governance through the collection and analysis of big data. The "data rush" is being compared to the gold rush and the oil boom as companies and governments spend billions to collect and analyze data (Hamm 2013). Utopian claims abound: big data is said to provide the means for governments to improve decision making, increase productivity, save money, become more efficient, improve health care, reduce fraud, get people to work sooner, provide more personalized services, prevent crises, and help society address a range of social and environmental problems, such as climate change and poverty. In short, it is said that big data will make us richer, healthier, safer, more civically engaged, improve government services, and lead to greater productivity (Manyika et al. 2011; Yiu 2012; Armah 2013; Microsoft 2013; TechAmerica Foundation 2012). There is often a dollar figure attached to big data promises. It has been argued that big data use could help the UK government save between £16 and 33 billion (Yiu 2012), that it could help the EU save between €150 and 300 billion a year, and help the US save $300 billion in health-care costs (Manyika et al. 2011).

To date critical literature questioning the political and social impact of big data is limited (Crawford, Milner, and Gray 2014; Helles and Jensen 2013; Gitelman 2013). Recent revelations about the US National Security Agency's PRISM surveillance program have drawn critique to various governments' use of big data as related to privacy, rights, spying, and security (Bauman et al. 2014; Deibert 2014). Little attention has been directed to how governments around the world are using data analytics in their day-to-day operations to inform decision making and policy development (Cook 2014; Bertot et al. 2014; Bhushan 2014; Margetts and Sutcliffe 2013). In the United Kingdom, the New Labour government oversaw the development of devices to connect data across services and departments (Ruppert 2012). More recently, big data is being tied to austerity measures as the coalition government investigates how data can be employed to reduce, target, and integrate programs and services. The American government is considered by many to be ahead of most other countries in its use of big data analytics. Big data is being used in security, law enforcement, education, and health care (Podesta et al. 2014). Like other G8 countries, the Canadian government has publicly endorsed the promise of governance through data. Data has been playing an ever-greater role as consumer marketing and political campaigning fuse. We do not know to what extent social media analysis and other forms of big data use are informing government decision making and policy development.

This chapter begins the process of detailing how the Government of Canada is using big data analysis now, and considers the political and social implications of this use. The specific research questions addressed are: How are the departments in the Government of Canada making use of data analytics? How is big data informing government decision making now? How might big data inform government decision making in the future? Research findings, I argue, raise important questions about big data and the computationalization of policymaking, the role of strategic ignorance, and the relationship of both to the intensification of neoliberal governance.

Method

This project employs semistructured interviews as the primary method of investigation. I also draw on government documents and research reports. Semistructured interviews with federal and provincial civil servants and private sector consultants working with government provide a means to track how and why government is using big data. To date, sixteen interviews have been conducted. Obtaining interviews with federal public servants has proven a major challenge. At the time of writing, interview requests had been sent to representatives from eighteen federal departments and three federal agencies; representatives from six federal bodies agreed to be interviewed and two of those representatives chose to engage in an email interview and provide written responses to questions rather than engaging in an oral interview. It has proven much easier to obtain interviews with provincial public servants. To date, five interviews have been conducted, with more planned. Interviews were conducted with five consultants who work with the federal government. In addition, three government documents provide details about big data use within the federal government. These include two reports from the Office of the Privacy Commissioner, "Checks and Controls: Reinforcing Privacy Protection and Oversight for the Canadian Intelligence Community in an Era of Cyber-Surveillance" and "The Age of Predictive Analysis: From Patterns to Predictions," and a report by the Standing Committee on Access to Information, Privacy and Ethics entitled "Privacy and Social Media in the Age of Big Data" (Dusseault 2013).

A semistructured interview format was selected as the best method for research as this fluid approach abandons a focus on standardization and complete control, and instead promotes open-ended dialogue (Deacon et al. 1999). The semistructured approach provides the flexibility to follow up interesting leads as they emerge. As one of the goals of the project is to consider the thinking behind big data use, questions are designed to draw out how data analysis and tools shape working practices, decision making, and become embedded as common practice. Although work investigating elite actors on a micro and qualitative level is rare, Davis (2007) and Herbst (1998) present two excellent examples to follow. By using interviews, the goal is to inductively build "grounded theory" by engaging continually and reflexively in data collection, initial interview analysis, and theorizing (Strauss and Corbin 1990). Theories are developed incrementally as interviews are continually transcribed, analyzed, and considered in relation to other interviews and key documents. In this way, certain findings throughout the course of the study "become solidified and others fall by the wayside" (Herbst 1998, 194). A similar list of questions was provided to all interviewees before the scheduled interview. Interviewees were asked about how big data analysis is being integrated into government processes, how it is now and might in the future influence decision making and policy development. They were also asked about whether or not analysis was conducted in-house or contracted out, and about data analysts working in government. Questions were asked about the analysis process, such as how research questions are generated, who does the analysis, and how information is reported and shared. There were also questions about perceived benefits, challenges, and limitations of big data analysis. Finally, questions were asked about national and international influencers

Table 2.1 Interview list.

Oral Interview	Field	Identifier	Interview Date
	Federal and Provincial Public Service	Public Servant A	2013
		Public Servant B	2014
		Public Servant C	2013
		Public Servant D	2014
		Public Servant E	2014
		Public Servant F	2014
		Public Servant G	2014
		Public Servant H	2014
		Public Servant I	2014
	Consultant	Consultant A	2013
		David Eaves, Public Policy Expert	2014
		Consultant B	2014
		Tasha Truant, Consultant Manager,	
		Goss Gilroy Inc.	2014
		Consultant C	2013
Written Response	Public Service	Treasury Board Secretariat	2014
		Communications Security Establishment	2014

and potentials and barriers to data analysis. Interviews were transcribed and responses were grouped thematically and analyzed. They were grouped into the following categories: what is happening in the federal government now, perceived benefits of big data analysis, concerns and limitations, big data literacy, big data versus traditional methods, the future of policy development, and the role of big data in international relations. The discussion of findings below begins by detailing some of the examples of current big data uses. I also summarize comments concerning the benefits, challenges, and limitations of big data use within government. Further, findings are considered in relation to the existing big data literature.

Findings

The federal government does not at this point in time have any documents that provide an overview of how big data is being used across government (Executive Office of the President 2012). Understanding how big data analysis is informing decision making requires compiling an overview of how it is being used within government to gain a comprehensive picture of the range and variety of applications. One of the objectives of the "Big Data and Canadian Governance" project is to develop such an overview. The information provided below is the beginning of this work, and as an ongoing project it remains incomplete. Examples are provided from various departments to illustrate the range of big data applications.

Big data is commonly explained in the IT sector in relation to volume, velocity, and variety. Volume refers to the increasing amount of data that streams from social media, from sensors, from transactions, and from machine to machine. Velocity refers to the speed of information coming in that people are trying to collect and respond to, often quickly. Variety refers to the variety of formats in which data is presented, including structured numeric data, and unstructured formats like texts, video, audio, or financial transactions. Combining this data in ways that can enable analysis is a major issue for government. Usefully, SAS, a business analytics company, adds variability and complexity to its definition of big data. Variability draws attention to data peaks; data loads can speedup and slowdown in relation to daily, seasonal, topical, and event-triggered peaks. Complexity refers to the need to connect, correlate, and link data from multiple sources (SAS 2014). This very broad definition of big data is useful when thinking through the broad range of data analysis that spans government departments. Some departments, such as Environment Canada and Natural Resources Canada, work with large volumes of data generated by environmental and spatial sensors. Health Canada works with a lot of administrative data sets. Other departments may analyze online transactions and public communications on social media sites.

In general, many of those interviewed view the federal government as more of a producer than a consumer of data. The Treasury Board Secretariat indicates that much of the federal government's focus at the moment is on open data, making more government data accessible to the public, than on developing the use of data analytics. Canada launched its open data site in 2011 and relaunched it with more publicity in June of 2013. Canada signed the G8 Open Data Charter in 2013, pledging to release high-quality and comprehensive data as early as possible. The Open Data Portal (data.gc.ca) at present hosts nearly 200,000 data sets. Some see the site as a step toward more open government, while others argue that the Conservatives are providing access to some information and promoting the idea of open data and open government while simultaneously making access to other types of government information more difficult (Ligeti and Smith 2014; Larsen and Walby 2012).

The intelligence community, as might be expected, is widely cited as being ahead of the rest of government in its use of big data analytics (Deibert 2013, 2014). When discussing how big data analysis is being used by the feds, public servants and consultants often responded that how the federal government is using big data and how intelligence agencies are using big data are two separate things; the point being that the latter must be considered and discussed separately. It is largely agreed that the federal government is in the early stages of using big data, while the intelligence community is highly advanced.

In the sciences, some of the bigger users of big data are Natural Resources Canada, Environment Canada, and Agriculture Agri-Food Canada, which generate a lot of data through their environmental sensing devices. Natural Resources Canada's work leading the Federal Geospatial Platform was highlighted as noteworthy. The goal of this project is to share geospatial assets. Environment Canada generates a lot of data through its work with Meteorological Services of Canada. The science departments are also in the process of trying to consolidate their data so that data can be accessed collectively and more easily shared.

Health Canada is using big data, for example, to develop early warning systems for monitoring pandemics. The extent to which Health Canada can make use of big data is limited by the fact that health falls under provincial jurisdiction and many health records are held provincially. The provinces vary in the extent to which they are big data ready. Public servants from one Canadian province suggest that it is a fallacy at present to talk about big data in the health sector because, although there is plenty of data, it is not integrated and so cannot be "crawled through." However, there is interest in moving toward a more integrated data solution (Public Servant G 2014). Logistically, many departments are wrestling with how to link data sets in a common fashion. In some cases, this will require addressing privacy and security matters. In many cases, there are strict legislative structures in place to ensure data is collected and maintained in accordance with specific obligations. Any move toward big data analysis will require respecting these legislative frameworks (Public Servant A

2013). In addition, new technological infrastructure will be needed to integrate data that will come in a variety of shapes and sizes. Consultant A notes that tight budget constraints in areas such as health are pushing public servants to integrate more data analysis into their policy and program development as they look for ways to make programs more effective and efficient.

Other big data initiatives include the Canada Border Services Agency use of predictive analytics to manage and mitigate risks. Human Resources and Skills Development Canada (now Employment and Social Development Canada) is developing and implementing the use of predictive analytics to save money by reducing client errors and fraud (HRSDC 2013). The aim is to detect Employment Insurance fraud and abuse through the analysis of multiple databases to detect people who have been overpaid. Files that are flagged by the system are then investigated. The program is undergoing a shift to this type of automated fraud detection and risk management through the use of analytical tools (Office of the Privacy Commissioner 2012). The National Research Council is said to be making great use of data to support research and business decisions. Revenue Canada, Statistics Canada, and Elections Canada have and continue to generate large data sets. Canada Post presently sells its compilation of address data to businesses for marketing and business intelligence. More work is needed to investigate how these government bodies are incorporating data analysis into their processes. Citizenship and Immigration Canada has created an immigrant longitudinal database and is linking its Permanent Resident Data System records to annual income tax returns to generate more detailed information than that provided by longitudinal surveys (Spencer and McNutt 2014). The Canadian Research Data Centre Network (CRDCN) manages and analyzes confidential data, making this data available to researchers to inform policy decisions. The network of centers provide access to confidential Statistics Canada records and an increasing number of administrative files such as files from the Canadian cancer registry, some provincial health records, and vital statistics. The CRDCN is trying to acquire more administrative data to enable greater data analytics (Spencer and McNutt 2014).

As of November 2013, the federal government did not have a program to do social media analysis, but public works had put out a tender for social media monitoring. At this point, it is unclear what this would entail. Through correspondence between the privacy commissioner and Tony Clement, the president of the Treasury Board, we know that some departments are collecting social media data (Wingrove 2014). Further, interviews indicate social media monitoring and analysis in relation to specific initiatives, and experimental uses by some departments to test its research value. Communications staff members are doing basic social media monitoring. For example, staff at one federal agency are monitoring and trying to influence social media outcomes in relation to specific campaigns.

The federal government is in the process of consolidating 1,500 websites to one portal over the next four years. When these are consolidated, one of the goals is to collect more data about how Canadians are accessing their information about government in order to provide better information and to also integrate Web and social media presence. The Government of Canada has also created Shared Services Canada with the aim of consolidating some of their basic systems. Their goal is to free up capacity by eliminating some of the redundancy happening in relation to IT delivery and maintenance, so that there would be more resources available to make use of big data analytics (Public Servant A 2013).

Interviewees repeatedly stress that the use of big data analysis in relation to policy development and decision making is in early stages. Consultants note that there is increasing interest among public servants and that more are becoming open to the idea of making use of big data, but there is a long way to go before use of this method of analysis reaches anything close to common practice. The consultant manager of Goss Gilroy Inc., Tasha Truant, is actively going to government departments and giving presentations about the uses of big data analysis. Truant says the goal is to try and get the word out about what these technologies and methodologies can do. For many, big data is new. Truant's company taps into public content already published on the Web. She argues that this type of big data analysis provides a list of benefits such as access to a large quantity of data, that it is a relatively less expensive method of research, and that this method does not present some of the biases introduced through other methods. One of the benefits of big data analysis, she argues, is the ability to access unprompted conversations by groups around certain topics. As an example, she notes that bringing immigrants into immigrant serving organizations for a focus group could introduce bias depending on the circumstances. Truant argues that it is possible to get a better read on immigrant attitudes and experiences by analyzing what is said online where huge diaspora communities are already talking about their experiences without any guidance. Further, she argues that big data analysis is one way to deal with decreasing participation rates in surveys. Others argue that monitoring unprompted social media comments and conversations on public sites does not plant questions and therefore introduce bias in the way that surveys do (Consultant B 2014). Others see potential benefits in big data as enabling public servants to make policies and services more responsive to real-time events, demands, and feedback. Eaves (Interview 2014) sees the potential for big data analytics to enable public servants to provide more customized services, provide better services according to citizen needs, and eventually enable real-time policy responses to health or food inspection reports. Analysts argue that big data can enable evaluations of the impact of projects and policies almost immediately, leading to more time-sensitive policy development.

At present, big data analysis is done by government employees and also contracted out. Basic social media analysis is being conducted and compiled by communications staff through social media platforms and services such as Hootsuite and Heartbeat. It is likely that the number of automated dashboard services will increase. These dashboard devices provide an easy and accessible way for communications staff to compile social media analytics. An analysis of the limitations and blind spots of these dashboard services would be useful. More detailed big data analysis is being conducted for a range of purposes. For example, it is being used to track how discourse around certain topics evolve online, who the key influencers are, how organizations are and are not changing debates, the impact of initiatives and programs, or how to meet increasing health needs in a better way. Approaches vary; public servants are sometimes going to analysts with specific questions or analysts are part of the process of formulating the analytical questions asked. Some are cautioning that there will need to be oversight the more big data analysis drives decision making.

One concern is the quality of the data itself (Busch 2014). There are issues with the very processes involved in trying to figure out how reliable the data is. As Leavey notes, "establishing information about samples, such as their demographic profiles and the provenance, reliability and timeliness of data is a challenge in itself. This makes correcting the data problematic" (2013, 16). Others have drawn attention to the question of authenticity online. The central question here is to what extent the information gleaned from social network analysis and other forms of online communication can be treated as "true," "accurate," and "authentic." The argument made by Manovich (2011) is that we know people behave differently in different environments and with different people, and in this respect, peoples' online behaviors are no different than their offline behaviors.

Given this, it would be a mistake to treat people's posts, comments, and other forms of information sharing as "transparent windows into their selves" (ibid.). The Canadian Privacy Commissioner has publicly warned that any social media data being used to inform government policy must be proven accurate, and that it is not clear that this obligation is being met (Wingrove 2014). Further, there is unease about the lack of information people have about the information that is being generated and/or collected about them and the ability of governments to protect people from harm if their personal data is released. More transparent debate is needed about what kinds of information governments plan to combine, analyze, and use (Eynon 2013).

There is a danger that an emphasis on data mining, data analysis, and data-informed decision making will transform the nature of government. The danger is that the public will be viewed as a set of subpopulations defined by risk profiles instead of a social body (Milakovich 2012). Another related danger is that, as data analysis approaches are largely being adopted from commercial uses, it is likely that citizens will be viewed and even treated as consumers and/or in connection to the particular subpopulation they are identified with rather than as citizens. One analyst noted that banks, for example, are restricted from targeting and offering special offers to people based on religion, age, or ethnicity, but that in a social media setting it is very easy for an analyst to figure out someone's age, religion, and ethnicity. Through social media analysis, it is possible to target groups and give some people special offers over others. He notes that this type of targeting and segmenting of groups of people could lead to unequal access to programs and services if incorporated into government and business practices (Consultant A 2013).

As noted by boyd and Crawford (2012), there is an assumption that the size of big data sets will lead to new and better information, and thus, insights. In part, this is related to the myth of objectivity and authenticity that surrounds big data analytics. However, in reality, subjective practices of selection continue. One of the dangers of big data analysis is becoming obsessed with the thing you know how to search for (Eaves 2014). Further, using big data for decision making and policy requires making sense of data and making sense of the data requires often complex models that few are able to design and understand. These models can be used to develop information that informs decision making, yet there are assumptions and biases involved, even at the model development stage, that are difficult for those outside of the process to question. In addition, these models are designed to work with the data that is available, not necessarily the question that is being asked. This presents a limitation on what can be done with the information generated. The potential for people to challenge decisions being made based on data and complex models is limited to the extent that they can actually challenge the models used to generate information and therefore trace the reasoning behind information generation. In this new big data world data scientists wield considerable power and there is a growing data analysis divide between those with the expertise to use and understand data analytics (Manovich 2011). Controllers of the information generated, owners of the vast data archives, and data miners who select what information to observe and ignore possess considerable political power (Gehl 2011).

How will data analysts be trained given the wide variety of skills they will need to possess? As discussed by Meyer (2013), data analysts working in policy development will need to be diplomatic. They will also need to have a good understanding of the areas they are working in so that they can grasp what seems to make sense and is plausible and not simply respond to what the data appears to indicate. It will be crucial that faulty conclusions based on false correlations are avoided. Further, these data analysts will need to be very skilled in asking questions of data and assessing the value of the data they have.

Of concern in relation to the development of social policy is the extent to which big data analytics may replace other forms of knowledge. One of the central claims about big data is that it provides us with a better picture of things because rather than relying on samples we can now have access to "more" and even "all" of the data in some cases (Mayer-Schönberger and Cukier 2013). Such claims mask how the data available limits the kinds of questions we can ask. Since we do not have data for everything, the data we do have can shape the kinds of questions we ask and the type of research conducted (Eynon 2013). Given the increasing pressure on governments to reduce costs we must be conscious of how the use of big data in this regard can sideline other types of research or the questions people ask. The importance of this is underlined in the Canadian context as the turn to big data is happening while other bodies of knowledge are eliminated or silenced. In the last seven years, the Canadian Conservative government has systematically cut agencies and institutions generating information that counter the government's neoliberal policy and legislative agenda. A few of the agencies and institutions that have been cut include: the Courts Challenges Program, the Canadian Council for International Co-operation, the Status of Women Canada, the National Council of Welfare, Statistics Canada's long-form census, and a wide range of environmental agencies including the Canadian Foundation for

Climate and Atmospheric Science. Also, scientists, academics, and bureaucrats are being systematically silenced. In a recent survey by the Public Service Alliance of Canada, 90 percent of scientists said they could not speak freely. One public servant described the chill across the civil service: "The current government is re-creating federal departments to serve the interests of its industry and business supporters and subverting the science. . . . Public servants with a conscience live in fear [of opening] their mouths to the media or the public" (PIPSC 2013). The turn to big data within government should be contextualized in relation to the turn away from other modes of generating information.

Big data analysis may facilitate neoliberal approaches by effectively erasing poverty. The effect could further be compounded by the elimination of the mandatory long-form census in Canada. The information gathered from this census provides detailed information about inequality and poverty in Canada. This information was used to justify funding for social programs and to also ensure money was directed where needed. The elimination of the mandatory long-form census has the effect of making the poor invisible and "easier to ignore" (McQuaig 2010). The use of big data for government decision making could contribute to a further erasure of poverty and even more unequal treatment of individuals (Meyer 2013; Lerman 2013). For a start, not everyone is online. Big data may both reinforce and even exacerbate existing social and educational inequalities. The people who leave data traces to be analyzed are likely to be those people of higher income and education who are online more and participate more on Twitter, the blogosphere, Google, etc. Also, it is a challenge to correctly weigh data for the wider population that does not have any kind of social media presence (Leavey 2013).

Three of the consultants interviewed and one public servant worry about the potential for big data analysis to exclude and marginalize particular groups of people. For Truant, potential exclusion and marginalization must be addressed in any research. She cautions that big data analysis should not be about replacing other forms of research, but about complementing other methods of investigation:

> The more we turn to online technologies to develop our policies and our programs the more we risk leaving out groups of people who are already marginalized, and we're already silencing people whose voices may not be all that loud in the first place. . . . To me, that's the thing I hope at the end of all of this I haven't contributed to. What it comes down to is we can't be lazy, we can't do it all online. Again it's one line of evidence amongst many. You still have to

go out there into the rural communities where people aren't online and talk to that person. . . . My answer is always "Look, it's not one or the other. It's about bringing this into what we're already doing and using it as one line of evidence.

The extent to which big data analytics will be added to other modes of investigation, and not simply replace them, will require continual monitoring particularly in this budgetary climate. Many IT companies are clearly marketing big data analysis as a cost-saving practice.

Some of the examples provided of uses of social media monitoring demonstrate how analysts are attempting to ensure their online samples are representative of offline realities. One public servant set out, through a pilot project, to test the extent to which online conversations were representative of offline dynamics (Public Servant B 2014). Public Servant B notes that online conversations, and the data gathered from social media monitoring, are only relevant when representative of real-world dynamics (Public Servant B 2014). Consultant B argues that analysts should take potential blind spots into account. This can involve identifying how and where the groups of interest are communicating and if their communication channels are accessible for analysis.

One of the major benefits of big data from a governmental perspective is that it enables probabilistic policymaking. This type of policymaking relies on developing rules and approaches based on ideas about what small groups of people will probably do rather than what they have done. A good example of this is the predictive policing in use in a number of cities across the United States. At this stage, it is unclear if predictive analytics are being used by the Canadian justice department, although it is known that cities across Canada are trying it. Toronto has tried predictive policing and the Vancouver Police Department is using predictive analysis (Silva 2012; Allen 2013). One of the dangers of predictive analysis and probabilistic policymaking is that it can lead to a "feedback loop of injustice" as groups identified as "at risk" or as likely to reoffend are increasingly watched and targeted (Margetts 2013). In this way, a reliance on future predictions to develop policies builds upon and reinforces present power dynamics. The effect of this is compounded by a turn away from causality to an emphasis on correlations. The big data argument is that we do not necessarily need to know why something is happening, just that it is happening (Mayer-Schönberger and Cukier 2013). This raises serious questions from a policy perspective, particularly when you consider it in relation to an issue like poverty, which is tied to a range of political, economic, and social factors. Eliminating causality from the equation can only contribute to the idea that poverty is a product of individual failing and an individual's responsibility.

The common view among interviewees is that government is still "testing the waters," but that the government will be moving toward more, and not less, big data analysis. As one analyst suggests, "it's hard to say what all of this will mean for the future of policy development, we're really only a couple of years into this" (Consultant B 2014). The cultures of policymaking, and whether or not these cultures change, will influence how big data analysis is and is not integrated into the policy process. High-ranking bureaucrats, as some note, have often achieved their position of authority through their political experience and instincts. There will need to be a change in mindset and a shift in policymaking practices by this group for big data analysis to be further integrated into government processes. "It's [going to involve] getting those folks to change their mindset, that they have to take policy advice from the pimple faced kid with the earring" (Consultant A 2013). One consultant argues that big data analysis may be threatening. "The notion that there is a whole bunch of data that might actually reveal some interesting insights threatens the group of people who don't have the skill sets to actually use and manage and play with that data" (Eaves 2014). Others note that there is always the question of whether or not higher-level decision makers care about the evidence when making policy decisions, and that this impacts the take-up and use of data analysis.

One interviewee argues that public servants and political staff worry about public perceptions. The fear is that the public is not making a distinction between data consultants and the analysis of already published content online, versus the more covert surveillance conducted by security agencies gaining much recent attention. One of the issues raised by consultants and analysts is that they are operating in a "murky, grey area" right now, as there are no federal guidelines about how the government should and should not be using social media analysis. Companies in Canada that do predictive analysis or use personal information have to follow the Personal Information Protection and Electronics and Documents Act. The Act does not provide the necessary oversight or guidelines for action in relation to the types of social media monitoring being done. In response to recent revelations about American, British, and Canadian intelligence surveillance practices, the Privacy Commissioner published a special report to parliament with a number of recommendations regarding government access and use of online communications (2014). The report recommends government develop guidelines for the collection, use, and dissemination of intelligence products using online sources and social network sites. The Privacy Commissioner also takes the position that just because personal information is available on the Internet, does not mean that this information is not personal. The commissioner cautioned that departments should not access personal information on social media unless they can demonstrate a direct correlation to legitimate government business. The report has had a chilling effect on users, and potential users, of social media data (Consultant B 2014). Further, interim Privacy Commissioner Chantal Bernier warned Treasury Board President Tony Clement in February 2014 that the government's collection of social media data might violate the Privacy Act. Minister Clement has said the government is conducting an internal review of these practices.

Cost is proving another barrier to big data integration. While consultants argue that big data analysis will save money, bureaucrats view big data as a new tool requiring new people to make use of it. Public Servant A describes the budget issue as one of capacity:

> As you know we are in a period of fiscal restraint and our budgets from an IT perspective do not grow on regular basis, nor do budgets for program delivery grow, so everybody is under the buzz word of constraint. Doing new things on that scale requires capacity, requires financial resources for computing capabilities and software and also the skillsets and the teams ready to focus on those, and that involves in today's environment having to make some tough decisions as to what will I stop doing if instead I want to work on this. I would say in the next five years we will see a growing move towards more big data.

She says the government's aim in integrating big data analysis will be to become more productive and efficient and provide better program and service delivery. She notes that departments are well aware of the potential to use big data but are limited by what they can do. Another public servant argues that it is difficult for government to do anything new in IT because of the increasing top-down control over expenditures. He argues that the increasing bureaucratization and control over decision making is dysfunctional and slows down and in some cases prevents innovation. Public Servant C is particularly troubled by how cost recovery models within various departments can be prohibitive to the sharing of ideas and information. His examples include one government body charging another to access its information, or IT staff being required to charge other departments for time spent in meetings. In combination, there is consensus that the future of big data – driven policy development depends largely upon how high-ranking policymakers and political staff respond to it as a tool. Their response is expected to be influenced most by how useful it seems, the outcomes of privacy debates, and if they conclude that the benefits exceed the costs.

Conclusion

This chapter presents an early sketch of big data approaches within the Canadian federal government. We are dealing with broad strokes and anecdotes of micro details. The ability to construct a systematic illustration of how big data analysis is being used by the federal government at present is limited by the sheer size of government operations and also by a lack of access to the information required. Nevertheless, this initial sketch raises some significant questions, concerns, and areas for future research. The lack of access to federal civil servants is an important methodological finding, and a problem that will need to be considered and addressed in future research if we are to better understand government practices and how they are changing. Interviews are a crucial social science research method, particularly when researching the present in order to consider future political and social implications. Interviews are also an important way to better understand how digital technologies are being used by elite actors and influencing the development of policy. What strategies can be used to unblock interview access? What other methods might we use to better understand the thinking and reasoning influencing the ways digital technologies are being integrated into government processes?

This research contributes to some of the epistemological concerns about the uses of big data. With the turn to big data, as raised by boyd and Crawford (2012), there is a concern about the computational turn in thought and research. As noted by boyd and Crawford, big data shapes the reality it measures by staking out new methods of knowing (2011, 665). Because of the sheer amount of information available, subjective decisions are made about what is measured and what is ignored. The "subtractive methods of understanding reality"—that is, the reduction of information flows into numbers that can be stored and then mined—produce very particular forms of information and computational knowledge (Berry 2011, 2). At issue is how this computationalization of reality, the "datafication" of reality, can lead to a computationalization of reason (Berry 2011), and moreover the congruence between the computationalization of reason and the intensification of neoliberalism. Epistemological concerns draw attention to how big data shapes the reality it measures through the subjective and value-laden decisions made about what to measure, the significance of results, and the value placed on big data findings as opposed to other methods of information generation. The process of converting our messy and unruly social world into numbers to be stored and mined, into data that can be collectively "crawled through" and compared, fits some frameworks of meaning better than others. In this way, the "datafication" of reality can privilege some lines of thought over others. Most importantly the datafication of reality may reinforce neoliberal frameworks of meaning over social justice frameworks.

Computational, or big data, decision making may reinforce neoliberal rationality, and therefore reinforce neoliberal calls for cuts and further marketization of government programs and services. This is particularly dangerous given the intensification of neoliberal governance since the financial crisis of 2007–08 (Mirowski 2013; Peck 2010; Hall, Massey, and Rustin 2013). The transformation of information about the social world in all its complexity into numbers, models, and calculations complements and reinforces the instrumental and market-based thinking of neoliberal rationality (Foucault 2008; Davies 2013). The problem, and cause for alarm, is the further dissemination of market values to all spheres of life given the role that neoliberal approaches have played in not simply increasing poverty and inequality (Coburn 2000; Navarro 2007; Ruckert and Labonté 2014; Jacobs and Lindsey 2014; Wacquant 2009) but encouraging attacks on the poor (Briant, Watson, and Philo 2013; Mooney 2011; Kendall 2011). The idea, as argued by Foucault and others, is that neoliberalism is not just a political and economic project, but also a project to change the way we think; neoliberalism becomes a method of thought, a grid of economic and sociological analysis (Foucault 2008, 218). The goal is for the rationalities of the market and its schemas of analysis, its decision-making criteria, to be extended to all facets of life (Couldry 2010; Brown 2005). These new tools complement ongoing attempts to quantify life, to make all decision making based on calculative reasoning. Information systems are shaped by value systems, and economic values, as opposed to social and personal values, are driving big data analysis (Baym 2013). Big data analysis supports and furthers governmental emphasis on efficiency, cost-benefit, productivity, quantification, and targets, continuing the neoliberal colonization of government practices since the advent of new public management strategies in the 1980s (Boltanski and Chiappello 2005; Lorenz 2012; Power 1999).

As the Canadian government increasingly integrates big data use in policy development processes, big data analysis must be placed within its wider informational context. In the Canadian case, this context is full of seeming contradiction: increasing government use of big data analysis, more social media monitoring, increasing efforts to make more data open to the public, increasing cuts to significant statistical services such as cutting the long-form census, cuts to key information bodies such as the National Council of Welfare, greater control of access to information, limits on journalistic investigation, and barriers to public servants speaking publicly. This context is important because while some sources of information are being eliminated or silenced, others are being pursued. As an example, information, such as the long-form census, provides government authorities with the high-quality socioeconomic data necessary to justify redistributive programs designed to increase social and economic equality. The census renders the poor "visible" in ways that social media monitoring cannot. The sheer fact of its elimination in the face of massive protest brings forth a reminder about the role of strategic ignorance in furthering the neoliberal project (Davies and McGoey 2012; Mirowsky 2013). As argued by Hayek, ignorance can be desirable and necessary to diffuse the authority of central planners by taking away the authority and reasons for action (Davies and McGoey 2012). The widespread claims of ignorance in the face of the 2007–8 financial crisis demonstrate the effectiveness of ignorance as strategy, and also its value to the neoliberal project (Davies and McGoey 2012). Going forward, it will be crucial to evaluate how government further integrates big data analysis, to consider its relationship to strategic ignorance, and to evaluate the extent to which big data analysis is used to supplement and complement research or to replace and reduce the expense of research endeavors.

References

Allen, Mary. 2013. "'Intelligence-led Policing' in Reach with Analytics." InsightaaS.com. September 24. Accessed July 9, 2014. http://www.insightaas.com/intelligence-led-policing-in-reach-with-analytics/.

Armah, Nii Ayi. 2013. "Big Data Analysis: The Next Frontier." *Bank of Canada Review.* Summer. Accessed July 9, 2014. http://www.bankofcanada.ca/wp-content/uploads/2013/08/boc-review-summer13-armah.pdf.

Bauman, Z., D. Bigo, P. Esteves, E. Guild, V. Jabri, D. Lyon, and R. B. J. Walker. 2014. "After Snowden: Rethinking the Impact of Surveillance." *International Political Sociology* 8(2): 121–44.

Baym, Nancy K. 2013. "Data Not Seen: The Uses and Shortcomings of Social Media Metrics." *First Monday* 18(10). Accessed June 10, 2014. http://firstmonday.org/ojs/index.php/fm/article/view/4873.

Berry, David. 2011. "The Computational Turn: Thinking About the Digital Humanities." *Culture Machine* 12: 1–22. Accessed July 10, 2013. http://www.culturemachine.net/index.php/cm/article/viewDownloadInterstitial/440/470.

Bertot, J. C., U. Gorham, P. T. Jaeger, L. C. Sarin, and H. Choi. 2014. "Big Data: Open Government and E-Government: Issues, Policies and Recommendations." *Information Polity* 19: 5–16.

Bhushan, Aniket. 2014. "Fast Data, Slow Policy: Making the Most of Disruptive Innovation." *SAIS Review of International Affairs* 34(1): 93–107.

Boltanski, L. and E. Chiapello. 2005. *The New Spirit of Capitalism.* New York: Verso.

boyd, d. and K. Crawford. 2012. "Critical Questions for Big Data." *Information, Communication & Society* 15(5): 662–79.

Briant, Emma, Nick Watson, and Gregory Philo. 2013. "Reporting Disability in the Age of Austerity: The Changing Face of Media Representation of Disability and Disabled People in the United Kingdom and the Creation of New 'Folk Devils.'" *Disability & Society* 28(6): 874–89.

Brown, Wendy. 2005. "Neoliberalism and the End of Liberal Democracy." In *Edgework: Critical Essays on Knowledge and Politics.* Princeton: Princeton University Press, 37–59.

Busch, Lawrence. 2014. "A Dozen Ways to Get Lost in Translation: Inherent Challenges in Large-Scale Data Sets." *International Journal of Communication* 8: 1727–44.

Coburn, David. 2000. "Income Inequality, Social Cohesion and the Health Status of Populations: The Role of Neo-liberalism." *Social Science & Medicine* 51: 135–46.

Cook, Thomas D. 2014. "'Big Data' in Research on Social Policy." *Journal of Policy Analysis and Management* 33(2): 544–47.

Couldry, Nick. 2010. *Why Voice Matters: Culture and Politics after Neoliberalism.* London: Sage.

Crawford, K., K. Milner, and M. L. Gray. 2014. Special Section Introduction: "Critiquing Big Data: Politics, Ethics, Epistemology." *International Journal of Communication* 8: 1663–72.

Davies, William. 2013. "Neoliberalism and the Revenge of the 'Social.'" *openDemocracy.* July 16. Accessed September 29, 2014. http://www.opendemocracy.net/william-davies/neoliberalism-and-revenge-of-%E2%80%9Csocial%E2%80%9D.

Davies, William and McGoey, Linsey. 2012. "Rationalities of Ignorance: On Financial Crisis and the Ambivalence of Neo-Liberal Epistemology," *Economy and Society* 41(1): 64–83.

Davis, Aeron. 2007. *The Mediation of Power.* London: Routledge.

Deacon, David, Michael Pickering, Peter Golding, and Graham Murdoch. 1999. *Researching Communications: A Practical Guide to Methods in Media and Cultural Analysis.* London: Arnold.

Deibert, Ronald. 2013. *Black Code: Inside the Battle for Cyberspace*. Toronto: McClelland and Stewart.

Deibert, Ronald. 2014. "Now we know Ottawa can snoop on any Canadian. What are we going to do?" *Globe and Mail*. January 31. Accessed May 3, 2014. http://www.theglobeandmail.com/globe-debate/now-we-know-ottawa-can-snoop-on-any-canadian-what-are-we-going-to-do/article16625310/.

Dusseault, Pierre-Luc, M.P. 2013. "Privacy and Social Media in the Age of Big Data." Report of the Standing Committee on Access to Information, Privacy and Ethics. Ottawa: Government of Canada. 41st Parliament, First Session, April. Accessed June 10, 2014. http://www.parl.gc.ca/content/hoc/Committee/411/ETHI/Reports/RP6094136/ethirp05/ethirp05-e.pdf.

Executive Office of the President. 2012. "Big Data Across the Federal Government." Washington: The White House. Accessed June 4, 2014. http://www.whitehouse.gov/sites/default/files/microsites/ostp/big_data_fact_sheet.pdf.

Eynon, Rebecca. 2013. "The Rise of Big Data: What Does it Mean for Education, Technology, and Media Research?" Editorial. *Learning, Media and Technology* 38(3): 237–40.

Foucault, Michel. 2008. *The Birth of Biopolitics: Lectures at the College De France 1978–1979*. New York: Palgrave Macmillan.

Francoli, Mary. 2014. Independent Reporting Mechanism Canada: Progress Report 2012–2013. Ottawa: Government of Canada. Accessed June 10, 2014. http://www.opengovpartnership.org/sites/default/files/Canada_final_2012_Eng.pdf.

Gehl, Robert. W. 2011. "The Archive and the Processor: The Internal Logic of Web 2.0." *New Media & Society* 13(8): 1228–44.

Gitelman, Lisa. 2013. *Raw Data is an Oxymoron*. Cambridge, MA: The MIT Press.

Hall, S., D. Massey, and M. Rustin. 2013. "After Neoliberalism? The Kilburn Manifesto." *Soundings*. Accessed June 5, 2014. http://www.lwbooks.co.uk/journals/soundings/manifesto.html.

Hamm, Dax. 2013. "How Data-Driven Society Can Benefit Us." *Huffington Post Business Canada* (blog). May 6. Accessed July 31, 2013. http://www.huffingtonpost.ca/dax-hamman/big-data_b_3215520.html.

Helles, Rasmus and Klaus Bruhn Jensen. 2013. Introduction to the special issue: "Making data – Big Data and Beyond." *First Monday* 18(10). Accessed June 10, 2014. http://firstmonday.org/article/view/4860/3748.

Herbst, Susan. 1998. *Reading Public Opinion: How Political Actors View the Democratic Process*. London: University of Chicago Press.

Human Resources and Skills Development Canada. 2013. 2013–2014 Report on Plans and Priorities. Ottawa: Government of Canada. Accessed July 7, 2014. http://www12.hrsdc.gc.ca.

Jacobs, David and Lindsey Myers. 2014. "Union Strength, Neoliberalism, and Inequality: Contingent Political Analyses of U.S. Income Differences Since 1950."

American Sociological Review. June 9: 1–23. Accessed July 2, 2014. http://asr.sagepub. com/content/early/2014/05/29/0003122414536392.

Keen, Justin, R. Calinescu, R. Paige, and J. Rooksby. 2012. "Big Health Data: Institutional and Technological Challenges." Conference presentation at Internet, Politics, Policy 2012: Big Data, Big Challenges, Oxford Internet Institute.

Kendall, Diana. 2011. *Framing Class: Media Representations of Wealth and Poverty in American*. Lanham, MD: Rowman & Littlefield.

Larsen, Mike and Kevin Walby. 2012. *Brokering Access: Power, Politics, and Freedom of Information Process in Canada*. Toronto: University of British Columbia Press.

Leavey, Jason. 2013. *Social Media and Public Policy: What is the Evidence*. Discussion Paper. Alliance for Useful Evidence.

Lerman, Jonas. 2013. "Big Data and Its Exclusions." *Stanford Law Review Online* 66: 55–63.

Ligeti, Arik and Marie-Danielle Smith. 2014. "Open Data, Restricted Access." *Capital News Online*, March 21. Accessed July 9, 2014. http://www.capitalnews.ca/index. php/news/open-data-restricted-access.

Lorenz, Chris. 2012. "If You're So Smart, Why Are You Under Surveillance? Universities, Neoliberalism, and New Public Management." *Critical Inquiry* 38(3): 599–629.

Manovich, Lev. 2011. "Trending: the Promises and the Challenges of Big Social Data." In Matthew K. Gold, ed. *Debates in the Digital Humanities*. Minneapolis: The University of Minnesota Press, 460–75.

Manyika, J., M. Chui, B. Brown, J. Bughin, R. Dobbs, C. Roxburgh, and A. Hung Byers. 2011. "Big Data: The Next Frontier for Innovation, Competition, and Productivity." McKinsey Global Institute.

Margetts, Helen. 2013. "The Promises and Threats of Big Data for Public Policy-Making." *The Policy and Internet Blog*. Oxford Internet Institute, University of Oxford. Accessed October 28, 2013. http://blogs.oii.ox.ac.uk/policy/promises-threats-big-data-for-public-policy-making/.

Margetts, Helen and David Sutcliffe. 2013. "Special Issue: Potentials and Challenges of Big Data." *Policy & Internet* 5(2): 139–46.

Mayer-Schönberger, Viktor and Kenneth Cukier. 2013. *Big Data: A Revolution That Will Transform How We Live, Work, and Think*. New York: Houghton Mifflin Harcourt.

McQuaig, Linda. 2010. "Making it Easier to Ignore the Poor." *Rabble.ca*. Accessed August 20, 2011. http://rabble.ca/columnists/2010/07/harpers-attack-census-bad-news-poor.

Microsoft. 2013. "Seizing the Power of Public Data to Transform Government." Microsoft and Socrata. Accessed September 25, 2013. http://www.microsoft.com/ government/ww/public-services/initiatives/pages/openness-interoperability.aspx.

Milakovich, Michael E. 2012. "Anticipatory Government: Integrating Big Data for Smaller Government." Conference presentation for Internet, Politics Policy 2012: Big Data, Big Challenges. St. Anne's College, Oxford University, UK. September.

Mirowski, Philip. 2013. *Never Let a Serious Crisis Go to Waste: How Neoliberalism Survived the Financial Crisis*. London: Verso.

Meyer, E. T. 2013. "Big Data and Public Policy Workshop." Oxford Internet Institute. Accessed September 30, 2013. http://people.oii.ox.ac.uk/meyer/2013/09/15/big-data-and-public-policy-workshop/.

Mooney, Gerry. 2011. *Stigmatising Poverty? The "Broken Society" and Reflections on Anti-Welfarism in the UK Today*. Oxford: Oxfam. Accessed September 20, 2013. http://oro.open.ac.uk/29714/.

Navarro, Vincente. 2007. *Neoliberalism, Globalization, and Inequalities*. Amityville, NY: Baywood Press.

Office of the Privacy Commissioner of Canada. 2012. "The Age of Predictive Analytics: From Patterns to Predictions." Research Group at the Office of the Privacy Commissioner of Canada. Ottawa: Government of Canada. Accessed July 1, 2014. https://www.priv.gc.ca/information/research-recherche/2012/pa_201208_e.asp#_ftn47.

Office of the Privacy Commissioner of Canada. 2014. "Checks and Controls: Reinforcing Privacy Protection and Oversight for the Canadian Intelligence Community in an Era of Cyber-Surveillance." Special Report to Parliament. Ottawa: Government of Canada, January 28. Accessed July 1, 2014. https://www.priv.gc.ca/information/sr-rs/201314/sr_cic_e.pdf.

Peck, Jamie. 2010. *Constructions of Neoliberal Reason*. Oxford: Oxford University Press.

Podesta, John, Penny Pritzker, Ernest J. Moniz, John Holdren, and Jeffrey Zients. 2014. *Big Data: Seizing Opportunities, Preserving Values*. Executive Office of the President. Washington, DC: The White House. Accessed June 10, 2014. http://www.whitehouse.gov/sites/default/files/docs/big_data_privacy_report_may_1_2014.pdf.

Power, Michael. 1999. *The Audit Society*. Oxford: Oxford University Press.

Professional Institute of the Public Service of Canada. 2013. "The Big Chill, Silencing Public Interest Science, A Survey." Ottawa, Canada. Accessed October 15, 2013. http://www.pipsc.ca/portal/page/portal/website/issues/science/bigchill.

Ruckert, Arne and Ronald Labonté. 2014. "The Global Financial Crisis and Health Equity: Early Experiences from Canada." *Globalization and Health* 10(2): 1–10.

Ruppert, Evelyn. 2012. "The Governmental Topologies of Database Devices." *Theory, Culture & Society* 29(4/5): 116–36.

SAS. 2014. "Big Data: What it Is and Why it Matters." SAS. Accessed July 9, 2014. http://www.sas.com/en_us/insights/big-data/what-is-big-data.html.

Silva, Luis. 2012. "High-Tech Crime-Fighting." *Toronto Star*, July 29. Accessed July 2, 2014. http://www.thestar.com/opinion/editorialopinion/2012/07/29/hightech_crimefighting.html.

Spencer, Byron G. and Robert McNutt. 2014. Science and Technology Consultation by Industry Canada, Canadian Research Data Centre Network, February. Accessed May 8, 2014. http://www.rdc-cdr.ca/sites/default/files/submission_to_industry_canada.pdf.

Strauss, Anselm and Juliet M. Corbin. 1990. *Basics of Qualitative Research: Grounded Theory Procedures and Techniques.* Newbury Park, CA: Sage.

Swanson, Jean. 2001. *Poor-Bashing: The Politics of Exclusion.* Toronto: Between the Lines.

TechAmerica Foundation. 2012. "Demystifying Big Data: A Practical Guide to Transforming the Business of Government." Washington, DC. Accessed September 20, 2013. http://breakinggov.sites.breakingmedia.com/wp-content/uploads/sites/4/2012/10/TechAmericaBigDataReport.pdf.

Wacquant, Loic. 2009. *Punishing the Poor: The Neoliberal Government of Social Insecurity.* Durham: Duke University Press.

Wingrove, Josh. 2014. "Ottawa Launches Data Collection Review." *Globe and Mail.* May 8. Accessed June 9, 2014. http://www.theglobeandmail.com/news/politics/ottawa-launches-data-collection-review/article18578578.

Yiu, Chris. 2012. "The Big Data Opportunity: Making Government Faster, Smarter and More Personal." *Policy Exchange.* http://www.policyexchange.org.uk/media-centre/blogs/category/item/the-big-data-opportunity.

3

Data Mining Research and the Disintegration of Society: The "Project X" Haren Riots

Ingrid Hoofd

We need [such classifications and calculations] because we have been dealing with increasingly high numbers of individual . . . entities whose activities and behaviours must be understood. . . .

Axel Bruns[1]

Understanding the "Accidental" Haren riots

On September 21, 2012, the small Dutch city of Haren in the Northern Province of Groningen experienced, for Dutch standards, an unexpected and unprecedented spate of rioting. The riot occurred after a sixteen-year-old girl's public Facebook announcement about her upcoming birthday party went viral via YouTube, Facebook, and Twitter, resulting in thousands of young people congregating near her home to join in the "celebrations." The party call was disseminated via the "Project X" meme—a meme referring to the title of an American comedy film about a Facebook party that got out of hand. The resulting riot caused millions of Euros in damages to property like cars and shop windows, and resulted in assaults against police officers as well as to the injuring of several people in Haren (*The Independent*, 2012). After the riots subsided, a commission was formed—consisting of several politicians and a couple of mass and new media scholars from the University of Twente and Utrecht University in the Netherlands—to investigate the cause and ways to prevent future riots. In March 2013, the commission published a large, general report entitled "Twee Werelden" ("Two Worlds"), and a more specific and well-researched report by

---

[1] "Entering the Age of the Generative Algorithm" (2014, n.p., author's emphasis).

van Dijk et al. (2013) on the role of the media entitled "De Weg naar Haren: de rol van jongeren, sociale media, massamedia en autoriteiten bij de mobilisatie voor Project X Haren" ("The Road to Haren: the role of youth, social media, mass media and the authorities in the mobilization for Project X Haren"). This latter report provides an extensive and in-depth analysis of the role played by mass and social media in the event, making use of data mining techniques to map out the relationship between the various phases of the riot and mobile phone and social media traffic. Around 500,000 tweets are subjected to computer analysis, together with more than 50,000 Facebook posts, in order to also identify major topics, tones of conversation, causal relations, and possible groups and networks in relation to the riots.

This usage of data mining by social scientists, in which computers are called upon to handle the exceptionally large data sets generated by computers, has become widespread in recent years. Many social science and humanities departments in major Western universities have boosted their funding and productivity thanks to the implementation of new digital tools. Indeed, the area that is now widely known as the "digital humanities" has transposed the supposedly dusty labors of traditional humanistic research into a more glitzy and up-to-date endeavor by harnessing the latest computing technologies and their calculative potentials for collection and interpretation. "Big data," in particular, with its promise of novel in-depth ways of understanding the world, appears to be the new buzzword in the corporate IT world, as well as in much cutting-edge social science and humanities research. Of course, a lot of this buzz has been the result of strategic ploys to keep certain non-Science, Technology, Engineering, and Mathematics (STEM) departments alive—a calculated endeavor that nonetheless also has the potential to rescue marginalized research. Many in the social sciences and humanities are moreover earnestly keen to dig into the treasure troves of big data and computer simulation for all kinds of worthy, and not merely strategic, purposes, for instance, comprehending the Haren riot. While such eagerness is understandable and indeed productive, this chapter suggests that we should remain apprehensive of uncritical uses and discourses around these new digital tools. Indeed, as a reaction to the uncritical eagerness with which digital tools have been embraced, especially in the social sciences, analyses that question such new media usage have also emerged. Excellent critiques of the incommensurability of computing and interpretation, by Jussi Parikka (2011) and Alex Galloway (2011) for example, build on a lineage of critical theories of technologies like those of Martin Heidegger, Paul Virilio,

Jean Baudrillard, and others. These critiques are, in fact, also considered by many to be part of "the" digital humanities.

In order to draw out the problems and limitations of how the Haren riots were analyzed by the social scientists involved in Project X Haren "Two Worlds" and especially in "The Road to Haren," this chapter aims to extend such critiques by first outlining some of the curious paradoxes of the digital turn in the humanities and social sciences. So, let me start with some preliminary questions. What could the foundational split in "the" digital humanities between hopeful or eager appropriation and skeptical or critical problematization—as I illustrated above—possibly tell us about the weaknesses and problems surrounding the increasing reliance on digital tools for understanding (Dutch) society? How might we come to appreciate the way in which new media technologies, with their "vaults" of big data, currently alter research in the social sciences and humanities in general and in unexpected ways? What are the moral and political implications of this research? Do data mining and opportunities for simulation through new media allow for better forms of knowledge about the social and society, or are they profoundly antisocial and anti-truth, vis-à-vis what Martin Heidegger in "The End of Philosophy and the Task of Thinking" (1977) already identifies as new media's oppressively cybernetic and calculative logic?

I hope to demonstrate through investigating these questions, and by reinterpreting "Project X" Haren, that the use of data mining in the social sciences exemplifies the *aporia*—the central tension between fostering an ideal society and the always ideologically and culturally specific tools and conceptions that such a fostering entails—that always-already lies at the heart of the humanistic enterprise. I will do so by illustrating how the "knowledge gained" about society by way of data mining methodology is itself principally an allegory (both a derivative and a silent justification) of the technical apparatuses it uses. This is because such knowledge is not only a mere outcome of this apparatus, but also because such knowledge points toward the near-perfect obscuring of this apparatus' central politics, which I call "speed-elitism." Speed-elitism is essentially the sublimation of the ideals of social progress into the contemporary tools of acceleration. It is an ever more pervasive ideology that intensifies and supplants the Eurocentric roots of technocratic capitalism by way of the dissemination of its central discursive and technical mechanisms. These mechanisms are the fostering of the humanistic ideals of "freedom" and "emancipation," as well as the ways in which these ideals are projected or "hallucinated" into the latest technological developments.

My main conclusion is that the realm of social representation has given way to the realm of algorithmic and object-oriented *functionality*, and I argue that this slippage is possible because acceleration and the utopian hope for a better society—a hope that governments and the social sciences alike translate into their managerial duties—have always been conjoined twins in the Western philosophical tradition. Due to this fundamental entanglement, the concept and construction of truth in academic work today hinges on the tension between modern technology's general propensity for speeding-up and slowing-down. It also hinges on the tension between calculation and change (as well as "calculating change") that those academic realms that concern themselves with the humanistic enterprise are doomed to shuttle between. After all, social "change" and individual autonomy over her or his life are central tenets of the emancipatory endeavor, but are also antagonistic forces. Especially the social sciences—but also to a large extent the humanities—*inhabit* this tension by assuming that the technological and methodological possibility of objectivity and "deep" knowledge is given, while also performing the idea that true objectivity, or at least a morally or scientifically "better" state of affairs, should *parse out* all assumptions or limiting techniques. Eventually, these accelerated tensions then increasingly generate "more true" as well as more questionable renditions of the social and of "reality" through, for instance, object-oriented computer programming and algorithms that generate aesthetically pleasing graphs and visualizations. The etymology of "algorithm," which shows the word as originating from a contraction of the name of the Arab mathematician Al-Kwarizmi and the Greek αριθμος (number), indeed already reveals the kinship of data processing techniques to arithmetic and calculation with their subsequent connotations of objectivity, purity, and elegant factuality (Klein 1966, 149). This means that the "knowledge gained" from data mining and simulation should first and foremost be understood as an aesthetic procedure, the primary political function of this procedure being to *mask* the complicity of computing functionality in technologically stratifying society.

On top of this, I propose that the obsession with "analytical depth" using new media today marks the general displacement and simulation of the ideals of humanist and liberal representation, due to the ongoing acceleration of the political by new media technologies. In other words, the social sciences are here implicated in an increasingly displaced and potentially deluded ideal of social change and scientific progress toward the utopia of complete knowledge and ultimately a questionable ideal of moral and political community or society.

This accelerated displacement therefore resides at the heart of contemporary forms of hope but also of despair under the neoliberal globalization of information and communication technologies and their mechanisms of inclusion and exclusion. In turn, national governments partake in this illusion of the possibility of totally managing and understanding populations and social problems, leading to a downward spiral where "increasing control drives things out of control." What this means is that the turn toward big data and digital tools *compromises* research in the social sciences in two consecutive ways, of which the latter way constitutes an intensification and displacement of the former. First, research is compromised—as always—by the political-economic-cultural conditions and the institutional politics in the Netherlands in which such research is necessarily embedded. Since the possibility of scientific and empirical research has taken as its necessary starting point the general knowability of the world, such politics has by and large rested on a Eurocentric and positivistic epistemological framework for which media technologies provide the materialization of the communicative ideal. Second, the form of today's research is compromised by the aesthetics of acceleration inherent in new media tools and technologies. Such inherent qualities are, for instance, their heavy reliance on algorithms and the connotations of elegant truth of algorithmic mathematics. Put differently, data today are compromised not only through media rhetoric and ideology, but also through the *sedimentation* and transformation of that rhetoric into the interpretative uses of algorithmic media. The inherently speed-elitist qualities of these tools are, in effect, an intrinsic aspect of the aggravation of contemporary inequalities and the ways in which the social sciences play a part in dissimulating the complicity of their tools in this aggravation.

The "mining" metaphor in data mining also assumes a kind of archaeological effort, digging into the "depth" of texts, which Jacques Derrida famously unsettles in *Archive Fever*. Derrida here notes that "the technical structure of the archiving archive also determines the structure of the archivable content even in its very coming into existence and in its relationship to the future," and that "the archivization produces as much as it records the event" (1998, 17). At issue is therefore not simply *that* new media archive stuff, but that this media archive pretends to be a neutral tool or storage place—discreet from human subjectivity and interpretation or even overarching sociopolitical relations—in which the presented data supposedly "speaks for itself." But the archive and indeed all media, in fact, makes possible what Derrida terms a "commencement" or a narrative of origin and progress (as well as the general obsession with classification and recording), and a "commandment" through which it seeks to validate and in turn institutionalize law and authority, also by way of hiding its own logic and exorcizing what resists archivization (1998, 1). This supposition of depth or "excavation" by way of data mining, both in the technological collection and analysis of data, therefore harbors a specific phenomenological understanding of the term "data," which Alex Galloway flags in "Are Some Things Unrepresentable?," entailing the conception (or misconception) of data as raw facts or "givens" (2011, 87). Galloway thus usefully proposes that thinking of data as its synonym "information" suggests that there is always a "form" or an aesthetic aspect at work in the generation of data (2011, 88).

Keeping this close relation between the aesthetic aspect of in-formation and the formation of society in mind, this chapter calls attention to the ways speed-elitism currently aids but also hampers traditional scientific research and complicates traditional methodology. The latter complication should be taken as the more urgent object of analysis of the social sciences today. It also proposes that Heidegger's work, as well as Baudrillard's and Virilio's, indeed took this methodological complication to task by thematizing as well as exemplifying it. Speed-elitism, which this chapter argues constitutes the ideological nexus of this complication, needs to be understood as the new near-totalizing and highly questionable economic and technological *condition of possibility* for much academic research and theory today. This chapter uses speed-elitism, then, as a shorthand for those techniques that foster the reproduction of dominant discourses and technologies of acceleration, which often express themselves in a worship of technological progress, connectivity, heightened mobility, and border crossing. The borders crossed are, for instance, the one between computing and the humanities, but also those between supposedly preestablished and discreet concepts and semantic items like "youths" versus "adults," or "digital natives" versus "the rest of the grown-up population." A central objective behind such border crossings lies in the seemingly benevolent bridging of all kinds of gaps through the implementation of tools and techniques of communication in order to open up all segments of society to increasing digital surveillance, oppression, control, and commercialization. At issue here is that such crossings made by academics and government officials are understood to be driven by a moral imperative, such that any critique of these objectives or imperatives—e.g. against the use of "big data" or digital tools for the "betterment" of society—initially appears as an immoral or regressive injunction. Nonetheless, again, such critiques are possible due to the fundamentally aporetic nature of the humanistic enterprise, which sought to universalize a particularly Eurocentric idea of the ideal democratic, representative, enlightened, and transparent society.

The mediated suppression of social despair and disintegration

The origin of the productive use of digital tools in the social sciences can to a large degree be located in the development of the cybernetic feedback model set up by Claude Shannon and Warren Weaver's famous attempts at "noise control" for electronic signals transmission in *The Mathematical Theory of Communication* (1963), which became a major inspiration for American communications departments. Shannon and Weaver's endeavor was part of the attempt to achieve predictability in engineering, which, as Axel Bruns notes, is also the prerogative of contemporary algorithmic machines (2014, n.p.). This resulted in the problematic equation of finding solutions for mechanical disorganization with ways of eliminating noise by technological means—in other words, to ensure that media communicate with as little inhibition as possible, thus guaranteeing mediated transparency, coherence, and truth. Computing today, as an extension of this logic of supposed transparency, likewise hides its internal operations by presenting functionality in the form of believable simulations of, for instance, "society" or "community." What we see emerge therefore in the social sciences is a new kind of politics that is intimately intertwined with the largely invisible aesthetics of acceleration and simulation of these data systems. It thus becomes vital that we better grasp how the cybernetic attempt at purging "noise" and the resultant simulation of sociality is directly related to the violence of social exclusion and fragmentation under speed-elitism. This central concern with either eliminating or revealing "noise" can in turn, I suggest, be connected to the fundamentally progressive *spirit* of the social sciences and the humanities, which has been usurped in the general push for acceleration. I understand spirit here as *irreducible to* yet also *constitutive of* sociality, rationality, and indeed of technological calculation and communicative transportation. This recuperation of the spirit of the humanistic spirit in social and human research is hence essential vis-à-vis the complicities that the digital humanities and social sciences currently inhabit yet dissimulate, and can according to Parikka be understood as a re-appreciation of "noise," or rather, that which is irreducible to yet constitutive of communication as such (2011, 273).

This cybernetic purging of noise, which Parikka usefully flags—posited as a technocratic solution to the "problem" of media communication and representation that the social sciences too uncritically have adopted—affects the very possibility of political representation and community in contemporary, supposedly democratic societies (like the Netherlands) in negative and unexpected ways. Indeed, this chapter proposes that due to this purging of noise, governments are becoming increasingly blind to the negative fallout of contemporary technocracy. It concurs with Bruns' claim that "algorithms fold into one the analysis of data and the production of order" (2014, n.p.) but notes that *disorder too* is an unintentional by-product of these tools. This means that the "Project X" Haren research, despite—or perhaps *because* of— all its good intentions and thorough investigations to aid in understanding the riots and providing recommendations, also participates in the speed-elitist drive to keep the *actual* cause of the riots concealed. It does so by failing to address the more fundamental role of new media ideology and technology in Dutch society, beyond mere instrumentalist concerns with the virality and speed of social media message dissemination ("The Road to Haren," 11, 33, 74, and especially 118–24).

Recognizing the fundamentally altered relationship between "reality" and representation in our era of technological acceleration, which emerges in Heidegger's work as the moment of the work's enunciation as well as its central concern, will help us better grasp this fundamental role of the media. In "The Origin of the Work of Art," Heidegger proceeds by asking after the essence of the work of art (a medium that does not hide its aesthetic dimension) by skillfully working through a number of productive confusions (2002, 4–19). These confusions concern the status of form and content (or matter), usefulness and uselessness, appearance and essence, depth and surface, and outside and inside. Showing that our understandings or experiences of the artwork cannot be disentangled from a certain limiting artificiality or aesthetic function, Heidegger suggests that thinking itself—as much as it is also a craft—must rely on such limitations as well. This means that any "truth" is always-already "artificial," and that any claim to objective reality amounts to a representation, which in one sense brings the object closer but in another sense makes it withdraw or disappear. Heidegger chides Western thought for assuming or pretending it can achieve a fully objective representation and a total communicative transparency in its scientific and philosophical endeavors. He especially proposes via an etymological approach typical of his work, that the slippage or mistranslation from the more revealing, "original" Greek terminology around being and object-hood (ουσία and συμβεβηκος) to the Latin terms *substantia* and *accidens* has been the origin of what he calls the "rootlessness of the Western tradition" (2002, 6).

At this point, I would like to suggest that the dual or ambiguous status of representation as "accurate" yet "removed" from its object—which Heidegger neatly uncovers in the "The Origin of the Work of Art"—precisely returns with a vengeance under speed-elitism, and that this fundamentally uproots the possibility for a representative politics. In this sense, we can conjecture that the young people who congregated in Haren (and many other economically marginalized Dutch people too) no longer feel politically represented; their only "connection" to a semblance of "society" is provided by the very technologies that equally obscure their concerns and desperation. The fact that the "Two Worlds" report suggests that there is a generational gap between youths and older people only serves to exacerbate this, as it leads to an argument in favor of connecting the rest of the older population to social media as well (2013, 21). Data mining in particular can be understood as the paradoxical upshot of the harnessing of change and risk through such "social" media—"social" being a term that arguably itself dissimulates the disintegration of the social—for neoliberal capital. My position on this, besides relying on Heidegger's critique of communicative transparency, is also inspired by the insights of Baudrillard and Ulrich Beck on simulation and risk society. Beck in *World at Risk* (2009) and Baudrillard in "For a Critique of the Political Economy of the Sign" (2001) both claim in their own divergent ways that contemporary capitalism creates and in turn expropriates sites of tension, difference, and risk. In *World at Risk*, Beck suggests that the general covering up or dramatization of risk results in a politics of anticipation, exemplified by apocalyptic narratives and dubious scientific models that are themselves thoroughly implicated in the ongoing financialization and militarization of democratic societies and of the globe. While Beck proposes this analysis in relation to ecological narratives and responses, I suggest that his point about scientific modeling is equally applicable to any perceived threat that apparently requires a form of preemptive policing, especially through new media technologies. Baudrillard, partly in line with Beck, similarly argues in "For a Critique of the Political Economy of the Sign" that, under our contemporary form of capitalism, the symbolic realm and the capitalistic reliance on information flows have collapsed into one another. The resulting simulation of truth relies on the representational fallacy of an empirical reality or a mode of thought that resides outside the capitalist logic of reproduction through social destruction and fragmentation.

Capitalism, or the main economic logic driving current "democracies" like the Netherlands, today seizes the ambiguity of *scientific* representation as such by incessantly calling upon and usurping the hope for a more meaningful cohabitation to which the seriously engaged social sciences and digital humanities—including, no doubt, the commendable Dutch media research team—respond. This acceleration of scientific representation is possible because the impossible scientific utopia of pure objectivity and of the unmediated representation of reality is enacted through the fantasy of technological superiority that stimulates capitalism. It is here that the tension between calculation and change, in the very desire to technologically predict and classify events and groups, leads the digital humanities into an immediate kind of *aporia* or internal division that is typical of the humanistic tradition in which Heidegger also participates; it wants to foster positive social change, but this very endeavor is produced in response to and as an offshoot of speed-elitism. In Heidegger's work, this emerges as an appearance of mere philosophical description and progressive questioning that is actually smartly crafted on the supposed authenticity (or "transparent truth") of Greek and Germanic conceptions. Nevertheless, this chapter proposes, in contrast to Beck and Heidegger, that such risk management engenders an increasingly obscure quality or aspect of contemporary society—of which the "Project X" riots can in fact be read as a symptom—so that such risk management can never harness social change over an infinite amount of time. It is for this reason that Heidegger's "The Origin" opens up to its own deconstruction. This means that the representations, or rather, the seemingly neutral *presentations* of data and logical reasoning in the "Project X" Haren report on the role of the media do not inform us about the social or the real, but function as a smokescreen in order to dissimulate the contemporary disintegration of the social and the real due to high-tech neoliberalism. "The Road to Haren" contains a plethora of charming graphs and many "cauliflower-like" drawings of social media traffic typical of the imagery generally generated by networked media (2013, 26). But these drawings, as Galloway reminds us in "Are Some Things Unrepresentable?," are quite simply stylized versions of the Internet's own underlying network architecture (Galloway 2011, 87).

What we can infer from this, is that our entire political economy is increasingly built on an accelerated *modeling* of the spheres of language, culture, politics, and the economy; in fact, these spheres have imploded into one another by virtue of the digital media, through which all forms of communication become financial transactions. This new semiotic-economic sphere today crucially relies on the reproduction of the ideals of communicability to which the social sciences and the digital humanities predominantly—though never entirely, because they can always also question such grounds—subscribe. Any general nostalgia for the origins of this social reality and attempts to "unearth" it are then the main mechanisms for the fragmentation and individualization of persons in this economy, also in the Netherlands. This is because both the "accuracy" and the "removedness" from the object of nostalgia is accelerated and intensified today; and Heidegger's work indeed exhibits such a hint of nostalgia for a more authentic Germanic or Greek basis for thinking and ethics, even if it is done in a self-aware fashion. The "Two Worlds" report seems to be relieved that there is not some larger close-knit community of young people behind the Haren riot (2012, 14). The fact that the partygoers were *not* known to each other should have made the writers think about how a pervasive individualization, as a worrisome form of social fragmentation, appears to be at play here.

This "invitation" to use digital media for progressive analysis is therefore paradoxically an outflow of the duty of the digital humanities and social sciences to move society forward, and the culmination—in the sense of both *telos* and termination—of this humanistic duty ascribed to the contemporary tools of acceleration. Social sciences and humanities studies that mobilize digital or data mining tools are then an acceleration of the humanities insofar as they intensify its ideals, but also displace them; in other words, the ideal of total representation and visibility emerges as its own antithesis. The latter thus eventually produces a general incomprehensibility covered up by "recommendations" consisting of educating the police and parents about social media utilities, like privacy settings, and the government monitoring (and even intervening in) social media usage ever more intensively ("The Road to Haren," 119 and 123; "Two Worlds," 31). Another recommendation put forward is an ever-stricter regulation of alcohol sales and consumption, claiming that alcohol was a "vital factor" in the riot ("Two Worlds," 32). We should note here likewise that fostering (superficial) *change* (with an eye to maintaining the basic economic status quo) is one of the key aims of the current neoliberal paradigm, but also of progressive intellectual movements that increasingly organize themselves through the media, like those that were engaged for "Project X" Haren. Social science methodology around social media has for many years now emphasized the facilitation of collection and collectivity that these media provide for—whether this facilitation entails the creation of a more sociable community, or entails the creation of a coherent and understandable reality or society through data mining tools. It is therefore no surprise that mass and social media research constituted such a major aspect of the "Project X" Haren investigation, even though one could likewise hold that transportation research should have been a major aspect because most rioters took public transport to the small Dutch city.

In light of this, it might be revealing to trace back where, how, and in what forms the reliance on data gathering through various modern media have informed or run parallel to the development and goals of the digital humanities and social sciences—indeed, when questions of humanity and sociality became scientific questions as such. I lack the space to address this tracing in its historical totality here, but want to indicate for now that the above research assumption maintains that the social scientific and the digital humanities' involvement with new media can, or will, facilitate a "changing society for the better." Paradoxically, also its inverse, namely a straightforward rejection of these media—one need only to think of the recent arguments made by pundits like Evgeny Morozov in *The Net Delusion* (2011)—professes to the same logic, because it relies on a fantasy of autonomous agent-driven change for social betterment as well. Here too, the foundational split returns in the guise of a supposed choice for or against social media use.

Let me illustrate this with a quick example, after which this chapter will move on to present a brief alternative reading of the "Project X" Haren riots. The always possible confusion between form and content, or "superficial" aesthetics and "deep" essence that Heidegger uncovers in "The Origin," gives rise to all kinds of interesting politicized arguments by digital humanities scholars. One such fascinating argument, which constitutes an exemplarily optimistic interpretation of computing, emerges in Steve Stagg's "How Feminist Programming Has Already Happened: Exploring how feminist ideals are represented in existing languages." This chapter is sharing this brief piece here not to poke fun at the suggestion that coding and algorithms can be "feminist" (why not, after all, if feminism is itself a profoundly slippery and unbounded territory), but in order to highlight how its confusion makes possible the contemporary production of liberal-humanistic arguments, and their complicity in functional managerialism, in general. In short, Stagg argues that the popular programming language Python demonstrates a "feminist" logic because it works in a "non-binary" and "non-rationalistic" way (Stagg 2004, n.p.). This is according to him due to the fact that first, the binding choices in Python are only decided at runtime and not a compiling time (which is the usual way in which most object-oriented coding is executed because it saves calculation time). Secondly, Stagg argues that this "non-rationalistic" feminist logic emerges through the connotations of some of the commands and operators that Python uses, thus reading this programming language in an enchantingly poetic way. If one takes Stagg's elegant argument at face value though, it appears to make a curious slip. Computer code is namely by its very nature rationalistic since it always follows a yes/no or 0/1 calculative automation; object-oriented computing has from its inception taken the logic as set out by a mathematical binary system first discussed by Gottfried Leibniz and implemented via software coding by John von Neumann (Heim 1993, 93). Such a system by definition leaves no room at all for fuzzy stuff, misinterpretations, or gray areas. Object-oriented programming languages like Python sprang from a rational worldview; in order to function they have to assume that the world of its computational objects is the total world. This is, of course, inherent in the very idea of cybernetics, the fundamental purpose of which, as I discussed earlier, was to banish noise or slippages.

One might nonetheless counter that Stagg's piece is not meant to be factual, but should be read metaphorically. Indeed, one could always read any coding language as a metaphor for something or even as a poem (an interesting precursor could be what is called ASCII art); reading indeed always involves some kind of displacement. But this poetic reading would still not constitute that piece of code's primarily *automated* politics, which operates solely on the functional or *executable* level. On the functional level of code, there is no "interpretation" by any subject reading a text; there is only one executable possibility, whereas our interpretation of a text differs with each and every reading. In other words, Stagg and those hopeful feminists who finally found a "feminist" programming language confuse the aesthetics of Python with its politics—a confusion that is also facilitated by the invisible and inaudible slippage between "language" (as literary text) and "language" (as computer code). Programming language is therefore also purposely invisible to the mere user because its very definition is automation, so that any coding malfunctions can only ever emerge as bad programming. In other words, coding and algorithmic functions exemplify the fundamentally stealthy ways in which contemporary technological power operates in general under speed-elitism, in which representation has become the inverse or *negation* of "automated" reality. It is here that Stagg's elegant claim becomes unwittingly malignant, because it serves in the end to obscure the profound complicity of computing technologies with the violence of speed-elitism. The perception of this complicity nonetheless cannot be completely stamped out from our understanding because this complicity *has* an identifiable founding moment which can be etymologically and historically traced back.

The rioters as technocratic "war machines"

Dwelling on the etymology of "data" and its kinship to that of the gift or dowry (Klein 1966, 468), as well as to "date" helps to highlight a perhaps uncanny quality of computer data that Stagg's misreading, despite itself, gives rise to. This etymology reveals, in particular, the quality of displacement—derivation or allegory—at work in computer data mining, because it points to something being "taken away" from its proper time and place. What is more, its etymology reveals that this displacement harbors an excess (a gift) that continuously *haunts* data mining methodology as well as the contemporary economic and scientific endeavor in general, despite all well-meaning attempts to stamp it out. Baudrillard likewise proposes in "The Theorem of the Accursed Share" that the very quest to technologically eliminate unpredictability and negativity precisely results in their resurrection, as such negativity and unpredictability are endemic to any attempt at total systemization (1993, 121). Extending this claim, I argue that this excess currently reappears in the form of a sort of "accursed share" that the social sciences of the hopeful and the critical perhaps seek to purge from (Dutch) society, namely an *interpretative violence turned mechanical* that is today intimately entwined with modern technology.

With the consumption of political differences and controversy in the media that is symptomatic of speed-elitism in mind, I will now turn to an alternative reading of the "Project X" riots. Obviously, it would be a mistake to assign any kind of attempt at political organization to the rioters actions; any sort of sophisticated political analysis or statement indeed seems radically absent from the rioters' mass and social media sound bites ("The Road to Haren," 27–28). Also, in terms of their marginalization, the rioters were not disenfranchised workers or excluded poor migrants, but highly mobile and communicative gangs, tweeting, and texting their plans and movements via Blackberry, Facebook, and iPhone. As such, they represent political non-representation in combination with technological privilege. We may conclude then that if these riots represent anything, it is the immorality of consumer capitalism and the ways it requires constant technological movement, violence, and transgression. This is not to say that social media did not play some kind of decisive role in the riots, but that to assign to these media the mere role of "instrument" misses a much more important aspect of how the riots might connect to the general restructuring of society. One could claim therefore that the riots were themselves an aspect of what Virilio would in rather militaristic terms call a situation of "total mobilization" under current technocratic conditions. Virilio's *Speed and Politics* allows us to trace an important part of the historical backdrop of such riots to bourgeois industrialization as well as German fascism. This chapter reads Virilio here as to suggest an uncanny parallel between the riots and Joseph Goebbels' successful attempt to move the masses by way of images, not texts, and instill in them a thirst for "plundering for plundering's sake" (Virilio 1977, 5). Virilio illustrates that German fascism of the 1930s indeed promised personal means of transport to the masses by way of the Volkswagen of the *Deutsche Arbeitsfront*, a technology of acceleration and movement that would keep the people ready to be mobilized at any time. Under industrialization, the emerging economic tactic of intensive penetration, or what he in *Pure War* calls "endo-colonization" (Virilio and Lotringner 2008, 95), parallels a militaristic attempt, through altering logistics and circulation, to foster change while eliminating chance, as well as rendering the populace transparent. In many ways, the mass uprising paradoxically started to function as a "Removal of the masses . . . a permanent exploitation of the masses' aptitude for movement as a bourgeois social solution" (Virilio 1977, 28).

Taking this premise from Virilio, I argue that, as progressively more populations become the objects or targets of the speed-elitist economic order, the Haren rioters inhabited this logic by themselves turning into unguided projectiles and loose cannons, targeting and transgressing a variety of physical borders throughout the city of Haren and causing their own version of collateral damage in an embodiment of what Virilio in *Speed and Politics* calls the global logic of "displacement without destination" (Virilio 1977, 40). The Haren rioting can then be read as the accident of acceleration exemplified on a small scale. To comprehend the riots as a mere local problem caused by a generational gap ("Two Worlds," 24) and by alcohol consumption (ibid., 26 and 32) ignores that this accidental violence has become the global world order's essence in a telling reversal of the Aristotelian distinction between the accidental and the essential that Heidegger also discusses in "The Origin." As Baudrillard describes it in

"The Implosion of Meaning in the Media," it is the ubiquitous circulation of imagery in the media that has essence (or reality) and accident (or representation) implode into the media and in turn has the social implode into the masses (Baudrillard 1994, 80), so that the masses start to simply *display* the logic of a global order in which destruction has simply become the flip side of innovation. This chapter concurs with Baudrillard that if this riot activity appears irrational, then this is precisely because it mirrors the irrationality of that very order. The new and mass media have also an intrinsic relation to one another, because the rioters transformed themselves into a spectacle primarily *for* the media— and the Dutch news media indeed had a field day with the riots ("The Road to Haren," 56)—because, even if they are that order's disposable objects, one of their goals was simply *to be registered* or seen at all. Not surprisingly then, their "empowerment" through these media and transportation tools is caused by and was immediately followed by their very surveillance, incarceration, and demonization at the hands of the police and the Dutch state. Such demonization, in turn, once more serves to obscure the fact that the rioters simply mirror the technocratic state as well as global speed-elitism. As Virilio puts it somewhat opaquely in *Speed and Politics*: "These militant fanatics are only the logistical agents of terror, members of the 'police'" (Virilio 1977, 20) since the "militarization of society makes every citizen a war machine" (Virilio 1977, 90) and machines, like soldiers, can be decommissioned at any time.

Thus, the Haren rioters exemplify the logic of speed-elitism by partaking in a near-pornographic mediated manifestation, by way of which speed-elitism "makes its enemies its best customers" (Virilio 1977, 65) through the consumption and dissemination of that spectacle as some kind of moral degeneration of youth today, as well as the mobilization of the Haren riot's imagery in an utterly superficial and, at times, dangerously moralistic, quasi-political *spiel* in mass media and government debate. Moreover, as consumers of that spectacle on our television and computer screens—the riots were, as I mentioned, extensively covered in the mass media and on YouTube—we in turn implicate ourselves in the violence of speed through the technological consumption of destruction. Visual media after all exemplify how "the frontal view pulls the trigger" (ibid., 124). This obsession with the spectacular image depleted of its radical content found its culmination in the highly aestheticized imagery that the "The Road to Haren" report generated of the rioters' Twitter feeds (Boeschoten 2012). This imagery tells us nothing about the dire state of democracy and community in the Netherlands, and everything about the supposedly sublime beauty of the new media themselves. It is telling here, also, that the "Project X" social media meme takes its cue from a movie by the same name, since "reality" here indeed increasingly gets *modeled* on the logic of the media (rather than the other way around under the older representative regime, in which the media are supposed to represent reality). "The Road to Haren" report in fact chides the movie content for letting the protagonists get off too lightly (2013, 10) while providing no interpretation whatsoever about why a large proportion of young Dutch moviegoers might be fascinated by the movie and its depiction of the authorities as dubious entities (2013, 9). "Blaming" the movie for falsely presenting a morally twisted plot therefore allows the illusion to persist that actual Dutch society is morally organized. The report also fails to think through the relationship between the immorality of technocratic capitalism and the ways in which such immorality is condensed into the movie's characters, and also in the fact that the social media graphs and drawings appear as utterly devoid of morality. Baudrillard mentions in *Simulacra and Simulation* that it is "the social itself that . . . is [increasingly] organized along the lines of a disaster-movie script" (1994, 40); and while *Project X* the movie is supposed to be a comedy, it nonetheless tragically mirrors the disaster that is technocratic society.

Fatalities: The ghostly return of the humanist spirit

In light of this reinterpretation of "Project X" Haren, how could the social sciences and the digital humanities move away from their complicity in speed-elitism? Indeed, what kind of understanding might finally help us divert the negative fallout and social accidents of economic acceleration? It is useful at this point to return to the works of Heidegger, which exemplify the humanist *aporia* so pivotally. The interpretation of the media as progressively distancing or obscuring potential elements of experience that this chapter has mounted also echoes Heidegger's reflections on the vicissitudes of calculation for thought and experience in "The End of Philosophy and the Task of Thinking" as well as in "The Question Concerning Technology." In the latter, Heidegger of course suggests that modern technologies increasingly conceal the never-neutral ways in which what is presented is fundamentally revealed through the never-neutral technological form. Heidegger asserts that contemporary technology marks the completion or death of philosophy in its logical culmination, the techno-sciences, of which the digital humanities likewise take part, as we have seen above. In Heidegger's view, every conceptualization will end up as a mere calculated digit in the new cybernetic space of flows. Philosophy can become that culmination because it has itself always assumed the ideal of transparent communication through the belief that its concepts and models are transcendental truths. This completion of philosophy, according to Heidegger, hence means that "Cybernetics transforms language into an exchange of news, . . . scientific truth is equated with efficiency, [. . . and] the operational and model-based character of representational-calculative thinking becomes dominant" (1977, 434). In "What Calls for Thinking," Heidegger cautions that this kind of thinking, whether it takes the form of rationalist philosophy or social scientific empiricism, is in fact not thinking at all, but merely the unthinking performance of a predefined path of interpretation that has become ignorant of its grounding gestures that only allow it to "reveal" in ways reducible to the cybernetic logic. So, in order for digital media tools to appear as transparent or noise-free, so that the social sciences can "harness" them for their research, their fundamental aspects—namely the ways in which they are implicated in a representational regime intertwined with the modern economic and social organization, hierarchization, and classification of all of society's creatures— need indeed to be suppressed or set aside as secondary. This indictment reveals the problem behind Stagg's hopeful feminist renditions and the "Project X" reports' recommendations, which both still blindly profess to the idea that new and social media can be "used for the better." Alex Galloway also usefully argues that under the contemporary regime of incessant control and calculation any "visualization is first and foremost a visualization of the [media's] conversion rules themselves" (2011, 88). This chapter agrees with Galloway that such visualizations, like those provided by sophisticated data mining software, indeed lead to a "form of blindness" toward the technical apparatus as well as to the current mode of economic production (2011, 95).

However, the problematic that Galloway uncovers, is, if we follow Heidegger's line of thinking in "The Origin," similarly applicable to other representations and interpretations of data that are nonvisual; in fact, any claim to "deep reading" may be subject to such a contention—even those made by Baudrillard, Parikka, and Galloway themselves. They are, after all, analyses that seek to carry forward the liberal utopian hope for a more just social world, just like this chapter ultimately aspires to do. The paradox of the situation is, hence, that the aggravation of global violence and disenfranchisement today is an unfortunate effect of—not in spite of—all the well-meaning academic engagements with data mining tools and other similar social science efforts. And yet, we *cannot help but enact* our responsibility today *through this very complicity*. Baudrillard in *In the Shadow of the Silent Majorities* qualifies this contemporary paradoxical situation therefore as "fatal" not only because the digital humanities engage in the creation of fatalities by way of their "fatal speed," but need themselves to (or have already) *become* the fatalities of their own analyses (2007, 74). Despite their relative ubiquity then, the digital humanities and social sciences, mirroring the subsequent worsening of the crises of capitalism, show themselves likewise to be "fatally wounded" in their simulatory and data mining efforts. It might be revealing at this late stage in the chapter to delve into etymology one final time. The English "speed" has its origins in the Germanic *spowan*, which means "to prosper" or "to succeed" (Klein 1966, 698). This, in turn, has its roots in the Latin *sperare* or "to hope." The Western philosophical tradition indeed, as this chapter has illustrated, appears to find in the tools of speed a prime reason for hope. Interestingly, though, the Dutch saying *haastige spoed is zelden goed* combines two versions of speed, namely "haste" and "speed." While this on the surface seems to be a pleonasm, the Germanic root of *haast* means rather "with force" or "zealous," as well as "almost there" in its adverb form. This interestingly relates to how Heidegger, as John Llewelyn suggests in "Announcing the Other," understands the word *Gegenwart* as a "waiting against" or as having an anticipatory quality in *Being and Time* (2004, 47). *Haastige spoed* can therefore be read as a "hurried hope that seeks to force fate," a fate that connects the tools of acceleration back to the spirit of the humanities and social sciences.

So where does this ultimate confusion that lies hidden in Germanic languages (of which Dutch language and culture also derives) which Heidegger has propelled, or rather was being propelled to execute, ultimately leave us? If we follow Derrida's claim in *Archive Fever* that the archive exemplifies our fear of death—that is, it is symptomatic of the desire for some semblance of everlasting, universal authority—and as much as the death drive always seeks to destroy what Baudrillard terms the "accursed share," there must inevitably be a lot of destruction and repression going on in Dutch and Western European society. It is in this sense that data mining methodology in the humanities is an allegory of the tools it uses; this use maintains the fantasy of a total truth as well as the overall destruction of truth and the social, *and this can be shown*: this new political logic is becoming more and more pervasive today, and we as socially engaged academics hastily need to formulate an adequate response to this state of affairs.

Even so, we could conversely claim that the assessment of social fragmentation and the destruction of thought by critics like Heidegger and Baudrillard inhabits a nostalgia for an "original" collectivity and understanding, as well as an access to reality via more "direct" human experience that never was—a nostalgia that is therefore just as much an effect of new media's sped-up aesthetics. Similarly, while Galloway and Parikka rightly critique the role of simulation in this new control regime, they also perform their academic duty to represent "the givens" (Galloway 2011, 87) more accurately. It is therefore finally the metaphor of *displacement,* not only in Heidegger's work, but in *this* chapter that allows for such normative claims to be made; *as if* a corruption exceedingly infests and accelerates a more original, true, or authentic situation. The concept of speed-elitism functions as the primary metaphor or displacement, rendering the world both "closer" and "more removed." So too, in this chapter, the *spirit* of the quest for truth remains forever irreducible to its formation. And so, the spirit survives, together with the unresolved ghosts of the riots, which the "Project X" Haren researchers, despite their commendable efforts, tried to lay to rest.

References

Baudrillard, Jean. 1993. *The Transparency of Evil. Essays on Extreme Phenomena.* Trans. James Benedict. London: Verso.

Baudrillard, Jean. 1994. *Simulacra and Simulation.* Trans. Sheila Faria Glaser.
Ann Arbor: University of Michigan Press.

Baudrillard, Jean. 2001. "For a Critique of the Political Economy of the Sign." In Mark Poster, ed. *Jean Baudrillard, Selected writings.* Stanford: Stanford University Press, 60–100.

Baudrillard, Jean. 2007. *In the Shadow of the Silent Majorities.* Trans. Paul Foss.
Los Angeles: Semiotext(e).

Beck, Ulrich. 2009. *World at Risk.* Trans. Ciaran Cronin. Cambridge, UK: Polity Press.

Boeschoten, Thomas. 2012. "#projectx Haren op Twitter: explosie van tweets." Accessed March 8, 2014. http://www.youtube.com/watch?v=3lOIDI2ntYA.

Bruns, Axel. 2014. "Entering the Age of the Generative Algorithm." Accessed June 20, 2014. http://snurb.info/node/1890.

Commissie "Project X" Haren. 2013. "Twee werelden: hoofdrapport commissie 'Project X' Haren." Accessed December 10, 2013. http://www.rijksoverheid.nl/ documenten-en-publicaties/rapporten/2013/03/08/twee-werelden-hoofdrapport- commissie-project-x-haren.html.

Derrida, Jacques. 1997. *Archive Fever: A Freudian Impression.* Chicago: University of Chicago Press.

Galloway, Alex. 2011. "Are Some Things Unrepresentable?" *Theory, Culture & Society* 28(7/8): 85–102.

Heidegger, Martin. 1977. "The End of Philosophy and the Task of Thinking." In David Farrell Krell, ed. *Basic Writings: from Being and Time 1927 to The Task of Thinking 1964.* New York: Harper & Row, 427–49.

Heidegger, Martin. 1977. "The Question Concerning Technology." *Basic Writings: from Being and Time 1927 to The Task of Thinking 1964.* Trans. David Farrell Krell. New York: Harper & Row, 307–42.

Heidegger, Martin. 1977. "What Calls for Thinking." *Basic Writings: from Being and Time 1927 to The Task of Thinking 1964.* Trans. David Farrell Krell. New York: Harper & Row, 365–92.

Heidegger, Martin. 2002. "The Origin of the Work of Art." *Off the Beaten Track.* Cambridge, UK: Cambridge University Press, 1–56.

Heim, Michael. 1993. *The Metaphysics of Virtual Reality.* Oxford: Oxford University Press.

Independent, The. 2012. "Teen's 'Facebook party' turns into riot in Netherlands." Accessed March 7, 2014. http://www.independent.co.uk/news/world/europe/teens-facebook-party-turns-into-riot-in-netherlands-8165681.html.

Klein, Ernest. 1966. *A Comprehensive Etymological Dictionary of the English Language.* Amsterdam: Elsevier.

Llewelyn, John. 2004. "Announcing the Other." *Emmanuel Levinas: The Genealogy of Ethics.* London: Routledge, 51–60.

Morozov, Evgeny. 2011. *The Net Delusion: The Dark Side of Internet Freedom.* New York: Public Affairs.

Parikka, Jussi. 2011. "Mapping Noise: Techniques and Tactics of Irregularities, Interception, and Disturbance." In Erkki Huhtamo and Jussi Parikka, eds. *Media Archaeology: Approaches, Applications, and Implications.* Berkeley, CA: University of California Press, 256–77.

Shannon, Claude and Warren Weaver. 1963. *The Mathematical Theory of Communication.* Baltimore: University of Illinois Press.

Stagg, Steve. 2013. "How Feminist Programming Has Already Happened: Exploring how feminist ideals are represented in existing languages." Accessed March 7, 2014. https://medium.com/@stestagg/how-feminist-programming-has-already-happened-9e4fb507ddb9.

van Dijk, J., T. Boeschoten, S. ten Tije, and L. van de Wijngaert. 2013. "De Weg naar Haren: De rol van jongeren, sociale media, massamedia en autoriteiten bij de mobilisatie voor Project X Haren." Accessed December 10, 2013. http://www.rijksoverheid.nl/documenten-en-publicaties/rapporten/2013/03/08/de-weg-naar-haren.html.

Virilio, Paul. 1977. *Speed and Politics: An Essay on Dromology.* Trans. Mark Polizzotti. New York: Semiotexte.

Virilio, Paul and Sylvère Lotringer. 2008. *Pure War.* Trans. Mark Polizzotti. New York: Semiotexte.

4

Look at the Man Behind the Curtain: Computational Management in "Spontaneous" Citizen Political Campaigning

David Karpf

Introduction

The rise of digital communications media has been heralded as having fundamentally transformed citizen political engagement. Any individual can now create a petition, start a hashtag, upload a YouTube video, or launch a Facebook group, potentially reaching millions and launching a successful movement for change. Whether we label it "clicktivism," "connective action," or "hashtag activism," there is a prevailing sense that digital technologies have imbued everyday citizenship with more power than ever before.

Websites like Change.org, MoveOn.org petitions, and We The People (petitions.whitehouse.gov) are particularly interesting digital-civic spaces, which allow individual citizens to create their own petitions, with the potential to "go viral" and spark global movements that pressure media and political elites. Jennifer Earl and Katrina Kimport label these digital platforms "warehouse" petition sites (Earl and Kimport 2011), evoking the image of a neutral venue where citizens can house their own petitions and stumble upon others. The warehouse imagery is part of a broader trend that celebrates the rise of organization-less organizing in the digital age (Shirky 2008; Bennett and Segerberg 2013). Petitions can be created for free. Under the right circumstances, they can cascade from a single author to millions of supporters. There are clear case examples of digital petitions influencing decision makers (Goldberg 2014; Wright 2012). Short-term affiliation networks now appear more powerful than long-term lobbying campaigns.

The "warehouse" concept emphasizes an enduser – centric view of digital politics. There is a danger, however, that viewing petition websites as "neutral platforms" obscures more than it reveals. Petition sites themselves are complex advocacy organizations, employing central staff of online organizers who meticulously craft the user experience on their platforms. *Divergent organizational logics* guide the design of the leading petition sites, influencing which petitions are created, promoted, and celebrated. Petition signatures are a type of political *data*, and the production of these signatures involves a range of *compromises*. Far from signaling the decline of intermediary political associations, distributed petition platforms offer an intensely mediated experience, driven by a hidden, analytics-focused reasoning.

This chapter opens up the black box of distributed "warehouse" petition platforms. It assesses both the inputs and outputs of the three largest distributed petition sites in the United States—Change.org, MoveOn.org petitions, and the White House's "We The People" site. Combining qualitative affordance analysis and descriptive case studies with an exploratory quantitative data set of the featured petitions at each site over a one-week period, the chapter reveals how the simple label "warehouse petition site" masks tremendous variation in the types of citizen campaigns that are promoted by each of these organizations. The comparative analysis highlights both shared and divergent features in the software, substantially challenging and extending existing theories of citizen-led, "spontaneous," or "viral" political mobilization. It also indicates the different types of citizen petitions that are highlighted by Change.org and MoveOn.org petitions, while drawing attention to the dormancy that results from the White House site's lack of highlighting or promotion. Centrally, this chapter reveals the habits and routines that these platforms encode, and the competing ways in which they influence the makeup of the citizenry and of the political sphere.

The chapter uses guiding cases, each illuminating the terrain of citizen petition campaigning, while also introducing the reader to the three large petition sites contained in this study. After offering individual observations of each site, I give a side-by-side comparison of the visual and textual cues contained on each site's homepage and petition-creation page. This serves to trace the input process at each site and reveals key similarities and differences. I then turn to the output process at each site, assessing what kinds of petitions each site features on its homepage, as well as the volatility of the "featured" sections and the signature totals at each site. By comparing both the inputs and outputs of the three petition sites, I provide evidence of substantial diversity among the large-scale websites that, to date, have been lumped together as "warehouses" and treated as neutral venues for unorganized citizen mobilization.

Change.org to the rescue: Trayvon Martin and "GOTP" campaign techniques

The tragic killing of Trayvon Martin sparked what is now one of the best-known cases of online citizen mobilization in the United States (Graeff, Stempeck, and Zuckerman 2014). The initial outrage surrounding the death of Florida teenager Trayvon Martin stemmed from the lack of general public outrage. The old media slogan, "if it bleeds, it leads" did not seem to apply in the case of this black teenager gunned down while walking home from a convenience store. His (white) killer, George Zimmerman, was immediately released without charges, but this attracted scant media coverage. After nearly two weeks of mainstream media silence, Martin's parents started a petition on Change.org, titled "Prosecute the Killer of Our Son, 17-Year-Old Trayvon Martin." The Change.org petition "went viral," attracting over two million signatures nationwide and sparking offline actions like the "million hoodie march" in New York City. In the following month and a half, Martin's story attracted national media attention, eventually leading to the local police chief's resignation and second-degree murder charges brought against Zimmerman (Graeff, Stempeck, and Zuckerman 2014).

The social movement mobilization surrounding Trayvon Martin would seem like a textbook example of what Jennifer Earl and Katrina Kimport term "social movement theory 2.0," what Clay Shirky calls "organizing without organizations," and what Lance Bennett and Alexandra Segerberg call "crowd-enabled connective action"—voiceless citizens, ignored by the media, turn to alternative, new media channels to fashion a short-term networked protest that demonstrates real power over media and political elites. Traditional interest group intermediaries like the NAACP are barely present in the narrative. Martin's parents did not turn to Jesse Jackson or Al Sharpton for help. They turned to the Web and started their own petition; millions responded.

This is rightly lauded as a success story in digital activism. There is indeed something qualitatively different about the social movement mobilization surrounding Trayvon Martin, and that difference demands new theorizing. Our theories have focused almost entirely on the end users of these petition platforms. Lost is an assessment of a deeper set of patterns, created at the intersection of organizational logics and new media/big data technological affordances. Change.org is not a passive intermediary, and Martin's parents did not stumble upon it by accident. Seemingly "spontaneous" moments such as this are influenced behind the scenes by a new class of savvy digital-organizing professionals. Change.org's role as a petition platform is far more active than our most prominent theories of digital activism would lead us to suspect. Like the fictitious Wizard of Oz, these organizing professionals facilitate fierce public spectacle while remaining hidden from view.

Trayvon's parents, Tracy Martin and Sybrina Fulton, were not the first to launch a Change.org petition on this topic. As Graeff, Stempeck, and Zuckerman (2014) make clear in their detailed assessment of this case, the petition was originally launched by Howard University alumnus Kevin Cunningham, after he saw a Reuters story about Martin's death on a listserv. Initial signatures came through listserv-based petition sharing, and were amplified by activist organizations like ColorofChange.org and Black Youth Project. Early petition activity drew the attention of Change.org staff, who evaluated the potential of this campaign and then reached out to Martin's parents and spoke with them about crafting the petition language that would eventually "go viral" through blast emails to Change.org's nearly 10 million members. Change.org staff refer to this technique as "Get Out the Petition," or GOTP—a reference to "GOTV" or Get Out the Vote mobilization that occurs in the last few days of an electoral campaign. As Graeff, Stempeck, and Zuckerman note in *First Monday* (February, 2014), "Change.org employee Timothy Newman brought the Trayvon petition to the attention of a cadre of targeted celebrities with potential for interest in the story and asked them to share the petition with their fans. Newman's activity elicited supportive tweets from celebrities such as Talib Kweli, Wyclef Jean, Spike Lee, Mia Farrow, and Chad Ochocinco, creating a 900 percent spike in social media traffic to the petition between March 12 and March 15, suggesting that targeted lobbying of celebrities led to increased online action in the form of petition signing."

Change.org is a for-profit organization, a "benefit corporation" (or "b-corp"). B-corps are a recent development in the American business landscape. According to Rick Cohen, they "incorporate public purposes such as comprehensive and transparent social and environmental performance standards into their corporate charters" (Cohen 2010). Such organizations are distinct from traditional non-profits or nongovernmental organizations (NGOs); they seek to turn a profit and continually grow. But they include provisions in their corporate charters to indicate that investors should not expect pure profit-maximizing behavior. Change.org seeks to maximize social change, rather than investor dividends. Nonetheless, this b-corp designation carries with it an underlying set of internal business logics: to succeed, Change.org staff must facilitate ongoing growth. Some issues have more list growth potential than others. Change.org has constructed a sophisticated system for identifying and promoting the "growthiest" issues.

The early Trayvon Martin petition was flagged through a backend "dashboard" that staff use to monitor petition activity. Early spikes attracted staff attention, and then staff meticulously tested and refined the messaging to increase the petition's broad appeal and probability of success. All of these practices have a heavy analytics component, similar to the "computational management" practices that Kreiss (2012) observed in the 2008 Obama campaign. Change.org and its peer organizations treat this petition activity as a form of member sentiment, using their petition platforms as "analytics engines" for identifying potential issue campaigns that can build their membership base, fill their coffers, and expand their political influence. The result of all this computational work is a refined petition that can attract additional signatures (thus adding to Change.org's revenue base) and become an object of mainstream media attention (improving Change.org's brand recognition in the process).

As we will see below, the for-profit business logic of Change.org leads it to highlight different petitions than the nonprofit logic of MoveOn.org. Both organizations rely on similar petition systems, but they promote different types of campaigns, which in turn leverage different types of outcomes. The Trayvon Martin victory is evidence of how digital-technological affordances can be leveraged in novel ways, but it is hardly a case of spontaneous citizen mobilization.

MoveOn.org effect 2, electric boogaloo

If the Trayvon Martin mobilization is noteworthy for the hidden role that organizations play in citizen-generated petition campaigns, then this next example is noteworthy for the pronounced role citizen-generated petition campaigns now play in established organizations. Founded in 1998, MoveOn.org is responsible for pioneering a new brand of nimble, reactive left-wing "netroots" activism (Karpf 2012). The MoveOn.org model of political activism has spread internationally through the Online Progressive Engagement Network (OPEN)

(Karpf 2013). OPEN's MoveOn.org-style organizations now represent over one percent of the national populations of Australia, Canada, the United Kingdom, and Germany, and OPEN startups have been launched in Ireland, India, and several other countries. For many journalists, scholars, and practitioners, MoveOn.org is synonymous with online citizen mobilization (Hayes 2008; White 2010; Sifry 2014).

Though MoveOn.org predates Change.org by nearly a decade, it has recently undergone a dramatic organizational change to incorporate the affordances of Change.org-style petition platforms. In a December 4, 2012 article entitled "MoveOn Moving On," political reporters Amanda Terkel and Ryan Grim outlined MoveOn.org's "radical new approach" to strategic direction-setting, "ced[ing] large elements of its strategic planning directly to its more than 7 million members." Outgoing Executive Director Justin Ruben described the change as follows:

> "The old way of doing things, you could think of it as there are three steps in the campaign process," Ruben said. "Step one, listen hard to what members want. Step two, figure out what we can do on that. Step three, turn around and kick that back out to folks and say, 'Ok, if everybody stands on their head on Thursday, we'll get health care,' or whatever the strategy is that we've come up with. So the game here is to take that middle step, which is really the leadership step, and hand as much of it over to members as possible." (Terkel and Grim 2012)

The center of this organizational redesign is MoveOn.org petitions, previously known as SignOn.org. Launched in 2011 as a Change.org-like offshoot of MoveOn.org, SignOn.org allows individual MoveOn.org members to create their own petition-based campaigns. An initial goal of the SignOn.org tool was to enable more small-scale and locally based MoveOn.org campaign activities. Members are encouraged to create their own campaigns through a monthly email. A necessary disclaimer on the site indicates that, "MoveOn Civic Action does not necessarily endorse the contents of petitions posted on this site. MoveOn.org petitions is an open tool that anyone can use to post a petition advocating any point of view, so long as the petition does not violate our terms of service." If a member-led petition attracts substantial activity, MoveOn.org staff consider "boosting" it, by emailing the petition to a subset of the organization's eight-million-strong member list. These subsets are determined through predictive analytics, either based on zip code or propensity-to-sign (similar petitions). For nearly two years, SignOn.org was a bottom-up offshoot of the MoveOn.org model.

Moving forward after the 2012 presidential election, SignOn.org merged into MoveOn.org petitions, migrating from an *offshoot* of the MoveOn.org model to the *core* of the MoveOn.org model. It represents a major advance in "listening hard to what members want" and a dramatic shift in the role assigned to central staff in developing individual tactics and strategies. The flowcharts below (Figures 4.1 and 4.2) illustrate the old and new MoveOn.org models.

In the old MoveOn.org model, listening to the membership occurred through a mix of weekly member surveys and *passive democratic feedback* obtained through email A/B testing (Karpf 2012). A/B testing—sending out two variants of the same message ("A" and "B") to random subsets of the overall list, then measuring for statistically significant differences in response rate—allowed MoveOn.org to compare different campaign topics, campaign tactics, and issue frames on a day-to-day basis. But A/B testing also produces a "local maxima problem" (Siroker and Koomen 2013; Pariser 2011); it gives MoveOn.org information about which of the staff-generated campaign are most popular, but provides no member input into which potential campaigns ought to be tested to begin with. Staff may be focused on national domestic issues (filibuster reform or judicial nominations, for instance), while members may independently be interested in local issues (natural gas "fracking" activities, for instance). MoveOn.org petitions offers a signal of strong member commitment, which in turn can guide

Figure 4.1 Old MoveOn.org decision process.

Figure 4.2 New MoveOn.org decision process.

the priority-setting process for the national organization. By placing priority on member-led campaigns, MoveOn.org creates an escape route from the local maxima problem.

When a single national or international crisis is dominating American politics (e.g. the 2013 US federal government shutdown or the Newtown school shooting), both decision processes converge upon the same outputs. But in normal times, some of the most active members (and allied organizations) will identify issues that are not on the core staff's radar. MoveOn.org petitions lets these participants create petitions on whichever topics matter most to them. MoveOn.org members effectively vote with their feet through signing and forwarding petitions. The result is an expanded issue agenda for the organization, and a new style of member listening, as monitored through the backend analytics dashboard. MoveOn.org staff can then trace emerging issues at the local and national levels as members launch petition campaigns and attract their peers' support. The organization is developing a suite of additional tools that enhance member engagement and allow these bottom-up campaigns to move beyond simple petitions.

As with Change.org, there is an organizational logic underlying this internal redesign. But it is a *different* logic. As a for-profit "b-corp," Change.org seeks to build an international user base and become "the google of modern politics" (Finley 2013). In so doing, it attempts in all cases to grow. Change.org eschews direct political stances—it is against hate groups, but otherwise wants to be the neutral home for teacher unions and school privatization advocates alike. MoveOn.org, on the other hand, is seeking to deepen the progressive power base by expanding its reach among members. Milan de Vries, MoveOn.org's Director of Analytics, has publicly stated that the organization "does not care about list growth when choosing which petitions to promote" (De Vries 2014). MoveOn.org petitions is a tool for activating and engaging an explicitly partisan membership base that will then donate and volunteer for (Democratic) candidates that MoveOn.org endorses. Change.org seeks to remain nonpartisan and stay out of the day-to-day scrum of American politics.

We The People's neutral administrative logic

Mimicking the success of the UK's Downing Street e-petition system (Wright 2012), the Obama administration announced the launch of its own distributed petition platform, petitions.whitehouse.gov (or We The People) in fall 2011.

Unlike platforms like Change.org or MoveOn.org petitions, the promise of this site was that it would offer a direct pipeline from citizen petitioners to government decision makers. The US Constitution guarantees the right of the people "to petition the Government for a redress of grievances." As technology journalist Alex Howard notes, We The People "formally [brings that constitutional right] into the digital age" (Howard 2011). The White House further promises that any petition that exceeded a specific viability threshold within a single month would be guaranteed a governmental response. That threshold was initially set at 5,000 signatures, but was then extended, first to 25,000 and later to 100,000. The promise and potential of the White House petition site is unique: it provides a direct avenue for citizens to petition their government and gestures at delivering on the promise that political decision makers are, in fact, listening.

In the two and a half years since We The People was launched, over ten million individuals have registered for accounts on the system, representing a population roughly the size of Ohio. Over 200 petitions have received governmental responses, and a handful of these have prompted genuine policy change. In one such case, over 114,000 citizens signed a petition urging the government to support unlocking cellphones, fostering greater competition between cellular providers. The Obama administration agreed and directed the Federal Communications Commission to issue new regulations (Compton 2013). But perhaps the best-known petition was a humorous request from Star Wars fans to "build a Death Star." The Administration issued a tongue-in-cheek response, titled "This isn't the petition response you're looking for," that estimated the cost of a Death Star at 850 quadrillion dollars and asked: "Why would we spend countless taxpayer dollars on a Death Star with a fundamental flaw that could be exploited by a one-man starship?" Lest the reader conclude that this is entirely trivial, it bears noting that the Death Star petition response received an avalanche of positive media, informing the broader American public of the availability of petitions.whitehouse.gov. The White House also published the recipe for the first beer brewed on the White House grounds, at the urging of over 12,000 petitioning home brewers. The Administration likewise used a tongue-in-cheek 2014 petition to "deport [Canadian pop star] Justin Bieber and revoke his green card," to highlight the importance of comprehensive Immigration Reform legislation.

The 10-million-plus accounts at We The People is a comparable figure to MoveOn.org petitions (MoveOn.org has an online list of over eight million members) and Change.org (Change.org has nearly 70 million members, but is global in scope). But by every other available measure of participation, the White House site dramatically lags behind these two competitors. As I described in a 2014 article in *TechPresident*, We The People has become a "virtual ghost-town," whose residents register a single visit but never make a return visit (Karpf 2014). With 10.25 million users and 15.86 million total signatures, the average "member" of the We The People community signs only 1.5 petitions. And this average is influenced by the well-known power law distribution of online activity (Hindman 2009), with a small group of active users signing many petitions and the vast majority signing only one or two.

The major limitation of We The People is written into the site's internal organizational logic. Not all petitions receive a timely reply, and the Obama administration clearly prefers to answer petitions that cast it in a positive light and offer comic relief, like the ones just mentioned. Popular-but-controversial petitions regarding the fate of government whistleblower Edward Snowden, the status of the Muslim Brotherhood, or abuse of power in the Department of Justice languish for years unanswered. Moreover, where Change.org and MoveOn.org employ a variety of techniques to promote repeated user activity, We The People only provides a neutral, static petition site. Both MoveOn.org and Change.org identify and promote promising petitions through email, Facebook, and Twitter channels. Both sites develop profiles of user preferences, and seek to match site visitors with attractive petition campaigns. Phrased another way, Change.org and MoveOn.org are in the business of "picking favorites" among the petitions on their sites. While both Change.org and MoveOn.org have organizational incentives to grow their user base and encourage frequent signatures, the White House's primary incentive is to *avoid trouble*. If We The People were to highlight petitions through social media and mass email channels, it would invite media controversy and outraged citizen counter-mobilization. The Executive Branch can create a venue for citizen petitions, but it does so under the expectation that it will remain a neutral arbiter. The limitations of that neutrality render the site less vibrant as a result.

Each of these three petition sites encourage citizens to launch and share their own petitions. This section has offered brief case examples of how the respective for-profit, nonprofit, and administrative logics of the three sites lead them to *use* the citizen petitions in different ways. The next section will offer a side-by-side comparison of how they frame petitions and guide civic actors as they engage in online politics.

Comparative affordances

Both Change.org and MoveOn.org have made distributed/member-led campaigns a central feature of their workflow, while the White House petition site provides a direct pipeline for citizens demanding a response from the Obama administration. Existing scholarship (Earl and Kimport 2011) would lead us to expect these petition sites to be practically interchangeable: each provides the same rudimentary tools for American citizens petitioning the government. The illustrative cases from the previous section provide at least anecdotal evidence of how the sites differ. But what systematic evidence of these differences can we detect?

Following Kavada (2012), one useful method for better assessing these organizations is to compare the features of their online user experience, also known as "feature analysis." By examining the affordances of their Web platforms, we can assess the managed end-user experience that these organizations are seeking to create. What types of message, topic, or content are promoted, and what types are discouraged? Is there clear evidence of what I am terming "for-profit," "nonprofit," and "administrative" organizational logics? In this section, I analyze the landing pages and petition-creation pages for all three organizations. Feature analysis is particularly worthwhile with these organizations, because all three have engaged in heavy website optimization and testing meant to improve the user experience. Virtually every component of their websites has been tweaked to improve some form of user engagement. If the three sites are attempting to promote the same types of user engagement, then we ought to observe some degree of mimicry in the user experience. The differences revealed through their websites provide trace evidence of intentional choices—proof of divergent organizational logics that dictate alternative efforts to define the contours of the public and of politics. Figures 4.3, 4.4, and 4.5 are screenshots of the Change.org, MoveOn.org, and whitehouse.gov landing pages.

Let us begin by considering Change.org and MoveOn.org. A few similarities demonstrate the central role of user-generated campaigns across the two organizations. Both Change.org and MoveOn.org place their logo and slogan in the upper left corner—MoveOn.org brands itself as "Democracy in Action," while Change.org is "the world's petition platform." Both sites also provide action-oriented breaking topics, as well as log in and search functionality. Both highlight victories they have facilitated. Both present a prominent red button at the top of the page labeled "start a petition."

Figure 4.3 Change.org's landing page (recorded October 18, 2013).

Change.org's site is more image-heavy, petition-heavy, and victory-boasting than MoveOn.org's. The black-and-white images in the upper portion of the Change.org page are photos from victorious campaigns. If the mouse cursor is placed over a black-and-white image, it rolls over to text describing the campaign victory. Prominent text proclaims, "happening now, 196 countries, 234,748,960 signatures, thousands of victories." At the bottom of the page, they explain how it

Figure 4.4 MoveOn.org's landing page (recorded October 18, 2013).

works: "Start a petition to change anything → Ask friends to sign and spread the word → Win your campaign like thousands of others." This language is positive and encouraging, making the work of social change seem blissfully simple.

MoveOn.org's site, by contrast, features a video titled "MoveOn leaders in action." The video highlights MoveOn.org members who created successful petitions aimed at Congress and local legislatures. It features four members telling their stories, as well as positive testimonials from Representative Jackie Speier (D-CA 14) and Senator Kirsten Gillibrand (D-NY). The two columns of updated content on the site are "top posts" from its blog and "take action," which includes a donation request, an offline organizing event, and a petition. The site includes hyperlinked graphics that encourages users to start a petition, manage petitions, join a council, donate, follow MoveOn.org on Facebook, and follow MoveOn.org on Twitter. While these first two options are mirrored on Change.org's site ("start a petition" and "browse"), the last four are not. MoveOn.org councils are local volunteer units. As a nonprofit organization, MoveOn.org is funded

Figure 4.5 Petitions. We the people's whitehouse.gov landing page (recorded June 15, 2014).

by its members and prominently asks for their support. Change.org is a for-profit company, funded through sponsored petitions. It thus optimizes the end-user experience toward one goal: starting and signing petitions. MoveOn.org has elevated online petitions to the most prominent space on the webpage, but also seeks to promote member engagement through other forms of activity, online and offline.

By comparison, the White House petition site promotes itself as "Your Voice In Our Government." Rather than featuring "victories," it features petition "responses." Rather than Change.org's "start a petition/spread the word/win" three-step process, We The People describes a "Browse open petitions → start your own → if it meets the threshold, it will receive a response." Notice how this softly reconfigures the expectations of the site's public; the language of social movements and mobilization is replaced by language of government responsiveness.

For users who take the next step and start a petition, the sites diverge still further. Figures 4.6, 4.7, and 4.8 are snapshots of the petition-creation pages at Change.org, MoveOn.org petitions, and We The People. All three pages are sparse, with an abundance of white space, and a few simple text boxes to fill out. Change.org provides a floating WYSIWYG (What You See Is What You Get) box on the right

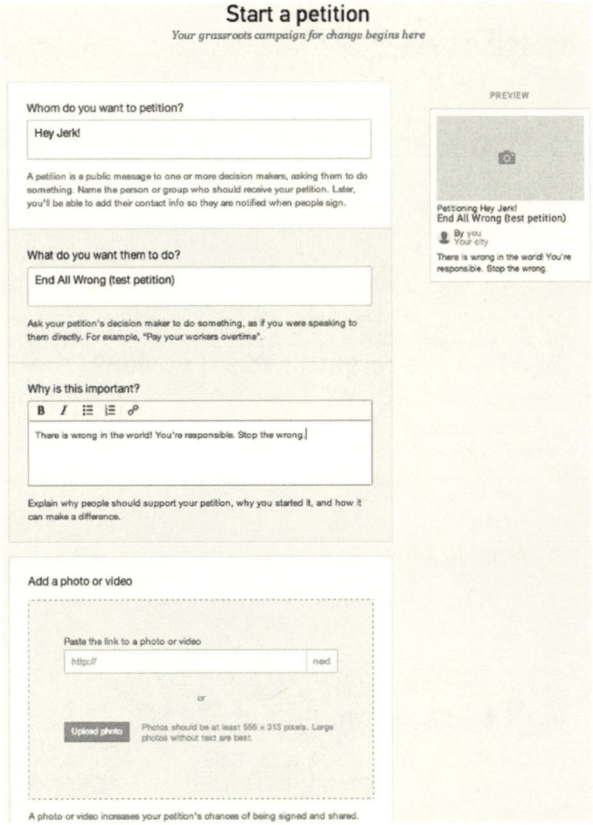

Figure 4.6 Change.org petition creator (captured October 18, 2013).

side, which reflects the user's text as it is entered. Petitions.moveon.org takes users to a separate "preview this petition" after the boxes have been filled out. Petitions.whitehouse.gov takes users through a four-step process: step one asks for a petition title and issue area; step two suggests existing petitions that might be duplicates; step three requests a petition description and key words; and step four provides a petition preview. All three sites thus emphasize simplicity. They render petition creation quick and easy, encouraging wavering petitioners to complete the process.

Beyond this service aim of ease and simplicity, there are three instructive design choices around which the sites diverge: the use of images, the rhetoric of the text boxes, and MoveOn.org's hover text. In these divergent design choices, we can see evidence that the site creators are trying to build different publics around different politics.

Figure 4.7 MoveOn.org petition creator (captured October 18, 2013).

Change.org prominently encourages users to add a photo or video. The photo/ video upload box is the largest on the page, and includes the instruction "A photo or video increases your petition's chances of being signed and shared." We see this reflected on Change.org's landing page (Figure 4.3), which features large photos for each featured petition, accompanied by small text denoting the title and total signatures. Neither MoveOn.org's nor We The People's petition engine features any such image upload option. Change.org petition images are given more space than the petition text, and offer iconic images of families, animals, and places that need our support. Where Change.org features personalized images of the person, animal, or place affected by the petition topic, petitions.moveon.org (Figure 4.9) feature a graphic indicating the state- or national-basis of the campaign, while directing attention to the collective action frame of the petition text itself. We The People, by comparison, prohibits both images and lengthy petition text, enforcing an 800 character limit on the description of the petition.

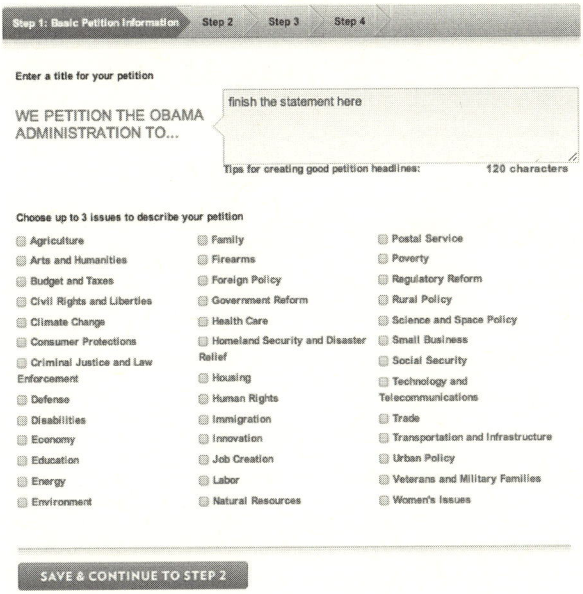

Figure 4.8 We the people petition creator (captured October 18, 2013).

Simplicity has its limits. Make the process *too simple* and you run the risk of encouraging ill-targeted, unfocused petitions. Change.org and MoveOn.org navigate this challenge in very different ways, as evidenced in the language of their respective three-step petition-creation processes. Change.org offers a Who-What-Why process (Whom do you want to petition? What do you want them to do? Why is this important?), with very simple descriptions ("A petition is a public message to one or more decision-makers, asking them to do something."). MoveOn.org offers a Start-Target-Why process (Start Your Petition? Who is the Target? Why are you starting the petition?), with more directed instructions ("What's the text of your petition? Try to keep it to 1–2 sentences"). MoveOn.org provides checkboxes for the targeting step, nudging petition creators to focus on "The White House or Congress," "Your governor or state legislature," or "Someone Else (like a local official or corporate CEO)." MoveOn.org's process thus funnels users toward traditional fields of political contention, while Change.org's process more vaguely defines petitions as "public messages" that can be sent to virtually anyone. As we will see in the next section, these divergent instructions at the petition-input stage correlate with marked differences at the petition-output stage. MoveOn.org petitions offer collective calls-to-action around traditional

Figure 4.9 Petitions.moveon.org (captured October 18, 2013).

political matters, while Change.org petitions offer personalized calls-to-action that fall outside the traditional political arena.

The petition-creation pages also provide a ripe opportunity for shaping the habits of civic activists. The petition-creation page offers a "teachable moment" of sorts: visitors are asked to creatively explain their intentions and voice their demands. The instructions on these pages inform us as to what sorts of claims, targets, and demands each organization views as "appropriate." MoveOn.org's page is particularly interesting in this regard. When a MoveOn.org visitor is ready to begin typing, and places their cursor on the text box, they are greeted with additional hover text that provides further guidance. Figures 4.10 and 4.11 provide screen capture of two examples, "choosing a target" and "petition background." This text could have been lifted directly from a strategic campaign planning manual ("think about who actually has the power to solve the problem or make the decision that you want," . . . "in 2–3 sentences, why should people be concerned about this issue? Is there a deadline? Have you been *personally* affected by the issue?"). MoveOn.org is nudging members toward brief petition language with clear titles, specific targets, and compelling language. Change.org, by comparison, provides fewer nudges; the suggestions it does provide are in the direction of compelling, media-friendly images. We The People, which also offers petitioning tips, offers dry, administrative suggestions like "Be sure the title clearly describes the goal of the petition" and "start by clearly articulating a

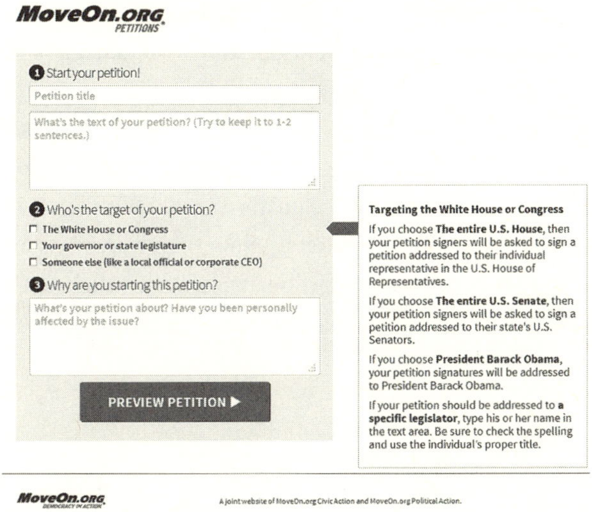

Figure 4.10 MoveOn.org national targets hover text (captured February 3, 2015).

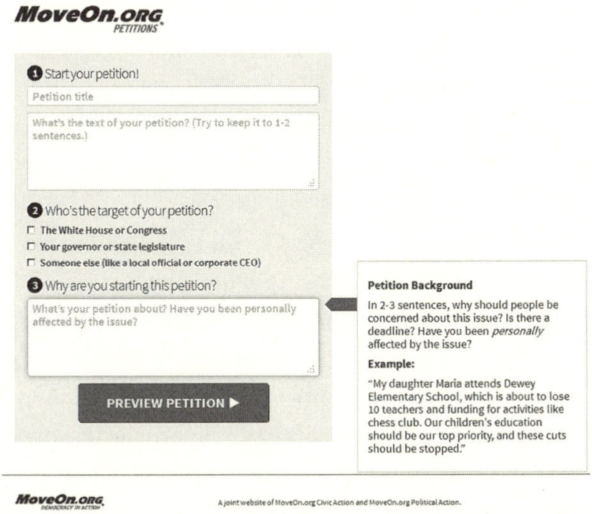

Figure 4.11 MoveOn.org petition background hover text (captured February 3, 2015).

position, and then include additional information or research." We The People is nudging members toward making their demands clear, not necessarily compelling.

Analyzing the features and rhetoric of these three public petition websites reveals broad similarities and nuanced differences. The similarities fall under the theme of ease and simplicity: each site is clearly designed to encourage visitors to create, sign, and share public petitions. But the differences emerge through comparison of how they define a petition, and what lessons and habits they encode in the petition-creation process. As we will see in the next section, the divergent user experiences at these sites correlate with markedly different petition activity at each site. Change.org receives the most petitions, and those petitions achieve the highest overall signature levels. But they do so by largely avoiding traditionally "political" matters. MoveOn.org petitions appear around a narrower band of issues, and often occur in partnership with progressive partner organizations. We The People petitions, meanwhile, are both brief and rare by comparison.

A week in the life of a distributed petition site

Change.org and MoveOn.org petitions are the two largest distributed petition websites. The embedded affordances of the two sites' homepages and petition-creation pages reveal the types of habits and practices that each organization seeks to promote. This next section offers a content analysis of the top ten petitions appearing over the course of a single week on the two sites. It reveals some stark differences in the output of the two sites, differences that are strongly linked to the affordances previously highlighted through examination of the input process for the two sites.

During the week of October 14–20, 2013, I recorded the top ten petitions on each of the two websites. This data set is the pilot version of a larger study, to appear in a forthcoming book. It included the petition's rank (1 through 10), title, author, organizational affiliation, number of signatures, signature goal, state versus national petition, and a brief summary of the subject matter. Data was collected in the early afternoon each day, at approximately the same time of day (2 p.m. EST). That particular week of October precluded me from including the We The People petition site in my data set: the US federal government had been shut down due to a budget impasse in mid-October, and the White House petition site was taken offline as a result. This is an instructive limitation: at the very time when American citizens may indeed have been *most* interested in petitioning their government, the government petition site was rendered inaccessible. External sites like Change.org and MoveOn.org petitions, however, remained active. I conducted a separate data collection for We The People during the month of April 2014. The dominant finding from that data set was the low number of total petitions (85, compared to 2,053 at MoveOn.org and 7,397 at Change.org that month) and low signature totals (average of 500 signatures per petition). These findings are reported in "How the White House's We The People E-Petition Site Became a Virtual Ghost-Town" (Karpf 2014). The descriptive findings are presented below.

Stability

Both petition sites demonstrated a surprising amount of stability during the week under study. Petitions rarely appeared or disappeared on a daily basis, and instead seem to be treated in a weekly rotation. Figures 4.12 and 4.13 display the relative stability of the top ten rankings on the two sites. Only sixteen MoveOn.org petitions and seventeen Change.org petitions appeared in the top ten rankings over the course of the week. For MoveOn.org, four petitions—"No Pay for Congress During the Shutdown," "Tell Ted Cruz to Stop Lying about Obamacare," "Tell PA Gov. Corbett: Apologize for Equating Same-Sex Relationships with Incest," and "Gov Rick Perry: Stop Denying Benefits to Same-Sex Couples Serving in Texas Military"—were in the top ten listings all week. Another two petitions—"Children Should be Safe in their Public Schools" and "Virginia House Representatives: End the Shutdown!"—were launched on Tuesday and remained on the list for the remainder of the week. Two additional petitions were on MoveOn.org's top ten list for four days, and another three petitions were on it for three days. For Change.org, three petitions—"Justice for Quinten," "Help me fight cancer and stop the shutdown," and "Let Jakiyah Keep Her Crown"—were in the top ten listings all week. Three petitions—"Review Ole Miss policies to ensure that LGBT students, staff, and faculty are fully covered by non-d . . .," "Amazon, Barnes and Noble, KOBO: Drop the clause of removing self-published Indie authors and Erotica," and "Minnesota Governor Mark Dayton: STOP WOLF HUNTING & TRAPPING IN MN"—appeared for four days, while nine petitions appeared for three days. Thursday appeared to be a breakpoint,

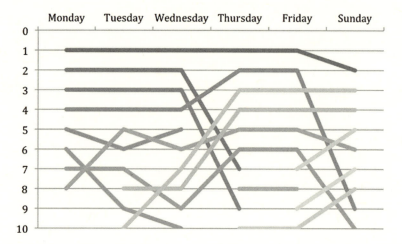

Figure 4.12 MoveOn.org petition ranking fluctuations (recorded October 14–20, 2013).

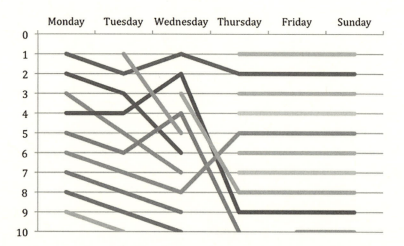

Figure 4.13 Change.org petition ranking fluctuations (recorded October 14–20, 2013).

with five new petitions featured that day, four of which were in the top six that appeared automatically on the front page. All four of those remained in the top six on Friday, Saturday, and Sunday. This appears to be part of a staff-driven curatorial routine, with staff leaving the rankings unaltered on the weekends.

The stability of the rankings is especially noteworthy given the particular events of that week. Several of MoveOn.org's petitions were related to the government shutdown. One of Change.org's petitions was loosely related to the shutdown as well. The shutdown ended on Wednesday, yet these petitions remained at the top of the rankings throughout the week. This, once again, suggests that the website rankings are not the primary interface that staff are monitoring. Staff at both organizations have confirmed through interviews that only a small fraction of petition traffic is driven through spontaneous visits to the website. Email and social sharing are much larger drivers of petition traffic.

Signature growth

The featured petitions at both sites boasted signature counts between the four-figure and six-figure range. Change.org petitions received, on average, far more traffic. The average MoveOn.org featured petition increased by 290.6 signatures per day, while the average Change.org featured petition increased by 4,758 signatures per day. Tables 4.1 and 4.2 reveal the increasing petition signatures at MoveOn.org and Change.org over the course of the week. Blank entries mean that the petition was not in the top ten that day. Highlighted entries denote particularly large increases in the petition count. Neither site ranks petitions solely based on signature totals, but it appears as though MoveOn.org's ranking algorithm relies more heavily on signature totals than Change.org's. In both cases, it appears as though petitions receive a large number of signatures *and then* are boosted to the top ten list, rather than arriving on the top ten list

Table 4.1 MoveOn.org petition totals (recorded October 14–20, 2013).

Column1	Monday	Tuesday	Wednesday	Thursday	Friday	Sunday
Justice for Q|	49,745	79110	94857	98,251	114,909	135,481
Tricare (Cran	37,023	40694	41,874			
The Honorab	8,562	9,696	10672			
Help me figh	140,733	145,993	148695	149,607	149,994	150453
Review Ole N	91,840	95,094	96716	97,772		
Let Jakiyah K|	19,986	27651	32,836	33,869	43162	44,815
Congress: Re	257,693	259,954	261,232			
Merck & BM!	504,217	504,592	504878			
Protect eleph	49,672	50,883				
Justice for Pu	286,114					
Amazon, Barnes and Nobl		11933	13,300		13,877	14126
Minnesota Governor Mark Dayton: STO			7623	8531	9121	9774
North Andover High School: Drop Erin Cox's Suspension				17,459	18,527	19522
M&M's Candies: Stop Using Artificial Dyes Linked to Hyp				11598	50759	59351
Good People of Pittsburgh: #KeepTheDuck in Pittsburgh				2885	4,753	5052
Ohio Parole Board and Governor Kasich: Free Tyra Patte				172,164	172,614	173,014
Please Grant Ryan Ferguson a New Trial or Freedom!				237,367	243266	245,946

Table 4.2 Change.org Petition Totals (recorded October 14–20, 2013).

Name	Monday	Tuesday	Wednesday	Thursday	Friday	Sunday
No Pay for Congress during the	444,845	449,435	450,828	452,417	453,473	453,963
Tell Florida not to block Obama	12,123	12,268	12,378	12,435		
Protect California: Don't Allow	7,618	7,719	7,773	7,820		
Tell Ted Cruz to Stop Lying abo(	6,404	6,596	6,680	6,945	6,945	7,003
9 House Democrats Who Forgo	5,139	5,168	5,199			
Oregon -- Tell HaagenDazs, Dre	3,145	3,145	3,187			
Tell PA Gov. Corbett: Apologize	2,900	3,026	3,064	3,091	3,116	3,143
Gov Rick Perry: Stop Denying B	2,595	5,278	5,477	5,555	5,606	5,654
Stop the Virginia Voter Purge!	2,021			2,135	2,152	
Washington -- Tell HaagenDazs	2,130					
Children Should be Safe in their Public Schools		3383	3,819	3,934	3,987	4019
Virginia House Representatives: End the Shutdown!		2001	3641	3,717	3,728	3733
No fracking in Allegheny, PA Parks!				1,263	1,346	1,409
Stop the Maryville Coverup					2,920	3241
Gov. Martinez: Send us a refund					2,111	2,275
Stop the Fast Food Swindle						36128,

and then benefiting from the increased exposure. This, once again, highlights the importance of email and social channels for generating petition signatures and shares—avenues of signature growth that are shut off to We The People's neutral administrative logic.

Additional trends

Four findings from this exploratory content analysis are worth highlighting further: (1) the petition titles and images on the two sites, (2) the average size of Change.org versus MoveOn.org petitions, (3) the issues covered by each site, and (4) the authors and affiliations of the petitions.

Several Change.org petition titles were unclear and nearly unreadable. For instance, on Monday October 14, the third-ranked petition at Change.org was "The Honorable Judge Wall, Middletown OH and the Ohio State Legislature: Pass tougher laws ag . . ." The petition is associated with an image of a sad-looking dog, giving readers some clue of the issue area. But readers have to click on the petition to find out that it is about a specific court case on animal cruelty. MoveOn.org headlines, by contrast, are punchy and direct (as MoveOn.org's hover text instructs). Here we see evidence of the power of affordances in the guided petition-input process. Change.org prioritizes personalized imagery, while MoveOn.org prioritizes clear, collective calls-to-action. A petition at Change.org with a great photo but an unclear headline can be selected as a featured petition. A petition at MoveOn.org with an unclear headline receives no such support.

Despite its title, the Judge Wall petition performed better at Change.org than 82 percent of MoveOn.org's featured petitions. The average featured petition at MoveOn.org had 49,885 signatures, while the average featured petition at Change.org had 106,531 signatures, more than a twofold difference. It would appear as though, if the goal of both organizations were solely to maximize signatures, then Change.org's strategy of encouraging a wide range of petition topics while leveraging images and videos outperforms MoveOn.org's strategy of promoting clear language and appropriate targets for traditional political issues.

But maximizing signatures is not the *only* goal of a petition site. Each organization also has to make decisions about which petitions are the most *important*. And here we may see reason for a normative critique of Change.org's output. Consider: in the week of October 14–20, 2013, the two topics that dominated the national media agenda were (1) the federal government shutdown and (2) the rollout of the Affordable Care Act. Five of MoveOn.org's top petitions focused on these two issues. American citizens who wanted to influence the government's position on the premier political issues of the day could reliably find an outlet in MoveOn.org petitions. Change.org, by comparison, stayed almost entirely silent on these issues. Only one Change.org petition was even loosely linked to the federal government shutdown ("help me fight cancer and stop the shutdown), and that petition was primarily framed around the personal plight of a single cancer patient.

Change.org's petitions discuss politics only in the broadest sense. Change.org's top petitions are aimed at revoking high school suspensions ("North Andover High School: Drop Erin Cox's Suspension and Reinstate Her as Team Captain"), child health and welfare ("Justice for Quinten"; "M&M's Candies: Stop Using Artificial Dyes Linked to Hyperactivity"), individual pleas for court pardons ("Please Grant Ryan Ferguson a New Trial or Freedom!"), or medical exemptions ("Merck and BMS: Save Locky's Dad. Provide Nick Auden access to the PD1 drug on a compassionate basis") and animal welfare ("Protect elephant, tiger, and orangutan habitats in Sumatra"). Though there is certainly a political *element* to these issues, they are each deliberately framed through a personal, rather than a collective, lens. Change.org is selecting the "growthiest" issues, and packaging them as media-ready stories of personal tragedy or human interest. In so doing, it removes itself from the realm of partisan political mobilization. MoveOn.org, by contrast, offers less signature growth but highlights opportunities for collective action around the most politically salient issues.

The difference between the two sites is further revealed by the authors and affiliations linked to the petitions. The top Change.org petitions are almost universally launched by everyday citizens with no affiliation to an outside organization. This may appear more "grassroots" at first glance, but it also precludes one valuable tactical use of an online petition. Affiliated petitions build the member list of an established organization, which in turn can contact signers and invite them to participate in additional political actions. The lack of affiliations among Change.org's top petitions give the site a "bottom-up" feel. By contrast, almost all of the top MoveOn.org petitions are affiliated with a MoveOn.org ally. The top petitions came from Laura Levitt of the Courage Campaign, Chris Bowers of DailyKos, Joe Dinkins of the Working Families Party, Peter Stocker of Friends of the Earth, and Roger Hickey of Campaign for America's Future. These affiliated petitions extend from the nonprofit logic of MoveOn.org's petition program. MoveOn.org features petitions that help augment the efforts of its progressive allies. By contrast, Change.org features petitions that help increase its total supporter list.

Conclusion: Divergent logics and escaping the warehouse metaphor

From the end user's perspective, Change.org, We The People, and MoveOn.org petitions are all just "platforms" on which a citizen can create their own digital petition. This "Do It Yourself" ethos often pervades scholarly and journalistic accounts of online citizen participation. If we treat online petition sites as a generic abstraction, then it is easy to miss the tremendous variation that can occur across these spaces.

But all platforms are not created equal. As this chapter has demonstrated, distributed petition platforms are crafted according to divergent organizational logics. MoveOn.org uses its platform to deepen and promote liberal activism around traditional US politics. Change.org uses its platform to promote a wider set of more media-friendly petition campaigns, fueling ongoing list growth along the way. And We The People uses its platform to highlight government responsiveness and generate positive attention to the Obama White House, while otherwise producing an intentional air of administrative neutrality. These organizational logics are rendered visible by studying both the input-side and output-side of their petition systems.

One lesson to take from this study is that the move towards "big data" and analytics involves a series of internal organizational compromises. Both MoveOn.org and Change.org rely heavily on data in their decision making. Data-driven activism does not necessarily move society in any one predetermined direction. Rather, computational data forms a new *object*, which in turn can be employed to help each organization move toward its goals. Change.org and MoveOn.org petitions promote different styles of political participation, not because one uses data and the other does not, but because they both employ data in the service of divergent organizational logics.

These distinctions are important and worthy of study because of the role they play in crafting the appropriate roles for citizens and determining which issues rise to political prominence. Change.org nudges users toward individual stories and images. MoveOn.org nudges users toward clear political targets and collective actions. We The People nudges users toward polite discourse with responsive government officials. All three of the sites can be termed a "success," but this is solely because each site uses citizen-created petitions for distinctly different ends. All three of these petition websites introduce a bias of sorts into the political sphere. They are promoting different ideals of citizen engagement, and their successes and failures model these ideals for the broader public.

To summarize: the nonprofit logic of MoveOn.org drives the organization to use online petitions to promote traditional political issues. The online petition is an entry point for MoveOn.org members to engage in extended activist campaigns that pressure government officials to adopt more progressive stances. The for-profit logic of Change.org drives the company to highlight online petitions that fall outside of traditional politics. As Change.org's CEO Ben Rattray put it in a 2011 keynote speech, "The thing about big problems is they exist for a reason." Rather than promoting petitions that focus on the "big" political problems favored by MoveOn.org, Change.org instead highlights smaller cultural issues with appealing personal narratives. The online petition is a form of civic signaling, which doubles as an engine for list growth and profitability. Finally, the administrative logic of We The People drives the Obama administration to highlight moments that cast the Executive Branch in a positive light. But, through its dual roles as the venue for and the target of these petitions, it also finds itself frequently hamstrung, unable to adopt many of the computational practices favored by MoveOn.org and Change.org. Ironically, in moments like the October 2013 government shutdown, when We The People could perhaps have made the biggest difference, the site was itself shuttered.

Altogether, this chapter provides illustrative evidence of the crafting influence that site architecture has on citizen petition campaigns. Very different petitions are produced on MoveOn.org petitions and Change.org. These petitions mobilize different publics toward different ends, in service of different organizational goals. While this is only an exploratory study—a precursor to a much larger, forthcoming data collection project—it demonstrates the compromises that political organizations make as they embrace bigger and bigger data. Contrary to what previous scholarship has claimed, petition websites are not "warehouses." They introduce biases, promoting some issue topics and strategies over others, and nudging citizen petitioners in the service of their divergent organizational logics. We must not forget that this is *crafted talk*. As it stands, the process by which citizen petitions are produced and promoted through the Web is a vital-but-opaque feature of the digital environment, a feature that demands greater scrutiny.

References

Bennett, Lance and Alexandra Segerberg. 2013. *The Logic of Connective Action: Digital Media and the Personalization of Contentious Politics*. New York: Cambridge University Press.

Cohen, Rick. 2010. "Nonprofit Newswire: The 'B' Corporation – 'Tax Preferred' Status?" *Nonprofit Quarterly Online*. July 20. Accessed June 10, 2014. https://nonprofitquarterly.org/index.php?option=com_content&view=article&id=4011:nonprofit-newswire-the-b-corporationtax-preferred-status&catid=155:daily-digest&Itemid=986.

Compton, Matt. 2013. "We The People Is Two Years Old." Blog Post, WhiteHouse.gov. Accessed June 10, 2014. http://www.whitehouse.gov/blog/2013/09/27/we-people-two-years-old.

DeVries, Milan. 2014. "Moving Beyond Petitions: How Organizations Can Harness Distributed Campaigns to Build Progressive Power." Panel presentation at Netroots Nation 2014. July 19. Detroit, MI.

Earl, Jennifer and Katrina Kimport. 2011. *Digitally Enabled Social Change*. Cambridge, MA: MIT Press.

Finley, Klint. 2013. "Meet Change.org, the Google of Modern Politics." *Wired Magazine*. Accessed June 10, 2014. http://www.wired.com/wiredenterprise/2013/09/change-org/all/.

Goldberg, Eleanor. 2014. "Here Are 7 Petitions That Actually Moved The White House To Take Action." *Huffington Post*. February 25. Accessed June 10, 2014. http://

www.huffingtonpost.com/2014/02/25/white-house-petitions-works_n_4848866. html?utm_hp_ref=tw.

Graeff, E., M. Stempeck, and E. Zuckerman. 2014. "The Battle for 'Trayvon Martin': Mapping a media controversy online and off-line." *First Monday* 19(2). http:// firstmonday.org/ojs/index.php/fm/article/view/4947/3821.

Hayes, Chris. 2008. "MoveOn at Ten." *The Nation* magazine. Accessed June 10, 2014. http://chrishayes.org/articles/moveon-ten/.

Hindman, Matthew. 2009. *The Myth of Digital Democracy*. Princeton, NJ: Princeton University Press.

Howard, Alex. 2011. "Commentary: Got a problem you want the White House to Fix? E-Petition it!" *NationalJournal.com*. September 9. Accessed June 10, 2014. http:// www.nationaljournal.com/tech/commentary-got-a-problem-you-want-the-white-house-to-fix-e-petition-it--20110909.

Karpf, David. 2012. *The MoveOn Effect: The Unexpected Transformation of American Political Advocacy*. New York: Oxford University Press.

Karpf, David. 2013. "Netroots Goes Global." *The Nation*. November 4. http://www. thenation.com/article/176700/netroots-goes-global.

Karpf, David. 2014. "How the White House's We The People E-Petition Site Became a Virtual Ghost-Town." *TechPresident.com*. June 20. http://techpresident.com/ news/25144/how-white-houses-we-people-e-petition-site-became-virtual-ghost-town.

Kavada, Anastasia. 2012. "Engagement, bonding, and identity across multiple platforms: Avaaz on Facebook, YouTube, and MySpace." *MedieKultur: Journal of Media and Communication Research*, 28(52): 28–48.

Kreiss, Daniel. 2012. *Taking Our Country Back: The Crafting of Networked Politics from Howard Dean to Barack Obama*. New York: Oxford University Press.

Pariser, Eli. 2011. *The Filter Bubble: How the New Personalized Web Is Changing What We Read and How We Think*. New York: Penguin Press.

Rattray, Ben. 2011. "How Hyperlocal Online Organizing Is Disrupting Traditional Advocacy." Keynote Speech, Personal Democracy Forum. Accessed June 10, 2014. https://www.youtube.com/watch?v=WV2XK46LkQE.

Shirky, Clay. 2008. *Here Comes Everybody: The Power of Organizing Without Organizations*. New York: Penguin.

Sifry, Micah. 2014. *The Big Disconnect: Why the Internet Hasn't Transformed Politics (Yet)*. New York: O/R Books.

Siroker, Dan and Pete Koomen. 2013. *A/B Testing: The Most Powerful Way to Turn Clicks Into Customers*. New York: Wiley-Blackwell.

Terkel, Amanda and Ryan Grim. 2012. "MoveOn Moving On: Progressive Powerhouse Launches Radical Strategic Overhaul." *The Huffington Post*. December 5. Accessed June 10, 2014. http://www.huffingtonpost.com/2012/12/04/moveon-changes_n_2240238.html.

White, Micah. 2010. "Clicktivism is ruining leftist activism." *The Guardian Online.*
    August 12. Accessed June 10, 2014. http://www.guardian.co.uk/commentisfree/2010/
    aug/12/clicktivism-ruining-leftist-activism.
Wright, Steven. 2012. "Assessing (e-)Democratic Innovations: 'Democratic Goods' and
    Downing Street E-petitions." *Journal of Information Technology and Politics* 9(4):
    453–70.

Part Two

Data Limit(ed)

5

Easy Data, Hard Data: The Politics and Pragmatics of Twitter Research After the Computational Turn

Jean Burgess and Axel Bruns

The implications of the computational turn

In the agenda-setting introductory chapter of his edited collection *Understanding Digital Humanities*, David Berry (2012) argues that the contemporary conjuncture in the history of the digital humanities constitutes a "computational turn." In Berry's formulation, this concept captures an historical moment that has both pragmatic and political dimensions. Berry defines it in terms of the use of computational technologies by disciplines in the humanities and social sciences, not only to "collect and analyze data with an unprecedented breadth and depth and scale," as Lazer et al. (2009) put it in their definitive statement on computational social science, but also "to shift the critical ground of [these disciplines'] concepts and theories" (Berry 2012, 11).

As the duality of this definition already shows, Berry's elaboration on the computational turn is much more than a procedural description of matters of fact affecting the self-identified digital humanities field. Rather, it is actually a provocative call to action directed at the humanities more broadly. Indeed, Berry draws on Presner's (2010) dramatic characterization of this situation according to which we were "at the beginning of a shift in standards governing permissible problems, concepts, and explanations, and also in the midst of a transformation of the institutional and conceptual conditions of possibility for the generation, transmission, accessibility, and preservation of knowledge" (Presner 2010, 10). While cautioning humanities scholars not to leave the design of research tools and environments to private industry, and noting that it is vital to examine the cultural assumptions and constraints encoded into both consumer- and programming-level digital technologies from Facebook to XML (10), Presner was clearly optimistic about Wikipedia as a model for digital transformations of the very structures of knowledge (11). At this point—four years on and counting—we note that in the context of an increasingly "platformed" (van Dijck 2013, 5–7) digital media environment that is "easier to use but more difficult to tinker with" (6), Presner's "transformation of the institutional and conceptual conditions of possibility" may entail as much closing down as opening up of scientific opportunities.

Taking these further complications into account and translating Berry's schema for understanding the implications of the computational turn in the field of sociocultural digital media research, the present chapter works from the premise that the computational turn has two main dimensions, which, taken separately and together, have significant implications for the competing futures of social media research in the humanities and social sciences.

The first dimension concerns the *practical* opportunities presented to humanities and social science researchers by computational approaches and methods. Here we are especially interested in the opportunities presented by the massive uptake and use of digital platforms for communication, the public availability of social media data that is generated by these activities, and new methods being developed to tackle the challenges of scale that result. In other words, this dimension describes the ways that computation can help to accomplish the pragmatic goals of empirical sociocultural research. It is no accident that in following this thread of analysis in this chapter, we focus almost exclusively on Twitter research. Indeed the comparative openness of Twitter as a platform (from both a user and a developer perspective) has both produced an unprecedented wealth of social media data and stimulated rapid and significant innovation in computational tools to gather, analyze, and visualize this data in the digital humanities and social sciences (see, for example, Weller et al. 2014). This openness has also, accordingly, provoked transformation and challenge in the institutional structures and conceptual frameworks of sociocultural digital media research (Rieder and Röhle 2012; Burgess and Bruns 2012).

The second dimension of the computational turn concerns the application of critical humanities and social science theories and methods to the material *politics* of computational culture. In the context of data-driven digital media research, this dimension entails an additional layer of reflexivity, because it requires critical approaches to the computational aspects of social media platforms themselves. For the purpose of this chapter, the second dimension requires that we attend to the means by which platforms shape and control access to the data we use to diagnose the patterns of personal and public communication that they mediate. Here we can point to the growing body of work we might variously describe as "software studies" (Fuller 2008; Helmond 2013; Bucher 2013), "platform studies" (Bogost and Montfort 2009), or the "politics of platforms" (Gillespie 2013) as a guide, with specific work on socio-technical elements of Twitter (van Dijck 2013) and Facebook (Gerlitz and Helmond 2013; Bucher 2012) as exemplars, as well as earlier work reflecting on the politics of empirical research on social media platforms (Langlois and Elmer 2012). In a parallel set of considerations, José van Dijck argues that a truly materialist approach to the politics of social media platforms—the "techno-cultural constructs" (2013, 29) that constitute so much of the digital media environment—increasingly requires the combination of Actor-Network Theory and political economy approaches (2013, 26–28). In what follows, we draw on both, albeit implicitly.

For digital media researchers working directly with social media data (whether big or small), these political and pragmatic dimensions of the computational turn are not easily separated. Given that we will always be at least affected by, if not actively engaged in, *both* of these dimensions in the simple act of carrying out our work, it becomes clear that the computational turn is already starting to have some fairly profound transformative effects on the field of digital media research. It not only transforms how we go about doing media and communication studies—for example, introducing into the field automated methods of data collection and computational techniques of analysis and visualization, redrawing and blurring disciplinary boundaries between the humanities, social sciences, and computer science; it also reconfigures the field itself, enlarging the scope of our potential objects of study—for example, requiring us to apply our analytical techniques to the study of the governing functions of APIs (Application Programming Interfaces) and the mechanics of hashtags, and not only the textual units of meaning they carry.

In the following section of the chapter, we draw out the relevant themes from a range of critical scholarship from the small body of digital media and software studies work that has focused on the politics of Twitter data and the socio-technical means by which access is regulated. We highlight in particular the contested relationships between social media research (in both academic and nonacademic contexts) and the data wholesale, retail, and analytics industries that feed on them. In the second major section of the chapter we discuss in detail the pragmatic edge of these politics in terms of what kinds of scientific research is and is not possible in the current political economy of Twitter data access. Finally, at the end of the chapter we return to the much broader implications of these issues for the politics of knowledge, demonstrating how the apparently microscopic level of how the Twitter API mediates access to Twitter data actually inscribes and influences the macro level of the global political economy of science itself, through reinscribing institutional and traditional disciplinary privilege. We conclude with some speculations about future developments in data rights and data philanthropy that may at least mitigate some of these negative impacts.

Platform politics and regimes of access

Each of the currently dominant proprietary social media platforms is profoundly political. They are socio-technical institutions that operate at multiple levels—technically, rhetorically, and culturally (Gillespie 2013)—to coordinate social and cultural interactions and expressions. As van Dijck reminds us, platforms are active mediators rather than neutral intermediaries, shaping "the performance of social acts instead of merely facilitating them" (2013, 29). At the same time, platforms are themselves shaped by use, and by the ways that they are represented in media, academic, and policy discourse. For researchers situated within sociocultural traditions but working with "big social data" (Manovich 2010) from social media, the politics of platforms are therefore ever-present as we go about what might otherwise appear to be purely instrumental exploitations of their affordances.

While a number of scholars are turning their critical attention to platforms understood in this way, the politics of the situation are often framed quite crudely—as a set of unilateral power relations between the platform, understood as a singular entity, and users, understood as a fairly homogeneous mass. But given the society-wide uptake of social media for a range of communicative purposes, it is important to differentiate these actors and the relations among them more carefully. We do so in this chapter by focusing on the politics of a particular set of relations—those that make up the field of computationally assisted academic research relying on Twitter data—around a specific issue: the scientific affordances of Twitter data and the regulatory regimes of access that govern such uses. Thus we bring into the picture the relations among the platform provider Twitter, Inc., the Twitter APIs, the third-party tools for accessing, analyzing, and sharing data, and the ancillary economies of data mining and data retail that have sprung up around these affordances, as well as a range of commercial and not-for-profit research institutions and individual scientific users of the Twitter API for research purposes. In doing so, we make explicit the material politics of social media data access and its socio-technical regulation as these relate to the wider critique of the politics of platforms (Gillespie 2013, 2014).

Part of the gradual but inexorable "making over" of Twitter from a social networking utility to a major media company (Burgess 2014) has been realized materially in changes to the technical and regulatory mechanisms that enable and constrain access to Twitter data, both for software development and research purposes. As Puschmann and Burgess (2014) have already discussed, social media data itself has become quickly commodified. Intermediaries who literally make it their business to package, sell, and analyze the collective interactions and expressions of millions of global social media users are emerging at a rapid rate. At the same time, the Twitter APIs have become less and less friendly to free-range data uses, including those of the third-party developer community that is arguably responsible for many of the innovations that give Twitter its unique culture, from the @reply and the hashtag to the search function and trending topics (Halavais 2014; Bruns 2011). But Twitter today is in the media business. It has been deliberately driven further and further away from being the neutral, transparent, and endlessly configurable "utility" that, back in 2009, co-founder Jack Dorsey famously declared he wanted it to be (McCarthy 2009) and toward being a managed advertising and interoperable media platform with a tightly controlled brand and user experience (Bilton 2012).

In this shift, the future monetization of data analytics—including scientific data analytics—drawing on social media data is clearly seen as an important commercial growth area. José van Dijck has framed this shift as one from a situation where the possible meanings and uses of Twitter were many and varied—which, borrowing from Bijker et al., she characterizes as a phase of great "interpretative flexibility" (2013, 68–69)—to a reduction in this flexibility, a pattern of enclosure marked in 2011 by new restrictions on and governance of API access (84–85). As van Dijck correctly deduces, the regimes of access to Twitter data have become more clearly articulated and more tightly managed in order to enable the monetization of data mining, which requires Twitter to have some controls over the entire pipeline of data, from the moment a tweet is uttered. Twitter's quasi-monopolistic licensing arrangements with, and then corporate acquisition of, data retailer Gnip in April 2014 (Messerschmidt 2014) are clear and relevant examples of Twitter's frequently remarked-upon corporate transition from a relatively free-range innovation platform to a much more managed, media-centric one, particularly since 2011 (Bilton 2012, 2013).

These significant changes in the ideologies and business models of social media platforms have been accompanied over the past five years by the increased "algorithmization" (Helmond 2013) of the social Web, including the very techniques and architectures that social media platforms run on—from search to content discovery to target behavioral advertising and beyond. Famously, the delegation of cultural and knowledge work like content curation, sorting, classification, and evaluation for fuzzy concepts like "relevance" is increasingly being delegated to algorithms (Gillespie 2014)—from Netflix's user-preference predictions (Hallinan and Striphas 2014) through to Google's search results (Hillis, Petit, and Jarrett 2013) to the Facebook newsfeed (Bucher 2012). Our culture and society are increasingly mediated not only by knowable, single algorithms (as the Google search algorithm may once have been), but now by mobile and dynamic assemblages of algorithms, creating an almost incomprehensible situation (even for the engineers who build particular parts of the algorithms, or for the companies who hope to profit from them). As Gillespie (2014) argues, the algorithmic turn is stretching the "black box" metaphor so loved by STS scholars well beyond its limit. Whether truly knowable or reverse engineerable by the platform providers, it is only the platform providers that have what Gillespie (2014) evocatively calls "backstage access" to "the public algorithms that matter so much to the public circulation of knowledge" (185). We suggest the same is true of the protocols and interfaces (such as APIs) that enable and govern public access to the data that constitute public communication after the computational turn.

While the cultures and meanings of Facebook and even Twitter are substantially and increasingly shaped by the algorithms used to search, curate, and suggest content to users, it is above all the Twitter APIs that play the most significant role in the mediating the function of Twitter as a platform for the purposes of third-party development, user innovation, and scientific research. But in comparison to, say, Facebook's newsfeed algorithms, there is far less critique of the politics of APIs. One notable exception here is Taina Bucher's (2013) study of the changing politics of Twitter's APIs, which includes valuable interview material garnered from conversations with members of the third-party developer community, demonstrating how APIs (including the Search and Streaming APIs that are essential to Twitter research) work as "quasi-objects" mediating the relations between actors and uses, and evoking "intense feeling" within the developer community.

But changes to the Twitter API have affected the research community as well. Bruns and Burgess (2015) have traced the ways that Twitter's changing business model, as instantiated through the API and associated rule changes, has impacted Twitter research over time. Gradual changes to what forms and volumes of data are available through the API, and at what retrieval speeds, have directly impacted academic research on the uses of the platform. For example, while during the early years of the platform researchers were able to request and gain "whitelisted," premium access to the API at the discretion of Twitter support staff, enabling them to retrieve a larger amount of data at greater speeds, such access (or the equivalent thereof) is now available only to the paying subscribers of third-party Twitter data resellers (such as Gnip or DataSift) and at significant cost, creating a "missing middle" in terms of data accessibility and putting small-scale data access facilitators out of business, at least where Twitter data is concerned (Irving 2014). Instead, Twitter's business model has relied progressively more on providing licensed data access to large players, in keeping with the rise of the "social data" market (Puschmann and Burgess 2014), further complicating not only the practical accessibility of the platform to researchers, but introducing new dimensions of the politics of such research.

This research becomes further entangled with the politics of platforms as social anxieties over corporate data mining and government surveillance mount. And matters are further complicated when corporate research crosses over into the public domain, raising serious questions about scientific research ethics after the computational turn. The most striking example here is the misnamed "emotional contagion" experiment run on the Facebook newsfeed without obtaining informed consent and without debriefing those users whose Facebook feeds were part of the experiment (Kramer, Guillory, and Hancock 2014; see also the follow-up on ethics from Kahn, Vayena, and Mastroianni 2014). As this controversy demonstrated, increasingly the tools, techniques, and methodologies of corporate data mining are becoming less distinct from academic ones; the same cannot necessarily be said of epistemological foundations, research motivations, and ethical considerations. The conversation on social media research ethics within the academic digital media research community is only just beginning (Zimmer and Proferes 2014) and is notably muted in contexts where large-scale Twitter data plays an important role and research teams might be operating in gray areas with respect to compliance with the Twitter Terms of Service, for example. Here we should note that privacy concerns are substantially integrated into the regulatory controls that Twitter, Inc. is deploying within its data retail business through Gnip. Simply handing over large amounts of money to Gnip is insufficient to gain access; rather, projects have to comply with Twitter's protocols for data use, instantiated in the licensing agreement between them as platform provider and Gnip as data reseller and additionally assessed on a case-by-case basis (Irving 2014), but not publicly available on the Gnip or Twitter websites.

We now turn to a more detailed narrative account of how scientific researchers—particularly those in the humanities and social sciences—have been using Twitter data, the way these regimes of access have shaped the kinds of methods and approaches that are possible (or even the kinds of questions that can be asked), and how changes to these regimes of access are introducing new challenges and limitations to such research. In so doing, we hope that a reflexive account from the perspective of researchers themselves can at least open up some of the "backstage" questions about the politics of Twitter data, if not their answers, as we reflect on the material aspects of the research challenges presented by attempts to negotiate data access and use via the Twitter APIs, Terms of Service, and disciplinary norms and expectations.

The changing scientific affordances of twitter data

As we have already outlined, Twitter's early history is characterized by—and indeed in many ways driven by—the existence of a strong and productive network of third-party developers and researchers providing a range of enhancements to the standard Twitter experience. Such enhancements included a variety of stand-alone Twitter clients that were more user-friendly than, or provided different functionality from, the standard Web-based Twitter user interface or Twitter's own smart phone apps—and even at this early stage offered some basic Twitter analytics, designed mainly to enable users to trace the trajectory of their own Twitter presence. On its own, the emergence of this ecosystem of Twitter enhancements can also be seen simply as the logical next stage of a history of platform co-design and co-evolution processes that for Twitter has always involved the company Twitter, Inc. and its lead users; even what are now regarded as some of the most basic interventions in Twitter's array of communication technologies—the @reply and the hashtag—were after all introduced by Twitter users and only subsequently incorporated into Twitter's core system (Halavais 2014; Bruns 2011).

As a fledgling social media service, emerging in early 2006 alongside the already well-established Facebook, and not receiving any substantial user and media recognition until early 2009, Twitter initially had a strong vested interest in facilitating widespread experimentation with its communicative features, and in working with third-party developers (themselves largely early adopters and enthusiasts) as they explored the technical and commercial viability of particular add-ons, thus identifying potential new applications for Twitter as a social media service. After all, any new uses for Twitter as a platform and, in particular, any "killer app" features that might position Twitter as an attractive alternative to Facebook, would also contribute considerably to Twitter's own viability as a platform.

Throughout these early days of Twitter's history, Twitter, Inc. therefore provided significant support and encouragement to the ecosystem of developers that gravitated to its platform. Central to such support was the provision of a relatively open and powerful API, which provided access to user profile and tweeting activity data. Notably, and owing also to the comparatively flat and open structure of the Twitter network itself, the Twitter API was considerably more powerful and less restricted than its Facebook counterpart. And while some restrictions did apply to the volume of data that ordinary API clients could access, Twitter, Inc. also operated a comparatively generous regime of API client "whitelisting," removing most of these restrictions for API users whose activities were considered *ad hoc* and of some value or interest to Twitter and its users.

While third-party Twitter developers made up the majority of the recipients of such whitelisted access, a number of scholarly and commercial Twitter researchers also benefitted from such generosity, and even the non-whitelisted API proved highly attractive to Twitter researchers. This is reflected in the substantially greater number of scholarly research papers published to date that draw on Twitter rather than Facebook API: in late 2014, a simple Google Scholar search for "Twitter" and "API" returns more than 560,000 results, compared to only 158,000 for "Facebook" and "API"). Indeed, much as the powerful Twitter API provided a general boost to the development of Twitter clients and other enhancements, it also led to the development of a number of widely used specialist Twitter research tools and applications.

The early tools for conducting Twitter research by gathering data from the API largely inherited the same spirit of enthusiasm and exploration as their generic counterparts; alongside the first Twitter researcher get-togethers under the auspices of leading academic conferences such as the annual Association of Internet Researchers conference, or in stand-alone events such as the Düsseldorf Workshop on Interdisciplinary Approaches to Twitter Analysis (DIATA), they contributed significantly to the emergence of a global network of Twitter researchers who shared their methods, approaches, and findings, and often also their data sets, with each other. Indeed, platforms such as TwapperKeeper.com—one of the most popular early tools for gathering Twitter data by tracking and archiving tweets that contained specific user-definable keywords or hashtags—explicitly encouraged such data sharing by making their archives publicly available not just to the originating researcher, but to all other users of the platform.

However, in their encouragement of such collegial and accountable research practices, which enabled researchers to test and verify each other's findings by working with these shared data sets, these tools also increasingly ran afoul of Twitter, Inc.'s stated Terms of Service for the API. In April of 2011, the company forced TwapperKeeper.com to shut down its public service (O'Brien 2011). TwapperKeeper.com functionality was instead made available only as part of the open-source package yourTwapperkeeper.com, which requires researchers to install the tool on their own Web servers and, in line with Twitter's Terms of Service, discourages the public sharing of the data sets it produces. This intervention by Twitter, Inc. thus had a considerable impact on the Twitter research community, both by limiting research activities to those researchers who had the capacity to operate their own data-gathering servers and by undermining researchers' ability to (legally) share and verify each other's data sets. Virtually all Twitter research tools and facilities that have emerged in the meantime (see Gaffney and Puschmann 2014, for a useful overview) similarly require researchers to operate their own servers, and provide data-gathering functionality that is broadly comparable to that of yourTwapperkeeper.com.

Subsequent to its shutdown of Twapperkeeper.com, Twitter, Inc. also began to circumscribe the functionality of the various elements of its Application Programming Interface considerably more tightly. Most centrally, it introduced a range of limits seriously restricting the number of calls to the user and search APIs (which provide information on user profiles and past tweets, respectively) that a Twitter client could make in each fifteen-minute window. Additionally, the search API also provides no more than the last 3,200 tweets for any given user or search term, while the Streaming API (which delivers a continuous feed of tweets matching a given search term) only delivers up to one percent of the total current throughput of the full Twitter Firehose—that is, of the full feed of all current tweets. Further, unrestricted access to the data, which these APIs are designed to provide (i.e., to older historical tweets or higher-volume current content) can now no longer be obtained by applying for whitelisted access. Rather, the only generally available method for gaining such access is to buy data at a substantial cost from one of a handful of authorized commercial Twitter data resellers, thus placing larger-scale access to Twitter data out of reach of most publicly funded research projects and institutions.

By contrast, what remains easily accessible through the standard, open APIs to Twitter researchers without the funds to buy data access are the Twitter feeds that can be generated by tracking a set of user-defined keywords or hashtags, provided that such feeds return a combined total volume of tweets that remains below the one-percent limit that applies to the Streaming API. The net effect of such access-shaping policies has been to push the emerging field of Twitter research to by and large focus on a relatively narrow range of research questions and comparatively isolated case studies, resulting in a dominant form of Twitter research that may be summarized without over-simplification as "hashtag studies," since it largely gathers and analyzes Twitter data sets defined by the presence of one or more set of hashtags. Such hashtag-centric research is undoubtedly valuable in its own right—it has variously shed light on the uses of Twitter in crisis communication (Palen et al. 2010; Mendoza, Poblete, and, Castillo 2010), political controversies (Maireder and Schlögl 2014; Hermida 2014), and second-screen viewing (Highfield, Harrington, and Bruns 2013), for example—but inevitably fails to place its findings in a broader, Twitter-wide context, since the very design of Twitter's API restrictions makes it virtually impossible for researchers to gather such contextual information. Indeed, even the one-percent limit of the Streaming API, which may affect data gathering for particularly active hashtags and keywords, is rarely recognized and problematized in the methodological discussion of hashtag studies papers.

Such a contextualization of hashtag studies in the wider context of Twitter activity is necessary and crucial. While it is useful, for example, to examine the volume and dynamics of user activities within a hashtag data set on a major crisis, such data sets miss out by design on any of the further ancillary public communication activities that happen around them, sparked by or leading to new hashtagged tweets. For example, users responding to a hashtagged tweet may themselves not include the hashtag in their responses, since they are now directly @replying to another user. Conversely, users may afford greater visibility to a tweet they encountered through their own network by retweeting it with an added topical hashtag. But neither of these subsequent or preceding activities will be visible in a hashtag data set. Similarly, while the volume of tweets captured in the data set may appear substantial, its full significance can be assessed only against the benchmark of the total volume of Twitter activity at the same time. Finally, the mere collection of hashtagged tweets itself provides very little indication of its likely impact on public communication on Twitter unless researchers can also draw on detailed information about the participating accounts and their positioning in the network of followers and followees: a hashtagged conversation may have taken place entirely between already tightly connected accounts, for example, or have brought together complete strangers; or it may have involved many virtually friendless accounts or a number of Twitter's most influential users. The contextual data underlying such further analysis is considerably harder to gather than the hashtagged data sets themselves; for a given hashtag data set, it would require the researcher to identify all participating accounts, and then to retrieve the public profile, recent tweeting history, and follower network information available for each of these profiles. Due to the significant limitations that apply to the relevant API access points for large hashtag data sets, this may be a slow and laborious undertaking.

Further, the continuing centrality of the hashtag data set as the first stage in any such research process also maintains an implicit assumption that hashtags do indeed continue to act as a core coordinating principle for Twitter interactions. But while this may be true for specific acute events (Burgess and Crawford 2011) and other forms of breaking news that lead to the rapid formation of an *ad hoc* public (Bruns and Burgess 2011) around emerging hashtags, that assumption is unlikely to be sustainable for most other forms of Twitter interaction. By contrast, the most common—and arguably least researched—form of public communication through Twitter is everyday interaction between users who simply encounter each other's posts because of unidirectional or reciprocal follower-followee relationships. Outside of crisis events, the routine monitoring of the Twitter feed, comprising all recent tweets made by the accounts followed by a given user, must clearly be considered the standard mechanism through which information is disseminated across the network.

To research the dynamics of such information dissemination and user interaction, then, would require a very different combination of data sets than is provided to users of the standard, open Twitter API. At minimum, researchers would need to define a population of Twitter accounts to be monitored; they would have to gather the follower-followee network information for all of these accounts; and they would have to monitor their public communication activities on an ongoing basis for the duration of the project. Most crucially, they would have to do so for a relatively large population of Twitter accounts (for example, all of the accounts in a specific region) in order to generate any meaningful insights that are not inherently skewed by the particular population of accounts tracked. In principle, any such data are also available from the open Twitter API; in practice, however, the API restrictions would make gathering them a slow and laborious process. Further, due to the continuing popularity of hashtag studies in the scholarly community, most of the data-gathering, -processing, and -analysis tools required for such work would have to be developed from scratch: the emphasis on hashtag studies, caused by Twitter, Inc.'s shaping of API access to privilege specific forms of data gathering over others, is thus self-reinforcing.

In essence, then, unless they can raise the significant funds required to buy data from commercial reselling services, Twitter researchers are today forced to limit their activities to working with the "easy" data that are readily available through the standard Twitter API services, or to engage with a clandestine network through which specific Twitter data sets, as well as methods and tools for circumventing the API access limits, are now being exchanged. Meanwhile, the "hard" data that require higher-level Twitter access and more powerful research facilities have become the sole domain of commercial research institutions and a handful of well-resourced research labs, which—often in collaboration with commercial partners—have managed to raise the funds required to buy access to the Twitter Firehose or similarly large data sets.

This has led to a certain stagnation in the development of Twitter research. Since the majority of Twitter researchers now emerging are still coming to terms with the research methods and approaches that are available to them, the chilling effects of a reduction of Twitter studies to mere hashtag studies are not yet widely appreciated and articulated. But the chilling effects of Twitter, Inc.'s restrictive policies do have a significant detrimental effect on both the quality and diversity of scholarly research investigating the uses of Twitter as a major medium for public communication today—and this ultimately not only affects the scholarly community and the public debates it contributes to and engages with, but also Twitter itself, as both a platform and a company. If very little intellectually hard research on Twitter is able to draw on large data sets, and most of the technically hard, "big data" Twitter research is conducted by commercial and market researchers, our understanding of Twitter as a media platform and of Twitter-based communication as a sociocultural phenomenon must necessarily suffer.

Conclusions

In this chapter, we have laid out the dual dimensions of the "computational turn" and how they become entangled with the practice of digital media research in the humanities and social sciences. We have focused particularly on some uses of critical software and platform studies for dealing with these entanglements at the very specific and concrete level of understanding how the Twitter API mediates access to Twitter data, and how changes to these "regimes of access" relate to the changing business realities and aspirations of Twitter, Inc., as well as to the "datafication" and "algorithmization" of the digital media business more generally. We focused particularly on the affordances of Twitter data for academic research and how these have been shaped and constrained by Twitter's regimes of access to data. Here we would like to emphasize that it is not only wholesale access per se, but also the differential availability of data—ranging from the various parts of the tweets and their metadata in hashtag and keyword data sets through to more comprehensive Twitter feeds, public profile information, and follower-followee networks—that shape the research questions that can be asked. Such constraining factors, resulting from the business decisions of Twitter, Inc., shift the emphases of the entire emerging field of "Twitter studies," which today tends to focus too heavily on @reply networks and hashtag publics because current API limitations privilege certain forms of access and use over others.

We therefore distinguish between "easy data" on the one hand—modestly sized sets of tweets and certain associated, predetermined metadata matching a keyword search over a short, recent period of time—and "hard data" on the other—more comprehensive, longitudinal data sets and/or any of the "missing" metadata. We have shown how access to the hard data bestows very considerable scientific advantages on those who have it, and suggested that it is problematic if there is a correspondence between scientific privileges of this kind and the prestige, wealth, and industry-connectedness already enjoyed by elite universities and research institutes—particularly in those cases where such research is conducted behind closed doors, to the benefit of industry but not to the collective benefit of the platform's differentiated user community.

On this basis we argue that there is now a growing divide between the majority of researchers who are forced to work with easy data—pursuing the low-hanging fruit in Twitter research because a lack of funding for data access and research tools development prevents them from doing anything else—and a minority of researchers and institutes who either have the funds to pay Gnip or DataSift, and whose research complies with the opaque corporate restrictions Twitter places even on its data-selling partners, or who have the technical skills to partially circumvent API restrictions and access the more difficult "hard data" about public communication on Twitter. Due to underlying differences in funding patterns, this divide is also one between different disciplinary perspectives: prominent commercial as well as university-based market research and computer science institutes dominate in the latter group (including the research labs associated with some of the world's biggest technology companies), while their poorer cousins from the humanities and social sciences, as well as from underfunded universities or those in developing countries without large research budgets, are more likely to be found in the former.

Whether intended by Twitter, Inc. or a collateral outcome of internal priorities, this growing imbalance significantly skews the trajectory of Twitter research, and thereby is likely also to affect the public perception of Twitter as a tool for public communication. Researchers who wish to dig deeply into the political economy of social media platforms—including those who wish to take up van Dijck's call to integrate Actor-Network Theory and political economy approaches when doing so—would do well to consider the regimes of access, politics of use, and economies of exchange that increasingly constitute the market in "big social data" research. Researchers more pragmatically concerned with access to Twitter data and the full range of (still circumscribed) scientific possibilities it affords—even if frustrated in their attempts to gain access—may nevertheless contribute to the global politics of knowledge, through public reflections and critiques of the regimes of access that emerge in relation to scientific uses of social media data.

Finally, while beyond the scope of our discussion in this chapter, it is possible that the politics of data access for Twitter and other social media platforms may have important legal and policy ramifications as well, especially in light of the growing "data rights" and information rights movements to which the growing debate around "data philanthropy" is contributing (see, for example, Stempeck 2014). Twitter's donation of the full historical Twitter Firehose to the US Library of Congress in 2010, as well as 2014's inaugural Twitter data grants program (Kirkorian 2014) are framed as examples of Twitter's largesse in data philanthropy; even third-party data reseller DataSift has announced humanitarian data science "partnerships" involving gifted data access (DataSift 2014).

Such grants are welcome, in principle, if they are truly philanthropic rather than merely an exercise in corporate public relations. The real impact of such initiatives to date is entirely negligible: the Library of Congress Twitter archive has yet to be made available to researchers in any meaningful and transparent fashion, and Twitter data grants were awarded to a paltry 6 projects from a total field of more than 1,300 applicants (Kirkorian 2014). Developments such as these should give us pause: why is it that commercial data retail companies are selectively making data "grants" to one-off projects (by proxy taking over the evaluative role of national science agencies and global not-for-profit organizations in selecting worthy initiatives to support), rather than developing widely accessible, affordable models of access to the public's data for public good? Given the strong demand for sustainable scientific access to social media data sets beyond what can be retrieved through their open APIs, it would be more responsible and appropriate for Twitter, Inc. and other providers to develop meaningful and affordable data access frameworks and pricing structures that address the growing missing middle in scholarly social media research, rather than operating what in essence amounts to a random data lottery.

References

Berry, David. 2012. "Introduction: Understanding the Digital Humanities." In David Berry, ed. *Understanding Digital Humanities*. London: Palgrave Macmillan, 1–20.

Bilton, Nick. 2012. "Is Twitter a technology company or a media company?" *Bits Blog* (*New York Times*). http://bits.blogs.nytimes.com/2012/07/25/is-twitter-a-media-or-technology-company/?_php=true&_type=blogs&_r=0.

Bilton, Nick. 2013. *Hatching Twitter: A True Story of Money, Power, Friendship, and Betrayal*. New York: Portfolio.

Bogost, Ian, and Nick Montfort. 2009. "Platform Studies: Frequently Questioned Answers." *Proceedings of the Digital Arts and Culture Conference.* http://escholarship. org/uc/item/01r0k9br.

Bruns, Axel. 2011. "Ad Hoc Innovation by Users of Social Networks: The Case of Twitter." ZSI Discussion Paper 16. https://www.zsi.at/object/publication/2186.

Bruns, Axel and Jean Burgess. 2011. "The Use of Twitter Hashtags in the Formation of Ad Hoc Publics." Paper presented at the European Consortium for Political Research conference, Reykjavík. October 25–27, 2011. http://eprints.qut.edu.au/46515/.

Bruns, Axel and Jean Burgess. 2015. "Methodological Innovation in Precarious Spaces: The Case of Twitter." In Helen Snee and Yvette Morey, eds. *Digital Methods for Social Science.* London: Palgrave Macmillan.

Bucher, Taina. 2012. "Want to Be on the Top? Algorithmic Power and the Threat of Invisibility on Facebook." *New Media & Society* 14(7): 1164–80.

Bucher, Taina. 2013. "Objects of Intense Feeling: The Case of the Twitter APIs." *Computational Culture* 3. http://computationalculture.net/article/objects-of-intense-feeling-the-case-of-the-twitter-api.

Burgess, Jean. 2014. "From 'Broadcast yourself' to 'Follow your interests': making over social media." *International Journal of Cultural Studies* [online first]. http://ics. sagepub.com/content/early/2014/01/13/1367877913513684.abstract.

Burgess, Jean and Axel Bruns. 2012. "Twitter Archives and the Challenges of 'Big Social Data' for Media and Communication Research." *M/C Journal* 15(5). http://journal. media.culture.org.au/index.php/mcjournal/article/viewArticle/561.

Burgess, Jean and Kate Crawford. 2011. "A Theory of Acute Events in Social Media." Paper presented at the Association of Internet Researchers conference, Seattle. October 11–13, 2011.

DataSift. 2014. "UN Global Pulse & DataSift Announce Data Philanthropy Partnership." http://datasift.com/press-releases/UN-Global%20Pulse%20Partnership/.

Fuller, Matthew. 2008. *Software Studies: A Lexicon.* Cambridge, MA: The MIT Press.

Gaffney, Devin and Cornelius Puschmann. 2014. "Data Collection on Twitter." In Katrin Weller, Axel Bruns, Jean Burgess, Merja Mahrt, and Cornelius Puschmann, eds. *Twitter & Society.* New York: Peter Lang, 55–68.

Gerlitz, Carolyn and Anne Helmond. 2013. "The Like Economy: Social Buttons and the Data-Intensive Web." *New Media & Society* 15(8): 1348–65.

Gillespie, Tarleton. 2013. "The Politics of 'Platforms.'" In John Hartley, Jean Burgess, and Axel Bruns, eds. *A Companion to New Media Dynamics.* London: Wiley-Blackwell, 407–16.

Gillespie, Tarleton. 2014. "The Relevance of Algorithms." In Tarleton Gillespie, Pablo Boczkowski, and Kirsten Foot, eds. *Media Technologies.* Cambridge, MA: MIT Press, 167–94.

Halavais, Alex. 2014. "Structure of Twitter: Social and Technical." In Katrin Weller, Axel Bruns, Jean Burgess, Merja Mahrt, and Cornelius Puschmann, eds. *Twitter & Society.* New York: Peter Lang, 29–42.

Hallinan, Blake and Ted Striphas. 2014. "Recommended for You: The Netflix Prize and the Production of Algorithmic Culture." *New Media & Society*. http://nms.sagepub. com/content/early/2014/06/23/1461444814538646.abstract.

Helmond, Anne. 2013. "The Algorithmization of the Hyperlink." *Computational Culture* 3. http://www.annehelmond.nl/wordpress/wp-content/uploads/2013/11/ Helmond_2013_CC_AlgorithmizationOfTheHyperlink.pdf.

Hermida, Alfred. 2014. "Contested Media Spaces: #idlenomore as an Emergent Middle Ground." Paper presented at *Social Media and the Transformation of Public Space*, University of Amsterdam, June 19.

Highfield, Tim, Stephen Harrington, and Axel Bruns. 2013. "Twitter as a Technology for Audiencing and Fandom: The #Eurovision Phenomenon." *Information, Communication & Society* 16(3): 315–39.

Hillis, Ken, Petit, Michael, and Kylie Jarrett. 2013. *Google and the Culture of Search*. New York: Routledge.

Irving, Francis. 2014. "The Story of Getting Twitter Data and its 'Missing Middle.'" *ScraperWiki Blog*. https://blog.scraperwiki.com/2014/08/the-story-of-getting-twitter-data-and-its-missing-middle/.

Kahn, Jeffrey P., Effy Vayena, and Anna C. Mastroianni. 2014. "Opinion: Learning as We Go: Lessons from the Publication of Facebook's Social-Computing Research." *Proceedings of the National Academy of Sciences* 111(38): 13677–79.

Kirkorian, Raffi. 2014. "Twitter #DataGrants Selections." *Twitter Engineering Blog*. April 17. https://blog.twitter.com/2014/twitter-datagrants-selections.

Kramer, Adam D. I., Jamie E. Guillory, and Jeffrey T. Hancock. 2014. "Experimental Evidence of Massive-Scale Emotional Contagion through Social Networks." *Proceedings of the National Academy of Sciences* 111(24): 8788–90.

Langlois, Ganaele, and Greg Elmer. 2013. "The Research Politics of Social Media Platforms." *Culture Machine* 14. http://www.culturemachine.net/index.php/cm/ article/viewDownloadInterstitial/505/531.

Lazer, David, Alex (Sandy) Pentland, Lada Adamic, Sinan Aral, Albert Laszlo Barabasi, Devon Brewer, Nicholas Christakis, Noshir Contractor, James Fowler, Myron Gutmann, Tony Jebara, Gary King, Michael Macy, Deb Roy, and Marshall Van Alstyne. 2009. "Life in the Network: The Coming Age of Computational Social Science." *Science* 323(5915): 721–23.

Maireder, Axel and Stephan Schlögl. 2014. "24 Hours of an #outcry: The Networked Publics of a Socio-Political Debate." *European Journal of Communication*. Online first, September 2. doi:10.1177/0267323114545710.

Manovich, Lev. 2010. "Trending: The Promises and the Challenges of Big Social Data." In Matthew K. Gold, ed. *Debates in the Digital Humanities*. Minneapolis: University of Minnesota Press, 460–75.

McCarthy, Caroline. 2009. "Twitter Co-Founder: We'll Have Made It When You Shut Up About Us." *CNet*. http://www.cnet.com/au/news/twitter-co-founder-well-have-made-it-when-you-shut-up-about-us/.

Mendoza, Marcelo, Barbara Poblete, and Carlos Castillo. 2010. "Twitter under Crisis: Can We Trust What We RT?" In *Proceedings of the First Workshop on Social Media Analytics* (SOMA'10), 71–79. http://snap.stanford.edu/soma2010/papers/soma2010_11.pdf.

Messerschmidt, Jana. 2014. "Twitter welcomes Gnip to the Flock." *Twitter Blog.* https://blog.twitter.com/2014/twitter-welcomes-gnip-to-the-flock.

O'Brien, Joe. 2011. "Removal of Export and Download/API Capabilities." *Archive of TwapperKeeper Blog.* http://twapperkeeper.wordpress.com/2011/02/22/removal-of-export-and-download-api-capabilities/.

Palen, Leisa, Kate Starbird, Sarah Vieweg, and Amanda Hughes. 2010. "Twitter-Based Information Distribution During the 2009 Red River Valley Flood Threat." *Bulletin of the American Society for Information Science and Technology* 36(5): 13–17.

Presner, Todd. 2010. "Digital Humanities 2.0: A report on knowledge." http://cnx.org/content/m34246/1.6/?format=pdf.

Puschmann, Cornelius, and Jean Burgess. 2014. "The Politics of Twitter Data." In Katrin Weller, Axel Bruns, Jean Burgess, Merja Mahrt, and Cornelius Puschmann, eds. *Twitter and Society*. New York: Peter Lang, 43–54.

Rieder, Bernhard and Theo Röhle. 2012. "Digital Methods: Five Challenges." In David Berry, ed. *Understanding Digital Humanities*. London: Palgrave Macmillan, 67–84.

Stempeck, Matt. 2014. "Sharing Data is a Form of Corporate Philanthropy." *Harvard Business Review*. http://blogs.hbr.org/2014/07/sharing-data-is-a-form-of-corporate-philanthropy/.

van Dijck, José. 2013. *Culture of Connectivity: A Critical History of Social Media* (Kindle Edition). New York: Oxford University Press.

Weller, Katrin, Axel Bruns, Jean Burgess, Cornelius Puschmann, and Merja Mahrt, eds. 2014. *Twitter and Society*. New York: Peter Lang.

Zimmer, Michael and Nicholas Proferes. 2014. "A Topology of Twitter Research: Disciplines, Methods, and Ethics." *ASLIB Proceedings* 66(3): 250–61.

6

Scraping the First Person

Greg Elmer

The problem shared by first- and third-person descriptions is obvious: namely, both are descriptions.

Graham Harman[1]

The WikiLeaks and Snowden files continue to generate heated debates over the motives and ethics of the protagonist leakers, the broader role of established newspapers in disseminating the leaked files to a worldwide audience, and of course the political fallout of the released content itself. Some three years after the initial WikiLeaks revelations, and almost a year after the first reports of Edward Snowden's leaked US National Security Agency's files hit the Internet and front pages of international dailies, the *New York Times* opened a new chapter in the debate over secret government files, reporting on the NSA's investigation into exactly how Edward Snowden was able to access and store some of the country's most highly classified files. NSA sources told the *Times* that Snowden "scraped data out of our system" and "we do not believe this was an individual sitting at a machine," but instead a "quite automated" process (Sanger and Schmitt 2014). *Time* magazine also chimed in, proclaiming that "Snowden Used Cheap Software to Plunder NSA Data" (Frizell 2014). As the headlines and reports reverberated across technology websites and blogs, the story rarely departed from the script: Snowden had beat the system by using a simple, cheap, and widely available software tool to easily copy the data from what many believed were incredibly complex and intensely guarded databases.

We should recognize, however, that the use of data scrapers is not restricted to those looking to blow the whistle on secretive government agencies or those

---

[1] From "Zero-Person and the Psyche." In David Skibia, ed. *Mind That Abides, David Skibia.* Amsterdam: Benjamins, 2009. http://dar.aucegypt.edu/bitstream/handle/10526/3384/Zeroperson. pdf?sequence=5.

looking to exploit proprietary data. Rather, data scraping, particularly on and across the Web—including social media platforms—has become big business. In the wake of the Snowden and WikiLeaks cases, such practices have raised ethical questions about the ownership of data, its broader circulation, and its use (or abuse) by a variety of independent and institutional actors. Take the example of Ireland-based budget airline Ryanair. In February 2014, the airline received a lot of bad press when a group of passengers were unable to print their boarding passes from the Internet. When the passengers telephoned Ryanair expecting this technical glitch to be quickly resolved they were instead charged a substantial fee to board their flight. Ryanair later explained to the *Guardian* that, against the advice of the airline, the passengers had booked their tickets through a "screen scraping" website, essentially a ghost company serving as an unofficial proxy to the airline (Brignall 2014). Such forms of data scraping point us far beyond and below the high profile Snowden and WikiLeaks examples, suggesting that the practice involves a broader process of integrating business practices, networks, and payment regimes. In the Ryanair case, the scraped data and mirror site were fully integrated into the airline's booking network, much like the site expedia.com.

While NSA investigators and Ryanair public relations staff sought to understand the implications of scraping within their own organizations and operational contexts, Google, one of the world's most influential corporations, was also coming to grips with the widespread use of such tools. In February 2014, Google's technical staff circulated a URL for a Web-based "Scraper Report" tool to its key clients. The Scraper Report added another indexical—or better *ranking*—component to the equation. Companies, institutions, and individuals were not only concerned about scrapers being used to lift or scrape content from their respective sites, but were also faced with the prospect that such scraped content might now outrank the original material and website on Google's search engine. In short, scraped-content sites were now more visible on Google than the originating sites.

Google's Scraper Report promised to remove the offending scraped sites by asking the original sites to list the URL on the site where the content was taken from, the exact URL on the scraper site, and the Google search URL that demonstrated the problem.[2] The ubiquity and blurry "ownership" of scraped

---

[2] https://docs.google.com/forms/d/1Pw1KVOVRyr4a7ezj_6SHghnX1Y6bp1SOVmy60QjkF0Y/viewform. Accessed May 15, 2014.

content would in short order, however, turn back on Google when users around the world used the Scraper Report and Twitter to post Google's own practice of "scraping" content from a host of sites across the Web, including such notable sites as Wikipedia (Abbruzzese 2014). Consequently, as one industry watcher noted: "Google's efforts to thwart Internet copycats known as 'scrapers' have backfired. Thus what started out with the best intentions has become Friday's Internet joke du jour after Google was caught using its *own* scraper to mine content" (ibid.).

Indeed, "scraper" is a contested and often exceedingly vague term, one that calls for a deeper understanding of Web architectures and economies. In the corporate realm, scrapers pose a challenge to the control over business models and brands, the acquisition of cheap to free content, online advertising, and ubiquitous data collection, profiling, and sales. By contrast, for the individual artist, scrapers are associated with the copying, reprinting, and publishing of their works. And by further contrast, in light of the Edward Snowden and WikiLeaks data controversies, scrapers have become synonymous with security breaches and intelligence theft. Moving beyond these limited and proscribed contexts, this chapter approaches the study of scrapers from a methodological perspective, investigating how such tools, processes, and nascent methods can be used to collect data sets from social media platforms and other digital properties. While social scientists and digital humanities and digital methods scholars have developed a mix of approaches and software tools addressing a wide range of problems, data scraping tends to originate from a common problem—that access to official, sanctioned, or authorized forms of data is restricted by design, cost, or neglect. Following the Snowden, Ryanair, and Google examples, this chapter also begins from the position that the lifting, copying, or otherwise "scraping" of data from the Web or other databases is increasingly entangled in broader networked technologies, protocols, and economies. It therefore questions the assumptions underlying recent attempts to develop an "architectural method" or "analytic of scraping" and seeks instead to understand the all-too-often "back boxed" algorithms and operational code of social media and digital media platforms by interrogating the "personalized" logics and formatting of content, data, and metadata.

Scraper analytics

Bernhard Rieder (2013) provides perhaps the clearest definition of a scraper analytic: the use of software tools to circumvent issues of data accessibility, both to the content itself and to the knowledge of the inner workings of largely proprietary social media platforms such as Facebook and Twitter. Including scraping among the broader "digital methods" of the digital humanities and computational social sciences (see Rogers 2013), Rieder writes:

> Data sets can be exploited to analyze complex social and cultural phenomena and digital methods . . . have a number of advantages compared to traditional ones: advantages concerning cost, speed, exhaustiveness, detail, and so forth, but also related to the rich contextualization afforded by the close association between data and the properties of the media (technologies, platforms, tools, websites, etc.) they are connected with; data crawling necessarily engages these media through the specifics of their technical and functional structure and therefore produces data that can provide detailed views of the systems and the use practices they host. (346)

Like Rieder, Marres and Weltevrede (2013) also suggest broader methodological goals beyond simple data extraction, claiming that scraping should be taken to refer not just to a technique but also to a specific "analytic practice," one that speaks as much about the source of its production (Web platforms, for instance) as it does about the extracted data itself. For Marres and Weltevrede, scraping not only provides a spatial—or better architectural—perspective on the relationship between Web platforms, shared objects, and their users; it also advances a temporal or "live" form of research methods (see also Back and Puwar 2013; Elmer 2012), one that provides insights on "research-in-the-making." Such a perspective no doubt proves helpful in research environments on Web/social media platforms where data is preformatted and generated in predictable flows, Twitter being the prototypical example. Marres and Weltevrede make a compelling case for how Twitter scraping—because of Twitter's constant stream of fresh data and lack of reliably accessible tweet archives—can enable and accommodate practices of "real-time" analysis in journalism, marketing, and policymaking. Putting aside attempts to "clean" data—that is, verify its biases or origins—Marres and Weltevrede encourage us to treat the Web "blindly," and thereby engage in a form of data aggregation from a multiplicity of sources, creating "continuous chains" that shed light on computational and algorithmic temporalities, again in the service of "live research."

In many respects, however, live research can only be enacted with access to live feeds, calling into question the overreliance upon feed-like platforms such as Twitter. Reider's project of providing access to semi-proprietary content has similarly focused on semi-private spaces on the Facebook platform. Here in this chapter, by contrast, we are looking to build upon Marres and Weltevrede's argument that scraping and analytical practices that flow from it, must be put in a cross-platform, comparative context if we are to glean the importance of preformatted data and metadata. There are commonalities among nearly all major social media platforms that we cannot simply overlook or reduce to the live feed or timeline. First and foremost, we consider social media—and any data scraped from its numerous platforms—as *first-person media*. From this perspective, social practices, conventions, interfaces, platforms, and shared objects are all governed by a logic of personalization.

By highlighting the means through which each form of data scraping and associated platform personalize their data—in effect, formatting data and metadata through the user platform—we here propose that an analytics of social media scraping can be found in rethinking social media from a *zero-person perspective,* one that focuses on the governance of *relationships* on and across social media practices, platforms, and objects. The notion of a zero-person perspective is in part derivative of Finnish grammar, which stresses an ecology of subjectivity, that is, it stresses the relationships forged between person and environmental context. In other words, "the zero person constructions express changes of state, emotions, perceptions, or other processes that affect human beings in particular situations" (Laitinen 2006). Thus, while recognizing the importance of the affective dimension of communication on social media, which is so central to the first-person perspective of social media writ large (as intensely personalized media), the zero-person perspective insists upon context and specificity. The chapter concludes with some speculative remarks on zero-person research trajectories, methods, and analytics.

Whether it is reported in the popular or technical press, leaked into the blogosphere, or openly promoted by new media companies themselves, there is no doubt that social media data is formatted and designed as *first-person media*—that is, the content of social media, and previously the World Wide Web, is intensely filtered and personalized through the "likes," friends, location, profile, browsing and posting habits, and other online behaviors of individual users. Do we really need a scraper analytic and associated methods to recognize that social media platforms and other digital media properties act, as I have elsewhere suggested, as "profiling machines" (Elmer 2004)? Or more to the point: what might a scraper analytic as a technique or method overlook or consciously displace by not beginning research with this fact in mind? Would the scraper analytic merely replicate preexisting Web logics that structure and govern Web content? To an extent, both Google's PageRank algorithm and Facebook's "Like" economy (Gerlitz and Helmond 2013) are rooted in the encoding of individual user and webmaster preferences and practices. Ultimately, does beginning the scraper analytic with the user platform, without recognizing its attendant first-person logic, risk turning such research into the very black box that it promises to deconstruct?

To expand upon the concern of the first person, we now turn to the three most common forms of data scraping—particularly from social media platforms—in an effort to understand how the first-person or personalized logics of such properties call into question, or otherwise overdetermine, the scraper method or analytic uniting the platform and user. The first goal of this review is simply to acknowledge that we cannot assume or develop overarching theories and methods of social media analysis based upon a singular notion or process of data scraping. And yet, while much effort has gone into developing tools and methods for scraping data from different platforms using different techniques, each instance remains enveloped—that is, aggregated—in and through first-person algorithms. The second goal of this section—which begins at screen scraping before moving to crawlers and API scraping—is to expand upon the critique of the user platform – based mode of scraper analytics and tools, again with the presumption that such an approach will render insight into the complex dynamics at play within the operating logics and code across social media platforms.

Screen and interface scraping

The history of data scraping is inherently tied to the first-person perspective. Screen or interface scraping is a process of extracting data from the HTML code that is visualized on user interfaces—the primary visual means through which data is personalized and customized for particular users. Many Web browser versions, including the very first mass-consumer graphics-enabled browsers, notably Netscape Navigator (1994), included a preference option that rendered the graphic interface into an HTML document (typically EDIT>View source code).[3] The broader process of extracting HTML code from multiples pages

---

[3] Contemporary browsers still maintain this browser preference, albeit with new nomenclature. Google's Chrome browser (version 35.0.1916.114, as of May 28, 2014) renders a page's source code through the preference pull down sequence *View>Developer>View Source*, whereas Mozilla's Firefox browser (version 29.0.1, as of May 28, 2014) through *Tools>Web Developer>Source Code*.

thus involved developing relatively simple computer scripts that automated this user-preference option. "Terminal Emulation" programs were initially designed, as the term suggests, to *impersonate* or otherwise represent host computer data (from servers) to user terminals (i.e., the computer screen, in today's technology). The concept was still in circulation and operation during the early formation of the World Wide Web, where common computer language was needed to render networked information (content and data) to computer terminals worldwide.[4] The development of graphic user interfaces thus initiated the process of separating operational data from computer terminals and screens. Though, at this early stage of web development, graphics interfaces/browsers— as we have seen with browsers and preference options—made screen scraping a relatively easy process to automate with computer scripts.

Terminal emulation programs did not, however, only emulate data and operations of computer servers; they also mimicked the command strokes of the users, through the use of I/O devices, most notably QWERTY keyboards. As Fulton (2014) suggests: "Screen scraping is a programmatic method to extract data from screens that are primarily designed to be viewed by humans. Basically the screen scraping program pretends to be a human and 'reads' the screen, collecting the interesting data into lists that can be processed automatically."

Screen scraping thus enacts a form of first-person data retrieval, in effect by mirroring the possible actions or interactions with the computer interface. The data extracted from the interface, in other words, is formatted, requested, or otherwise presented for the use of the individual computer user. The automation of such screen scraping likewise, technologically speaking, *emulated* user-centric forms of browsing, for instance the following of links and other user-designed navigational practices such as "next page" buttons to extract data from multiple Web pages. Thus, to summarize, early forms of screen or interface scraping can be said to emulate or otherwise "impersonate" the behavior of users, setting in place a logic that was to be followed by more complex scraping programs and ever more restrictive and proprietary, data-rich platforms. Such scraped data sets thus call into question not only the personalized structure of content and associated data and metadata, but also the behavioral practices attached to them—whether browsing, searching, or other forms of sifting through information.

---

[4] See the request for comments (RFC) on telnet terminal options from the Network Working Group in February, 1989. http://tools.ietf.org/html/rfc1091.

Crawler scraping—index and content

As the 1990s progressed, the Web soon emerged as a network dominated by sites, pages, and hyperlinks. Research seeking to map relationships, clusters, centers, and peripheries developed scrapers that not only captured and extracted HTML, but also "crawled" websites through their hyperlinks. The technique remains in use today. Snowden's capture of NSA data also deployed a so-called "web scraper," a bot-like program that searched for associated pages and files, offering not only context but a picture of the architecture or index of the scraped database. NSA officials likened the software to "Googlebot, a widely used web crawler that Google developed to find and index new pages on the web" (Sanger and Schmitt 2004).

As automated search agents, Web crawlers' collection of data occurred in a decidedly gray zone, not only defined by proprietorial issues and claims, but also exceptionally unstable and constantly evolving protocols that governed the limits and access of such "bots" to files and servers. Server-side programs were developed, some in conjunction with protocols such as robot.txt files that attempted to restrict the ability of crawlers and bots to collect specific data (Elmer 2009). Security-like protocols were henceforth installed to detect the repeat bot-visitor, which subsequently led to crawler programmers extending their requests to longer time periods (typically to 30–60 seconds) so as to avoid detection and server-side bans. More to the point, as automated programs, crawlers or bots were not designed to analyze or otherwise report on such protocols and roadblocks to site and page scraping; they merely archived the accessible Web from the geo-location of the researcher and host computer.

Such limitations on early crawlers or bots thus raise questions over the contours of the restricted Web, or compromised Web crawl data, those limited (filtered) by the personal settings, geographic location, and thus "first-person" perspective of the researcher, host computer, and consequently the "starting location" of their crawlers. The work of Ron Deibert et al. (2010) and others at the University of Toronto's Citizen Lab have, for example, widely documented the inaccessible Web, depending on the origins of one's IP address. The World Wide Web is, in this sense, a censored space with key aggregators and search engines like Google facilitating and maintaining the terms of restriction. Social media platforms have only multiplied the rules and regulations of data access of course. Countries such as South Korea have further required that its citizens complete extensive registration forms to enroll in global social media platforms such as Yahoo. Many users consequently seek anonymity by registering for US-based Yahoo accounts, once again pointing to a broader set of international policies, protocols, and personal practices that complicate or, as previously noted, "pre-format" scraped data through the geo-locationality of individual users, researchers, and site of research tools such as crawlers and scrapers.

API scraping

As a stand-alone entity of sorts, with much greater control over access to its data, the social media platform has greatly restricted the ability of crawlers and other automated scrapers to search and archive its many spaces, applications, and archives. And given the vast amount of personal comments, intimate details, and extensive profiles that users share and post on social network sites like Facebook, such restrictions arguably maintain essential privacy commitments to users. That said, while much has been made of the helpfulness of social media "application program interfaces" (APIs) as interfaces that make data access more convenient, little is known about how they filter, format, or otherwise make data available. Scholars and researchers ultimately cannot confirm the manner in which platforms such as Twitter and Facebook format their API-facilitated data requests or "scrapes." Such platforms also constantly change the backend code that governs and facilitates such requests with or without notice. Through interviews and reviews of technical reports, Bucher (2013) has nonetheless provided a helpful overview of the forms of digital practice that APIs encompass and govern. She writes:

> Web APIs encompass: a physicality in terms of the corporeal landscape of infrastructure and technology, through to the economic logics at work (i.e. business models, ownership, licensing of the APIs), functions and services (i.e. access to data), practices of users (i.e. forms of labor, play and collaboration), discursive formations (i.e. statements, knowledge, ideas), rules and norms (i.e. design principles, terms of service, technical standards), as well as social imaginaries and desires. As is apparent, APIs are complex phenomena.

While they are complex and opaque assemblages, social media APIs have not developed in a vacuum. Rather, both Facebook and Twitter developed their interfaces and associated functions in the years immediately preceding their public listing on stock exchanges. Is it so far-fetched to suggest that such functions were developed to increase the potential market value and profitability of these platforms and parent companies? Or to rephrase, can we assume that data scraped through social media platform APIs is unfiltered or otherwise disentangled from the logics that aggregate users, friends, user-generated content, interface visualizations and preferences, and so forth? Software studies scholars and critics such as Bucher and software engineers (Ko, Cheek, and Shehab 2010) suggest otherwise. As Bucher argues, "The Open Graph protocol [a protocol that Facbook uses to assign proximity and relevance of users and objects], the API and the 'Like' button cannot function effectively independently of each other. Together however, these infrastructural and medium-specific elements provide a foundation for the organisation and management of users and their connections". Ko, Cheek, and Shehab likewise argue that APIs are fully integrated—indeed were initially designed—to govern and encourage ever more intricate and granular forms of user surveillance and profiling. They write:

> Social networking websites let users build social connections with family, friends, and coworkers. Users can also build profiles for storing and sharing various types of content with others, including photos, videos, and messages. Updating user profiles with interesting content is a form of self-expression that increases interaction in such sites. To encourage this interaction and provide richer content, social-networking sites expose their networks to web services in the form of online application programming interfaces. These APIs allow third-party developers to interface with the social-networking site, access information and media posted with user profiles, and build social applications that aggregate, process, and create content based on users' interests. (37)

Scraping social media data through APIs thus calls into question not only the analytics of scraping and the claims that can be made from such data, but also the role that researchers can play in reproducing the terms of first-person media such as Facebook. Bernard Rieder of the University of Amsterdam has developed a series of tools to assist in the capturing, storing, and analyzing of API-generated data. Such tools have, unlike the stand-alone ones before them (screen scrapers and crawlers), been fully integrated into social media platforms themselves. Rider's Netvizz tool, for example, a scraper designed to collect data from Facebook groups, is itself hosted on Facebook, fully integrated into the platform's application ("app") architecture and algorithms. On deploying the scraper app, the researcher is informed that "Netvizz will receive the following info: your public profile, friend list, News Feed, status updates, groups and likes and your friends' likes." To conduct data scraping with Netvizz, the researcher, in short, is forced to participate in the work of the platform—the divulging of one's friend network, and all their attendant likes, comments, behaviors, etc. Such instances of API scraping thus raise significant ethical questions for the nature of research participation, consent, and privacy. Marres and Gerlitz (2014) nicely summarize the inherent danger of such approaches: "The risk . . . is that we end up essentializing the differences between the 'methods of the medium' and 'our own' sociological methods" (8).

Conclusions

While admittedly brief and selective, this historical and technological review of scraping research has nonetheless highlighted the centrality of the user in the data scraping process, first as the source of data (collecting the residual imprints of the user's computer-based behaviors and practices), next as a geo-located and limited crawler, and lastly, as a form of research that trades access to data for incorporation in the very reproduction of first-person data on, for instance, Facebook. That is, scraped data is not only formatted as first-person or profiled data; it is in the very first instance produced as human-machine-emulated data, thus providing the researcher with a recognizable perspective, a first-person perspective. We could also refer to this perspective as a socially embodied perspective, from the user "out" toward his or her networks, friends, pages, and so forth.

But where does that leave the social media researcher in need of data? While the recent Facebook controversy over researchers acquiring insider access to data (only to then turn such access into an experiment with the mood of users[5]) aptly highlighted the ethical pitfalls of sanctioned data access, it may also have reaffirmed the need for scraped data. Yet the first-person question persists, and it should not be dismissed as the "cost" of doing social media research, making it doable and relatively inexpensive. This is not merely a question of privacy, ethics, or collaboration with corporate entities. Rather, the first-person perspective of

---

[5]   http://www.theguardian.com/technology/2014/jun/29/facebook-users-emotions-news-feeds.

social media scraping calls into question the importance of position. Scraped data not only represents a particular perspective or view, it also highlights the source or position of that view—positions that are united by common social media platforms. By contrast, the goal of a zero-person perspective would therefore be to multiply the points of research, of not only perspectives but of positions, times, and connections, of which the user/social media platform is but one.

Importantly, this chapter does not make the case for an objective, observational, or third-person perspective in and across such networks and platforms. Nor is this an effort to cleanse the Internet, Web, or social media research of its human dimension. Quite the opposite; a *zero-person* perspective would need to take into consideration the affective flows and disruptions of networked life. A zero-person perspective is not automated; it is clearly not a "zero touch technology" that purports to remove the need for human intervention (Dunleavy et al. 2006). Rather, a move from the first to the zero person, would instead look to the connectivities and other signs of relationships—again chiefly among users, platforms, and mediated objects across social media and beyond—including data scraped, hacked, stolen, and aggregated by other parties and platforms operated by governments, private metrics firms, Google, and so on (see Redden in this volume).

Zero-person perspectives have also begun to emerge of late in the design of new social media platforms and logics, ones that purposefully move outside of personalized logics and points of view. So-called antisocial networks are an interesting attempt to move beyond the first person, though some like the app Cloak[6] merely serve as technologies that use personalized data to avoid social media friends. The app Rando, by contrast, actively seeks out relationships outside of first-person networks, for instance by enabling a user to sends photos to strangers.[7] While some might see anonymity in such connections (e.g. from the user sending out photos), the zero-person perspective would also note the moment of serendipity produced by receiving such photos. Scraping data associated with the photo themselves would also move a network or social media analytic outside of the premise of affinity (or its opposite) as the principal force of connectivity and meaningful relations. Such is the promise and possibility of a zero-person analytic.

---

[6]   https://www.getcloak.com/.
[7]   http://www.ustwo.co.uk/blog/introducing-rando/.

References

Abbruzzese, Jason. 2014. "Google Trolls Itself in Attempt to End Website Scraping." *Mashable*. February 28. http://mashable.com/2014/02/28/google-trolls-scraping/.

Back, Les and Nirmal Puwar, eds. 2013. *Live Methods*. Malden, MA: Wiley-Blackwell.

Brignall, Miles. 2014. "Reaching the Point of No Return with Ryanair but 'Screen Scraping' Was to Blame." *The Guardian*. March 8. http://www.theguardian.com/money/2014/mar/10/ryanair-book-online-error-screen-scraping.

Bucher, Taina. 2013. "Objects of Intense Feeling: The Case of the Twitter API: Computational Culture." Accessed December 1, 2014. http://computationalculture.net/article/objects-of-intense-feeling-the-case-of-the-twitter-api.

Deibert, Ronald, John G. Palfrey, Rafal Rohozinski, and Jonathan Zittrain, eds. 2010. *Access Controlled: The Shaping of Power, Rights, and Rule in Cyberspace*. Cambridge, MA: MIT Press.

Dunleavy, Patrick, Helen Margetts, Simon Bastow, and Jane Tinkler. 2006. "New Public Management Is Dead—Long Live Digital-Era Governance." *Journal of Public Administration Research and Theory* 16(3): 467–94. doi:10.1093/jopart/mui057.

Elmer, Greg. 2004. *Profiling Machines Mapping the Personal Information Economy*. Cambridge, MA: MIT Press.

Elmer, Greg. 2009. "Robots.txt: The Politics of Search Engine Exclusion." In J. Parikka and T. Sampson, eds. *The Spam Book: On Anomalous Objects of Digital Culture*. Cresskill, NY: Hampton, 217–27.

Elmer, Greg. 2012. "Live Research: Micro-blogging an election debate." *New Media and Society* 15(1): 18–30.

Frizell, Sam. 2014. "Snowden Used Cheap Software to Plunder NSA Data." *Time Magazine*. Accessed February 21, 2014. http://swampland.time.com/2014/02/09/snowden-nsa-cheap-software/.

Fulton, Kane. 2014. "Screen Scraping: How to Stop the Internet's Invisible Data Leeches." *TechRadar*. Accessed April 1, 2014. http://www.techradar.com/news/internet/web/screen-scraping-how-to-stop-the-internet-s-invisible-data-leaches-1214404.

Gerlitz, Carolin and Anne Helmond. 2013. "The Like Economy: Social Buttons and the Data-Intensive Web." *New Media & Society* 15(8): 1–18.

Ko, Moo Nam, Gorrell P. Cheek, and Mohamed Shehab. 2010. "Social-Networks Connect Services." *Computer* 8(August): 37–43.

Laitinen, Lea. 2006. "Zero Person in Finnish: Paradigmatic resource for construing human reference." In M. Helasvuo and L. Campbell, eds. *Grammar from the Human Perspective: Case, space and Person in Finnish*. Amsterdam: John Benjamins, 209–31.

Marres, Noortje and Carolin Gerlitz. 2014. "Interface Methods: Renegotiating Relations Between Digital Research, STS and Sociology" (unpublished manuscript).

Marres, Noortje and Esther Weltevrede. 2013. "Scraping the Social? Issues in live social research." *Journal of Cultural Economy* 6(3): 313–35.

Rieder, Bernard. 2013. Studying Facebook via Data Extraction: The Netvizz Application. In *Proceedings of the 5th Annual ACM Web Science Conference*, New York, NY, 346–55.

Rogers, Richard. 2013. *Digital Methods*. Cambridge, MA: The MIT Press.

Sanger, David E. and Eric Schmitt. 2014. "Snowden Used Low-Cost Tool to Best N.S.A." *The New York Times*. February 8. http://www.nytimes.com/2014/02/09/us/snowden-used-low-cost-tool-to-best-nsa.html.

7

Openness Compromised? Questioning the Role of Openness in Digital Methods and Contemporary Critical Praxis

Fenwick McKelvey

Introduction

In 2009, Google's Senior Vice President, Product Management, Jonathan Rosenberg circulated a memo about "the meaning of open." "At Google," he begins "we believe that open systems win." He goes on to describe how openness works as open-source code, open standards, and open information. He explains: "When we have information about users we use it to provide something that is valuable to them, we are transparent about what information we have about them, and we give them ultimate control over their information" (2009, n.p.). Openness at Google, he concedes, is still an ideal—Google *aspires* to be open. The dreams of Google, however, might unsettle critical Internet researchers who also share a critical praxis in making the Internet practicably open. This research seeks open information about the system and, at times, seeks to counteract the very work of Google in creating *an open information commons* unlike the commercial and commercializing engines of the Internet. How can both Google and critical Internet researchers both embrace openness despite clearly having different ends in mind?

This chapter asks if openness is indeed a critical response to "compromised data." Many scholars in this volume and elsewhere (see also DeNardis 2014; Gillespie 2010) have described the main issues surrounding compromised data online: proprietary code, restricted data, and opaque platforms. To counteract the forces compromising data, scholars as diverse as Lawrence Lessig (2006) and Michael Hardt and Antonio Negri (2004) have embraced openness as a critical praxis. Responses manifest as open data in academic research, open code in software production, and open society in democratic theory. Anonymous, Edward Snowden, and other leakers have also embraced openness as a way to challenge state and corporate power. Finally, the imaginary of openness has inspired Internet research to find ways to open up the Web, to find "potential critical fissures, openings, and possibilities for progressive social and political change" (Elmer 2006, 163).

Openness has only begun to attract critical attention, despite its seminal role in shaping the modern Internet and digital economy (Russell 2014). Much of the criticism comes from critiques of democracy under capitalism; the dreams of an open Web persist despite the realities of compromised data. Openness, communication, and publicity imbricate and are too easily adopted as values of neoliberalism and capitalism (Dean 2005; Tkacz 2012). Barney (2014) argues that "despite the tendency to equate communication and access to information with democracy itself, publicity is not the same thing as politics" (85). Publicity is not necessarily the antidote to apathy, but might exacerbate the problem, prompting a response, according to Barney, of "I know very well, but all the same . . . ." The risk is that "openness" stands in for serious debate and political engagement. Providing an "opening" may gesture toward a response without provoking one. As Jodi Dean (2005) describes, in "communicative capitalism" the speech itself matters more than its consequences. Being open runs the risk of being a stand-in for alternative approaches to technology by offering technical "fixes" that often obscure the political questions provoked of digital media.

This chapter aims to contribute to these critical reflections by focusing on the implications and consequences of openness-inspired digital methods for the ever-increasing "compromise" of data. Here, I define "digital methods" as tools designed to attend to the materiality of digital media—its data and its code—as opposed to digitized methods adapting social science methodologies to the Internet, for example, online surveys or interviews conducted over Internet Relay Chat (Rogers 2013). By attending to digital media, these methods simultaneously create knowledge about digital communication and the medium itself.

As much as digital methods have tried to find clarity in opacity and break secrecy, they have also had an uneasy relationship with information intermediaries—especially search engines and social media platforms—which have developed their own digital methods to mine, analyze, and control access to the web. The same opportunities for digital methods have also attracted companies trying to "listen in" on the conversation online (Crawford 2009). Internet research, in other words, is now a site of struggle and a means to expose power structures online. Digital methods compete with commercial forms of social research. Digital marketing, social media analytics, data brokers also make promises to open the Web. Of course, this sort of tension is not altogether new in communications research, which has had a close relationship with state propaganda efforts (Simpson 2003) and later with commercial marketing research (Smythe 1981; Streeter 1996). Still, I argue that those developing and using digital methods have to account for the power relations inherent in their design and implementation if they are serious about pursuing the agenda of online openness. Part of this challenge is to reflect on the history of digital methods.

The chapter addresses the question of openness through two of the most popular digital methods: Web archiving and platform studies. Web archiving has long tried to make the Web more open, while platform studies have focused on the restrictions of so-called open social media platforms. These sites of analysis affirm that openness is both a seminal concept for digital methods and one that might need to be refined, or outright abandoned, given its uneasy connection to compromised data. The chapter provides a review of these methods—how they work, their "exploits," and their relationship to openness—and concludes that critical Internet research might have to reorient itself toward a more experimental and less replicable mode of inquiry and engagement.

Digital methods and the value of opening

Faced with the power and complexity of new communications infrastructure and information technology, scholars have long tried to *open* up the black box of technology (Bijker et al. 1987; Latour 2005). Hackers, phreakers, and crackers have made similar responses to the same conditions, albeit from very different motivations. Even with their differences, scholars and hackers share a belief that openness supports a more democratic and accountable approach to technology. An open technology exposes its operation to users as well as keeps its use open-ended. Free software with its open code, access, and participation often exemplifies this alternative approach to technology.

Lawrence Lessig has been clearest in bridging hackers and scholarly theories of openness. In his introduction to the politics of code, he concludes: "If code regulates, then in at least some critical contexts, the kind of code that regulates is critically important" (2006, 139). By code, Lessig means the technical systems that regulate the Internet, such as the hardware, protocols, and software. Only one kind of code, for Lessig, is appropriate in critical contexts: open code. In a divide reminiscent of Karl Popper's (1971) own division between open/democratic versus closed/authoritarian governments, Lessig divides code between open code, "whose functionality is transparent at least to one knowledgeable about the technology," and closed code, "whose functionality is opaque" (2006, 139). Whether the code runs a Diebold voting machine or tracks trends on Twitter (cf. Gillespie 2014), code has to be open and transparent in order to be accountable. Openness provides more transparency and greater social accountability because it allows anyone to look at the source code, analyze the data, and access the findings.

Lessig draws on hacker culture and especially the Free, Libre, and Open Source movement (FLOSS) to justify the accountability of openness.[1] Openness, to FLOSS, is a mode of publicity—to borrow a word from Barney (2014)—for technology. Projects like the Linux operating system or the Mozilla Web browser use open-source licenses so anyone can read, modify, and contribute to the project. Anyone with technical skill can learn about the software through its open code and contribute back through its open development process. Open code is better because it is open to the public. A popular mantra by famed hacker Eric S. Raymond insists that "given enough eyeballs, all bugs are shallow" (Raymond 1999, 30). In other words, opening up code to the public leads to better products as opposed to closed or unpublicized code. Opening enlists the public in its development, better connecting a technology with its users and creating a more democratic technical culture.

Openness is a practice as much as a state of technology. Hackers and academics work to make and keep technology open, a relationship to technology that Christopher Kelty (2008) describes as recursive. Openness functions as an imaginary that inspires geeks to make the Internet *as open as they imagine it to be*, working against efforts to partition it. Openness as an imaginary has its roots in the early Internet. Most of the code, protocols, and even institutions of the early Internet tried to be as open as possible (DeNardis 2009; Russell 2014;

---

[1] The embrace of open source by academia marks an interesting return to a class of hackers cast out by the creep of proprietary code in the lab. In a strange inversion, the academic culture of open knowledge that inspired open source and free software is, in turn, influenced by these communities (Kelty 2008, 2013).

Gillespie 2006) or rather this supposed history inspires hackers to make technology open. (An alternative telling of the Internet's history could just as easily focus on its concentrated development in elite computer science and corporate research institutions.) Kelty suggests that, "for the last quarter century it has been the Internet that geeks have been most concerned to protect and to keep as *radically open* as possible—for it is now the sine qua non of any other software or network they or anyone else might build" [italics added] (2005, 202). Kelty calls this approach recursive since the vision of an open Internet propels the development of a future Internet.

Hackers have inspired Internet researchers to try their hand at writing code, which has ultimately given rise to digital methods (Blumenthal 2005). Digital methods attempt to open digital media to find new insights about society and power. Bruno Latour has been particularly articulate in connecting the praxis of digital methods with political accountability. He has explored how digital methods might "map" controversies in science and technology as they occur online[2] (Latour and Rogers 2012). Mapping, conceptually, aligns with Latour's attempts to redefine authority *as networked*. Latour gives the example of a professor of climatology who is asked to justify his authority and the certainty of his findings. While Latour first worried that the professor would insist on the infallibility of facts, the professor instead outlined the steps undertaken to produce his evidence: the methods, the practices, and the scope. The professor, in other words, traces the network that led to the creation of facts (Latour 2013, 2–3). Laying out the network of a fact, so to speak, implies accountability. Digital methods, to Latour, offer a way to draw these connections using Internet data.

Now that we have a sense of the logic of digital methods, the questions that follow are: What is the work of digital methods? How do they attempt to make technology more open? The next section of this chapter describes the work of digital methods as searching for "exploits" in systems. Methods use exploits to open and publicize technical system—a technical process that opens data. The search for exploits marks the point where digital methods have an uneasy proximity to the forces of compromised data. The section will describe how exploits are as open to information intermediaries as they are to researchers.

---

[2] For more details, see the Mapping Controversies Project: http://www.mappingcontroversies.net.

Digital methods and the exploit

Digital methods search for "exploits" in existing systems that might create openings for research. Galloway and Thacker (2007) contend that "informatic spaces do have bugs and holes, a by-product of high levels of technical complexity, which make them as vulnerable to penetration and change as would a social actor at the hands of more traditional political agitation" (2007, 82). Exploits are these bugs and holes. The term borrows from hacker nomenclature, where an exploit refers to vulnerabilities in technical systems that might break its security. Both hackers and digital methods see exploits as a means to learn about a system (albeit for different ends). Whereas a hacker's interest in the exploit might be more technical, digital methods use exploits for academic research. The exploit might remind us of Rogers' observation that, "computing may have techniques which can be re-purposed for research" (Rogers 2009, 3). Repurposing, to use Roger's term, studies how the digital encoding of information might be used in unexpected ways to reveal more information about the workings of a complex technical system.

Some of earliest methods to study the Internet demonstrate the search for exploits. It is now common to run a "ping" command to test an Internet connection, but the original Internet Protocol Suite never included the test. Instead, Mike Muuss (n.d.) developed ping using an exploit of these protocols in 1983. It measured the time taken to communicate between two nodes of the network (and round-trip time, RTT). Without a formal measurement, Muuss calculated the RTT by timing the delay in receiving an echo request using the Internet Control Message Protocol (ICMP). While ICMP had not been designed for measurement, Muuss realized that its Echo Request could measure RTT—an exploit of the protocol, so to speak. In 1987, ping inspired Traceroute to list the networks a message travels through to reach its destination. Traceroute sent a sequence of packets, like the Echo Request packets of ping, with varying Time-to-Live (TTL) values. The lower the value, the less distance a packet travels before causing a response. These responses allowed Traceroute to map how information travels across its various networks from sender to receiver. Traceroute, as a digital method, exploited the TTL function—beyond its original purpose to reduce network congestion of undeliverable packets—to create a tool for measurement and research. Both found ways to repurpose or exploit protocols for research purposes.

These early digital methods demonstrate two aspects of the digital methods research: how hackers have inspired research to write tools to study technical systems, and how these exploits became means to open up complex technical systems. Traceroute helped create some of the first maps of the early Internet, then known as the National Science Foundation Network (NSFNET). There had been hand-drawn maps of the Advanced Research Projects Agency Network (ARPANET) since the start, but the NSFNET proved too big to map conventionally (see Dodge and Kitchin 2001 for a detailed overview of Internet mapping). Burch and Cheswick (1999) ran millions of traceroutes to locations across the world. The results charted how information moved across NSFNET. The Burch and Cheswick study created one of the first maps of what we would now call Internet. Their map Internet research, like the FLOSS movement, had a recursive relationship with this openness. The Internet's openness allowed for innovative new methods and research sought to perpetuate this openness by adding back new knowledge about its networks.

While these examples come from computer science, Internet research has continued this search for exploits to make the Internet more open. The next section explores the tensions through Web archiving. Web archiving is the key method to understand the work carried out by Internet research in digital methods. Web archiving uses the traces of activity left encoded in the Web as a mirror to reflect trends in society and culture. At the same time, search engines and information intermediaries also use Web archiving to enclose the open data of the Internet and generate what this book calls "compromised data."

Opening up the black box of the Web:
Web archiving and its praxis

Digital methods attracted a critical mass as the World Wide Web came to be seen as part of everyday life and therefore an important site of study (for a more in-depth discussion, see Rogers 2009; Schneider and Foot 2004). Researchers could now focus on methods to study social activity encoded (or in-formation) in the language of the World Wide Web, the HyperText Markup Language (HTML). It is hard to know exactly when archiving started, since all Web browsing technically involves making a copy, but the Internet Archive popularized the method when it launched in 1996 (Kahle 1997). The Archive today allows users to browse the history of a website through its Wayback Machine that navigates its snapshots of Web pages or Web scrapes. The Wayback Machine partially fulfills the Archive's mission to provide "universal access to all knowledge"—a mission emblematic of a public perpetuating an open Web. The method has grown more popular as the website became part of everyday life—not simply a digital document, but a site of social activity.

Web archiving refers to the storing, indexing, and analysis of the World Wide Web. Archiving offsets the Web's "unique mixture of the ephemeral and the permanent" (Schneider and Foot 2004, 114). The Web is ephemeral, as it might be taken down at any time, yet "web content must exist in a permanent form in order to be transmitted" (Schneider and Foot 2004, 114). Web archiving exploits the open code and data of the HTTP and HTML standards. These protocols, like most Internet protocols, leave their code open or exposed (DeNardis 2009). HTTP transmits information as a raw, unencrypted code to be rendered by a browser on a local machine (much to the frustration of Web developers who find subtle differences between browsers when writing their code). Archiving works because HTTP and HTML do not prohibit making a copy of websites (in fact it required a user to download each website) (Schneider and Foot 2004). Tools known as "scrapers" read HTML pages, collect the necessary pieces, and save all the components as an accurate archive of the website.

Web archiving involves another kind of opening too, not necessarily a making open—the Web was already open—but rather a window to create knowledge and build upon it. HTML's open code provides a layer of metadata such as tags at the top of a file to identify a site to search engines and robots.txt files to understand the social activity it encoded (Elmer 2008). Once collected, a secondary analysis could analyze these codes, permitting alternative perspectives in the document. Hyperlink analysis has been the most popular method to discover these patterns (Park and Thelwall 2003). A website encoded its context on the Internet through hyperlinks. By collecting and parsing the links, Web archiving could situate websites and identify clusters of interest (or Web spheres) online. Richard Rogers, along with members of the GovCom organization, use their IssueCrawler to trace a network of organizations surrounding certain issues (Bruns 2007; Marres and Rogers 2005). The tool starts with a snowball sample of issue-oriented websites, such as environmental groups, and scrapes how these sites linked to other websites, gradually creating a network of relationships between groups based on their linking patterns. By contrast, the alternative

Web browser Web Stalker[3] renders websites as nodes in a network. Users might navigate the connections between websites rather than viewing the site itself. Hyperlink analysis then functions recursively to both create more data about the Internet and justify the need for open data by demonstrating the benefits of its open interpretation.

Web archiving has been highly useful in the social sciences and particularly, in my own experience, in political communication. Foot and Schneider (2006) used Web archiving to code and analyze American Presidential campaigns from 2000 to 2004 to see how campaigns actually used the Web either as a kind of static brochureware or to encourage more political participation (hint: its usually not the latter). Where Foot and Schneider use archiving to question how the Web might reshape politics, other iterations of archiving draw a connection between the method and greater transparency in politics. John McCain used a Web archiving tool to watch Barack Obama's policy positions, looking for when his opponent changed positions (Paul 2008). Wikiscanner, a scraper for Wikipedia, scraped its data and matched edits to locations on the Internet to determine if certain institutions had edited politicized articles. Did a candidate edit the Wiki of their opponent?

Web archiving has struggled over how to exploit open data without being exploitative. Debates hinge on the ambiguity of the publicity of technically open data. Almost any website can technically be scraped, but whether it *should* be scraped is another matter. For instance, did archiving break copyright law? Regional laws offer conflicting opinions since archiving could debatably fall under fair use or fair dealing. Part of the debate has focused on the matter of privacy and whether people knowingly publicized their information as open data (Hine 2005; Markham and Baym 2008). Should a personal blog post be scraped? Does a user know the ways their content might be repurposed when contributing it to the Web? Privacy guidelines have developed in institutional ethics review boards (Buchanan and Ess 2009) and in professional associations like the Association of Internet Researchers.[4] Researchers also argued the opposite for institutional cases—in a language similar to WikiLeaks—that some data should be made public. Elmer (2008) debated whether scrapers should, for example, follow a website's robots.txt, a file that specified what files a site did not want publicized or indexed by search engines. Robots.txt only ever functioned

---

[3] For the latest version, see: http://v2.nl/archive/works/the-web-stalker.
[4] For a complete review, see Buchanan and Zimmer 2012.

as an informal, good faith guideline and scrapers, ignoring the guideline, could actually find information meant to be hidden. While none of these debates have been resolved, they suggest that "openness" in practice raises basic questions about its meaning.

The open-endedness of Web archiving and hyperlink analysis hints at a darker side of exploits. By discovering and using exploits, do researchers ease the commercialization and enclosure of open data? Digital methods have a vexing relationship with the political economy of information that it promises to reform. Both open data and open methods leave their use open-ended, facilitating rather than resisting the digital enclosure. More than ease commodification, the logic of opening might obfuscate other critical praxis. The concern echoes a problem raised by Barney, that "the distribution of possibility and impossibility is a material question more than it is a question of information" (2014, 81). This suggests that the ideals of a more democratic approach to technology might not be best realized by an ethos of openness. Openness might simply add information rather than confront the forces that keep the data closed. As will be discussed in this next section, the dangers of this open-endedness seem clearly apparent in its appropriation by commercial forces.

The convenience of open data for the digital enclosure

Openness easily flows into new systems of commercialization. Langlois and Elmer (2009) noticed such a pattern on Wikipedia. Hundreds of websites wrap ads around Wikipedia text, repurposing noncommercial content to generate ad revenues. The literature describes this process of moving open data from not-for-profit to for-profit contexts as a *digital enclosure* (Bettig 1997; Boyle 2003). Open data seems to aid as much as resist this process. Search engines have recognized the value of openness of the World Wide Web and set about to mine it. Google exemplifies how open data has led to a new industry of information intermediaries that aggregate and mediate access to open data (DeNardis 2014). Their ability to do so depends on the same exploits as Web archiving. At its core, Google is a form of Web archiving, although its scale dwarfs academic research. Its engines (or spiders) scan the Internet, collect copies of websites, index their metadata and analyze the link between sites to determine relevance (Becker and Stalder 2009; Bermejo 2009; Vaidhyanathan 2011). The PageRank algorithm used to rank sites began as hyperlink analysis. PageRank, so closely associated with Google's success, is in principle a kind of hyperlink analysis.

The commercialization of data avoids the ambiguities of privacy and copyright found in academic research. Information intermediaries largely sidestep issues of privacy, describing their work as a kind of profiling that uses aggregated rather than personal information (Elmer 2004; Gangadharan 2012; Turow 2012). Furthermore, copyright provisions such as the Digital Millennium Copyright Act granted commercial search engines the legal impunity to index and cache information (Masanés 2006). Web scraping has also developed to support more commercial-oriented activities. Much of the development of sophisticated Web scrapers now happens through ScraperWiki. The website provides a simple but robust programming interface to collect data from websites. ScraperWiki, however, is a commercial operation aiming to sell to both academics and commercial firms alike; its scrapers can be used for profit just as much as for nonprofit research.

The success of these information intermediaries has rewired the Web, making it more difficult to scrape and diminishing its initial openness. The Web moved from 1.0 to 2.0. Its sites developed into social media platforms that converged "different technical systems, protocols and networks that enable specific user practices and connect users in different and particular ways" (Langlois et al. 2009, 419). Platforms ran using Javascript, server-side scripting, and databases to create dynamic websites that behave more like software than hypertext (van Dijck 2013; Gillespie 2010; Langlois et al. 2009). The digital enclosure then is twofold: both commodifying open data and producing new access in proprietary spaces. As the next section explains, the work of digital methods has become more difficult with platform studies. Current platforms resist scrapers and limit access. These changes point to a contradiction of the contemporary Web: it is less open, yet all the major digital empires from Apple to Google believe in openness—that open systems will win.

Platform studies and me-centricity

The transition to Web 2.0 has shifted digital methods away from Web archiving toward platform studies. Where digital methods in the past dealt with exploits in HTML and HTTP, new digital methods had to find exploits specific to platforms. This has proved to be more difficult. Platforms leave their data less exposed than

Web 1.0, limiting the possibility of using digital methods. Their underlying code changes faster than protocols or standards that have to be formulated, agreed upon, and petitioned for revision by international standards organizations (DeNardis 2009). Custom scrapers might be able to collect data for a while until an update breaks the scraping script. Even if a scraper works, it only captures the output and not the code running on the server, leaving researchers with only a partial understanding of the platform. A few open source tools managed to adapt Web archiving to platforms, especially blogs (Burgess and Bruns 2012; Elmer, Langlois, and McKelvey 2012; Karpf 2008), but the methods constantly struggled to keep up with changing platforms.

Though platforms differ from one another, tools for specific platforms share a common problem of overcoming the narrow perspective provided to researchers. Without access to the proprietary data feeds authorized by the platform, researchers suffer from what Langlois et al. (2009) describe as "me-centricity." Researchers never have access to the source code in HTML, nor to the whole platform, but only to their own specific vantage point.

The concept of me-centricity developed at the Infoscape Lab (Ryerson University, Toronto, Canada) during its studies of Canadian elections on social media platforms. The project queried Facebook to find the most popular political Facebook groups. Facebook results began to differ depending on the user. The same queries would give different results. Me-centricity eroded the lab's ability to discern popularity, as queries only returned personalized results. Platform me-centricity deflects this inquiry through ambiguity: researchers only see as much of the site as determined by the platform. It never discloses the logics that decide what appears in the search returns or, by extension, the newsfeed or in recommendations. The platform only appears to the researcher in its final form after customization and individualization.

Attempts have been made to address the methodological issues of me-centricity. Langlois and Elmer suggest that the problem concerns *what is available to the researcher* with limited access to corporate social media data and to the social media algorithms that organize life online." Since researchers cannot overcome their own perspective, Langlois and Elmer stress the need to focus on "digital objects" or "the elements that compose social media platforms in specific context: a 'Like' button is a digital object, for instance, as is a comment or any other kinds of text" (2013, 11). Similar to the exploits of HTML, attending to the function and design of digital objects allows researchers a glimpse at the workings of the platform. Gerlitz and Helmond (2013), for example, study the

"Like" button and its sharing functions. Feuz, Fuller, and Stalder (2011) focused on the outputs of platforms. They automated queries on Google to see whether results varied between user accounts. Their research compares search returns from different profiles to discover how platforms might construct different user perspectives. This comparative approach thus studies "a distributed machinery that is both wilfully opaque and highly dynamic" (Feuz, Fuller, and Stalder 2011).

As researchers attempt to overcome me-centricity, platforms have begun to provide their own conditional forms of access. APIs allow researchers to access the data generated from the platform. These tools also allow developers to create new apps alongside the platform or within the platform, such as Facebook Apps. APIs provide open-access, much to the concern of privacy critics, who worry that platforms share too much user data, but for specific reasons and usually for paying customers only. APIs also require users to abide by its Terms of Use that focus tools on the commercial-specific uses of the data—mostly platform apps or games. Some researchers do get access, but access is unevenly distributed according to a somewhat exclusive social network. Often friends of developers or well-funded researchers get access first (cf. boyd and Crawford 2012; Bruns and Stieglitz 2013; Ravindranath 2014).

Internet researchers now have to choose between a daunting do-it-yourself approach and relying on platforms for data. Platforms have partnered with new information intermediaries to sell data access, and a whole industry of social media analytics developed for research into platforms (Helmond 2014). Tools such as Adobe Social, SalesForce Marketing Cloud, Radian, and Sysomos all sell products to conduct research on social media, though such products are packaged for commercial rather than academic purposes. It is tempting to return to open-source values to critique these proprietary methods, since their sleek interfaces obscure methodological decisions. Certainly, the slick interface of social media analytic software and closed code may provoke fewer questions than the experiments, hacks, and ad hoc solutions celebrated by digital methods (Karpf 2012). Commercial tools are often easier to use, better supported, and bigger. Some excellent research about blogs came out of repurposing the Technorati (Farrell and Drezner 2007) and HitWise Competitive Intelligence (Hindman 2009). One might ask what is wrong with co-opting closed methods given these successful studies.

By using these closed methods, researchers run the risk of validating these compromised sources of data; indeed, platforms employ a rhetoric of an open Internet despite being a force for its enclosure. While the language of openness abounds in social media firm rhetoric (Gillespie 2010; van Dijck 2013), the 2012 protests against the US Stop Online Piracy Act (SOPA) demonstrated that numerous forces of compromised data actually rally in favor of an open Internet: Facebook, Google, and Twitter rallied against the SOPA bill. Openness seemingly complements their business models. Indeed, "the ideals of openness fit equally as comfortably in the spirit of entrepreneurial capitalism as they do in the liberatory impulse of the hacker ethic" (Russell quoted in Schrock 2014, 12–13). The conflation of openness with the market principles goes as far back as Karl Popper's embrace of an open society that celebrated the circulation of ideas akin to the circulation of goods and services in a free market (Tkacz 2012).

These forces of compromised access draw on the same rhetoric of openness as digital methods do. Google believes that open systems will win. Facebook releases its code as open-source. The open-endedness of the concept openness seems to be to the advantage of the forces of compromised data. As Schrock found in his study of HTML5, the "rhetoric of openness is deployed as a public relations tactic and to reconcile competing visions of stakeholders. It is important to not conflate these versions while understanding that definitions of openness are still in flux and have a polysemic quality" (2014, 11). Platforms seem to use the term openness to disguise their closed efforts. The dream of free communication persists, but is ultimately undermined by the realities of the structural advantage of the major tech players. The New World Information and Communication Order (NWICO or NWIO) debates at the United Nations sought to question how free and open communication function to support forms of media domination (Preston, Herman, and Schiller 1989).

In the end, the struggles of platform studies pose a problem to digital methods: Is openness an appropriate foundation for the critique of compromised data? Open data have become fuel for driving the engines of Google and other information intermediaries. Open code participates in innovation for spammers as much as for academics. All the while, open standards paradoxically serve to obfuscate systems and "open-access" has become so vague a term that companies employ it heavily while getting rich through data privatization and enclosure. In pointing to these limitations of openness, I aim to provoke, not condemn, research on the issue. The limitations of the concept of openness appear both in the praxis of digital methods and in its discursive and strategic articulation with the social platforms. Digital methods seemingly participate in the compromising of data as much as they attempt to contest it.

Is openness still relevant?

How might data be open without being compromised? Could openness be replaced with a normative stance with a clear direction, one that specifies the rights and conditions of circulation? Some open licenses have already moved in this direction. Creative Commons and the GNU Public License, version 3, restrict circulation in order to prevent its commercialization. GPLv3, for instance, stops the movement of code onto devices that prevent the modification of that code. The changes target companies, especially the smart TV maker TiVo, from benefiting from open code while locking down its devices. Michael Gurstein (2011) suggests that open data needs an added layer that stipulates its "effective use" to ensure "that opportunities and resources for translating this open data into useful outcomes would be available (and adapted) for the widest possible range of users" (n.p.). On the opposite end, data pirates have often called for a "grey commons" that does not recognize file ownership. Such a gray commons might be a counterforce to those commercial engines pulling data into proprietary data sets (Fleischer and Palle 2005; Sengupta 2006). Pirates instead pull all content into the open—a tension that might just as well feed back into commercialization. Either way, data is never left open.

How also might digital methods researchers change their praxis? One option would be reorient digital methods as tools for experimentation rather than openness. Foucault elaborates on this direction when he describes an experiment as

> work done at the limits of ourselves must, on the one hand, open up a realm of historical inquiry and, on the other, put itself to the test of reality, of contemporary reality, both to grasp the points where change is possible and desirable, and to determine the precise form this change should take. (1984, 46)

Experimenting uses methods as events in themselves. The event might not be about open data or access, but about creating openings in themselves and accepting the ephemerality of such openings. In contrast with hoping to make the Web permanently more open, digital methods might embrace momentary openings—flash bulbs in the dark. Critical engineering (Parikka 2013) and reverse engineering (Gehl 2014) both offer directions for this experimental method. Both developed as alternatives to openness that embrace the question of knowledge while better acknowledging power relations. Critical engineering, rather than taking transparency for granted, embraces the imperceptibility of code and how its tricks might expose "how infrastructure is in most cases less stable than it seems" as well as leaking "data on many fronts, intervening in negotiations of public and private" (2013, 15). To make open, in this sense, would not entail a release into openness, but a moment of uncertainty of being open like an error message appearing on a computer billboard exposing its code for a moment before being fixed. An experimental approach might resemble what Karpf (2012) calls "kludginess."[5] Could methods be tactical interventions rather than replicable methods?

I have been suggesting in this chapter that, by now, openness might be an exhausted concept. "There is no free software," says Chris Kelty at the end of his critical appraisal of modern open-source code, "and the problem it solved is yet with us." Free, Libre, and Open Source Software (FLOSS) no longer offers an alternative to commercial software production under capitalism, according to Kelty. We may have to look elsewhere for tactics of resistance. This same conclusion no doubt applies to digital methods contesting the forces described in this volume as "compromised data."

References

Barney, Darin. 2014. "Publics without Politics: Surplus Publicity as Depoliticization." In Kirsten Kozolanka, ed. *Publicity and the Canadian State: Critical Communications Approaches*. Toronto: University of Toronto Press, 72–88.

Becker, Konrad and Felix Stalder, eds. 2009. *Deep Search: The Politics of Search beyond Google*. Innsbruck: Transaction Publishers.

Bermejo, Fernando. 2009. "Audience Manufacture in Historical Perspective: From Broadcasting to Google." *New Media & Society* 11(1/2): 133–54.

Bettig, Ronald. 1997. "The Enclosure of Cyberspace." *Critical Studies in Mass Communications* 14(2): 138–58.

---

5 To kludge is to find a work-around or a messy solution to a problem.

Bijker, Wiebe E., Thomas P. Hughes, Trevor Pinch, and Deborah G. Douglas, eds. 1987. *The Social Construction of Technological Systems: New Directions in the Sociology and History of Technology*. Cambridge, MA: The MIT Press.

Blumenthal, Mark M. 2005. "Toward an Open-Source Methodology: What We Can Learn from the Blogosphere." *Public Opinion Quarterly* 69(5): 655–69.

boyd, danah and Kate Crawford. 2012. "Critical Questions for Big Data: Provocations for a Cultural, Technological, and Scholarly Phenomenon." *Information, Communication & Society* 15(5): 662–79. doi:10.1080/1369118X.2012.678878.

Boyle, James. 2003. "The Second Enclosure Movement and the Construction of the Public Domain, The." *Law & Contemporary Problems* 66 (Winter/Spring): 33–74.

Bruns, Axel. 2007. "Methodologies for Mapping the Political Blogosphere: An Exploration Using the IssueCrawler Research Tool." *First Monday* 12(5). http://firstmonday.org/htbin/cgiwrap/bin/ojs/index.php/fm/article/view/1834/1718.

Bruns, Axel and Stefan Stieglitz. 2013. "Towards More Systematic Twitter Analysis: Metrics for Tweeting Activities." *International Journal of Social Research Methodology* 20 (February): 1–18. doi:10.1080/13645579.2013.770300.

Buchanan, E. A. and Ess, C. M. 2009. "Internet Research Ethics and the Institutional Review Board: Current Practices and Issues." *ACM SIGCAS Computers and Society* 39(3): 43–49.

Buchanan, Elizabeth A. and Michael Zimmer. 2012. "Internet Research Ethics." *The Stanford Encyclopedia of Philosophy* (Fall 2013 Edition). June 22. http://plato. stanford.edu/archives/fall2013/entries/ethics-internet-research/.

Burch, H. and B. Cheswick. 1999. "Mapping the Internet." *Computer* 32(4): 97–98, 102. doi:10.1109/2.755008.

Burgess, Jean and Axel Bruns. 2012. "Twitter Archives and the Challenges of 'Big Social Data' for Media and Communication Research." *M/C Journal* 15(5). http://journal. media-culture.org.au/index.php/mcjournal/article/view/561.

Crawford, Kate. 2009. "Following You: Disciplines of Listening in Social Media." *Continuum* 23(4): 525–35. doi:10.1080/10304310903003270.

Dean, Jodi. 2005. "Communicative Capitalism: Circulation and the Foreclosure of Politics." *Cultural Politics* 1(1): 51–74. doi:10.2752/174321905778054845.

DeNardis, Laura. 2009. *Protocol Politics: The Globalization of Internet Governance*. Cambridge, MA: MIT Press.

DeNardis, Laura. 2014. *The Global War for Internet Governance*. New Haven: Yale University Press.

Dodge, Martin and Rob Kitchin. 2001. *Mapping Cyberspace*. New York: Routledge.

Elmer, Greg. 2004. *Profiling Machines: Mapping the Personal Information Economy*. Cambridge, MA: MIT Press.

Elmer, Greg. 2006. "Re-Tooling the Network: Parsing the Links and Codes of the Web World." *Convergence* 12(1): 9–19.

Elmer, Greg. 2008. "Exclusionary Rules? The Politics of Protocols." In Andrew Chadwick and Philip N. Howard, eds. *Routledge Handbook of Internet Politics*. New York: Routledge. http://www.loc.gov/catdir/enhancements/fy0808/2008003045-d.html.

Elmer, Greg, Ganaele Langlois, and Fenwick McKelvey. 2012. *The Permanent Campaign: New Media, New Politics*. New York: Peter Lang.

Farrell, Henry and Daniel W. Drezner. 2007. "The Power and Politics of Blogs." *Public Choice* 134(1/2): 15–30. doi:10.1007/s11127-007-9198-1.

Feuz, Martin, Matthew Fuller, and Felix Stalder. 2011. "Personal Web Searching in the Age of Semantic Capitalism: Diagnosing the Mechanisms of Personalisation." *First Monday* 16(2). http://www.firstmonday.org/htbin/cgiwrap/bin/ojs/index.php/fm/article/view/3344/2766.

Fleischer, Rasmus and Torsson Palle. 2005. *Presentation Entitled The Grey Commons at 22nd Chaos Communications Congress*. Berlin. http://www.youtube.com/watch?v=aLwQkzPY9-8.

Foot, Kirsten A. and Steven M Schneider. 2006. *Web Campaigning*. Cambridge, MA: MIT Press.

Foucault, Michel. 1984. "What is Enlightenment?" In Paul Rabinow, ed. *The Foucault Reader*. New York: Pantheon, 32–50.

Galloway, Alexander and Eugene Thacker. 2007. *The Exploit: A Theory of Networks*. Minneapolis: University of Minnesota Press.

Gangadharan, Seeta Peña. 2012. "Digital Inclusion and Data Profiling." *First Monday* 17(5). http://www.uic.edu/htbin/cgiwrap/bin/ojs/index.php/fm/article/view/3821/3199.

Gehl, Robert. 2014. *Reverse Engineering Social Media: Software, Culture, and Political Economy in New Media Capitalism*. Philadelphia: Temple University Press.

Gerlitz, Carolin and Anne Helmond. 2013. "The like economy: Social buttons and the data-intensive web." *New Media & Society* 15(8): 1348–65. http://doi.org/10.1177/1461444812472322.

Gillespie, Tarleton. 2006. "Engineering a Principle: 'End-to-End' in the Design of the Internet." *Social Studies of Science* 36(3): 427–57.

Gillespie, Tarleton. 2010. "The Politics of 'Platforms.'" *New Media & Society* 12(3): 347–64.

Gillespie, Tarleton. 2014. "The Relevance of Algorithms." In Tarleton Gillespie, Pablo Boczkowski, and Kirsten Foot, eds. *Media Technologies*. Cambridge, MA: MIT Press, 167–94.

Gurstein, Michael. 2011. "Open Data: Empowering the Empowered or Effective Data Use for Everyone?" *First Monday* 16(2). http://firstmonday.org/htbin/cgiwrap/bin/ojs/index.php/fm/article/view/3316/2764.

Hardt, Michael and Antonio Negri. 2004. *Multitude: War and Democracy in the Age of Empire*. New York: Penguin Press.

Helmond, Anne. 2013. "The Algorithmization of the Hyperlink : Computational Culture." *Computational Culture* 3. http://computationalculture.net/article/the-algorithmization-of-the-hyperlink.

Helmond, Anne. 2014, May 7. "Adding the Bling: The Role of Social Media Data Intermediaries." *Culture Digitally* [Web log comment]. Retrieved from http://www.annehelmond.nl/2014/05/07/adding-the-bling-the-role-of-social-media-data-intermediaries/.

Hindman, Matthew. 2009. *The Myth of Digital Democracy*. Princeton: Princeton University Press.

Hine, Christine, ed. 2005. "Virtual Methods: Issues in Social Research on the Internet." Berg. http://www.loc.gov/catdir/toc/ecip056/2005001815.html.

Kahle, Brewster. 1997. "Preserving the Internet." *Scientific American* 276(3): 82–83. doi:10.1038/scientificamerican0397-82.

Karpf, David. 2008. "Understanding Blogspace." *Journal of Information Technology & Politics* 5(4): 369–85.

Karpf, David. 2012. "Social Science Research Methods in Internet Time." *Information, Communication & Society* 15(5): 639–61. doi:10.1080/1369118X.2012.665468.

Kelty, Christopher. 2005. "Geeks, Social Imaginaries, and Recursive Publics." *Cultural Anthropology* 20(2): 185–214.

Kelty, Christopher. 2008. *Two Bits: The Cultural Significance of Free Software*. Durham: Duke University Press.

Kelty, Christopher. 2013. "There Is No Free Software." *Journal of Peer Production* 3. http://peerproduction.net/issues/issue-3-free-software-epistemics/debate/there-is-no-free-software/.

Langlois, Ganaele and Greg Elmer. 2009. "Wikipedia Leeches? The Promotion of Traffic through a Collaborative Web Format." *New Media & Society* 11(5): 773–94.

Langlois, Ganaele, Greg Elmer, Fenwick McKelvey, and Zachary Devereaux. 2009. "Networked Publics: The Double Articulation of Code and Politics on Facebook." *Canadian Journal of Communication* 34(3): 415–33.

Langlois, Ganaele, Fenwick McKelvey, Greg Elmer, and Kenneth Werbin. 2009. "Mapping Commercial Web 2.0 Worlds: Towards a New Critical Ontogenesis." *Fibreculture* 14.

Latour, Bruno. 2005. "From Realpolitik to Dingpolitik or How to Make Things Public." In Bruno Latour and Peter Weibel, eds. *Making Things Public: Atmospheres of Democracy*. Cambridge: MIT Press, 14–41.

Latour, Bruno. 2013. *An Inquiry into Modes of Existence: An Anthropology of the Moderns*. Cambridge, MA: Harvard University Press.

Latour, Bruno and Richard Rogers. 2012. "Digital Societies: Between Ontology and Methods." Goldsmiths Centre for the Study of Invention and Social Process, March 12. http://connectedfutures.com/blog/digital_societies_bruno_latour_and_richard_rogers_event_at_goldsmiths.

Lessig, Lawrence. 2006. *Code: Version 2.0*. New York: Basic Books.

Markham, Annette N. and Nancy K. Baym, eds. 2008. *Internet Inquiry: Conversations About Method*. Los Angeles: Sage Publications.

Marres, Noortje and Richard Rogers. 2005. "Recipe for Tracing the Fate of Issues and Their Publics on the Web." In Bruno Latour and Peter Weibel, eds. Cambridge, MA: MIT Press, 922–35.

Masanés, Julien. 2006. "Web Archiving: Issues and Methods." In *Web Archiving*, 1–53. Springer, Berlin, Heidelberg. http://link.springer.com/chapter/10.1007/978-3-540-46332-0_1.

Muuss, Mike. (n.d.). "The Story of the PING Program." Accessed March 31, 2014. Retrieved from http://ftp.arl.army.mil/~mike/ping.html.

Parikka, Jussi. 2013. "Critically Engineered Wireless Politics." *Culture Machine* 14. http://www.culturemachine.net/index.php/cm/article/viewDownloadInterstitial/514/529.

Park, Han Woo and Mike Thelwall. 2003. "Hyperlink Analyses of the World Wide Web: A Review." *Journal of Computer-Mediated Communication* 8(4).

Paul, Ryan. 2008. "What's the Diff? McCain Attacks Obama with Versionista." *Ars Technica*. July 17. http://arstechnica.com/uncategorized/2008/07/whats-the-diff-mccain-attacks-obama-with-versionista/.

Popper, Karl R. 1971. *The Open Society and Its Enemies, Vol. 1: The Spell of Plato* (Revised). Princeton: Princeton University Press.

Preston, William, Edward S. Herman, and Herbert I. Schiller. 1989. *Hope and Folly: The United States and UNESCO, 1945–1985*. Minneapolis: University of Minnesota Press.

Ravindranath, Mohana. 2014. "Twitter Grants Select Researchers Access to Its Public Database." *The Washington Post*. October 26. http://www.washingtonpost.com/business/on-it/twitter-grants-select-researchers-access-to-its-public-database/2014/10/26/48a1f532-5931-11e4-b812-38518ae74c67_story.html.

Raymond, Eric S. 1999. *The Cathedral and the Bazaar: Musings on Linux and Open Source by an Accidental Revolutionary*. Sebastopol, CA: O'Reilly.

Rogers, Richard. 2009. "The Internet Treats Censorship as a Malfunction and Routes Around It?: A New Media Approach to the Study of State Internet Censorship." In Jussi Parikka and Tony D Sampson, eds. Cresskill: Hampton Press.

Rogers, Richard. 2013. *Digital Methods*. Cambridge, MA: MIT Press.

Rosenberg, Jonathan. 2009. "The Meaning of Open." *Official Google Blog*. December 21. http://googleblog.blogspot.com/2009/12/meaning-of-open.html.

Russell, Andrew L. 2014. *Open Standards and the Digital Age: History, Ideology, and Networks*. Cambridge: Cambridge University Press.

Schneider, Steven M. and Kirsten A Foot. 2004. "The Web as an Object of Study." *New Media & Society* 6(1): 114–22.

Schrock, Andrew Richard. 2014. "HTML5 and Openness in Mobile Platforms." *Continuum*. August, 1–15. doi:10.1080/10304312.2014.941333.

Sengupta, Shuddhabrata. 2006. "A Letter to the Commons." In *In the Shade of the Commons: Towards a Culture of Open Networks*. Amsterdam: Waag Society, 19–21.

Simpson, Christopher. 2003. "U.S, Mass Communication Research, Counterinsurgency, and 'Scientific' Reality." In Sandra Braman, Lipika Bansal, Paul Keller, and Geert Lovink, eds. *Communication Researchers and Policy-Making*. Cambridge, MA: MIT Press.

Smythe, Dallas Walker. 1981. *Dependency Road: Communications, Capitalism, Consciousness and Canada*. Norwood, NJ: Ablex Pub.

Streeter, Thomas. 1996. *Selling the Air: A Critique of the Policy of Commercial Broadcasting in the United States*. Chicago: University of Chicago Press.

Tkacz, Nathaniel. 2012. "From Open Source to Open Government: A Critique of Open Politics." *Ephemera: Theory and Politics in Organization* 12(4): 386–405.

Turow, Joseph. 2012. *The Daily You - How the Advertising Industry Is Defining: Your Identity and Your Worth*. New Haven: Yale University Press.

Vaidhyanathan, Siva. 2011. *The Googlization of Everything*. Berkeley and Los Angeles: University of California Press. http://www.ucpress.edu/book. php?isbn=9780520258822.

van Dijck, José. 2013. *The Culture of Connectivity: A Critical History of Social Media*. Oxford: Oxford University Press.

8

Critical Reverse Engineering:
The Case of Twitter and TalkOpen

Robert Gehl

Introduction

Social media present the critical media scholar with a quandary. First of all, a growing number of scholars are faulting sites such as Twitter for their erosion of privacy, their desire to turn every thought into monetizable, quantifiable evidence of individual consumer desires, their reduction of human interaction to 140 character chunks, their promise of openness while viciously protecting their algorithms and data sets with lawsuits, and their susceptibility to (if not downright compliance with) government surveillance programs. On the other hand, it is difficult even for the most hardened social media critic to deny the pleasures of using these systems, of making friends and connections, and of bathing in a stream of new ideas as it flows across the screen. Nor can the critic deny social media's utility in political, cultural, and social organizing, their centrality in the erosion of mass media gatekeepers, or their part in the larger epistemological shift that is happening due to big data.

The critic's relationship to social media is thus compromised in many senses. For some, the sites compromise critical inquiry just as a virus compromises bodily integrity: critics become infected with laudatory love for viral videos, memes, trends, and the quantified self, ignoring the ways in which such practices reify existing power relations. For others, such sites are compromised, full stop: they cannot be trusted. For them, the dual-headed surveillance system, comprised of states and transnational corporations, is simply too dominant in corporate social media, and the only clear course is to get out. Revel or get out: these appear to be our options, and these options are largely reflected in the academic literature on social media.

However, there is another compromise to make with social media: build your own. When we use the Internet, we often forget that we are working with a network of universal machines, computers that can be modified to meet different goals. We are by no means locked into social media as it currently exists; we could champion—or even make—new social media systems. As the old saying goes, "another world is possible." To this end, I propose a methodology of "reverse engineering" to critique contemporary social media software as well as establish criteria for alternatives to that software. Drawing on the reverse engineering literature as it is found in fields such as engineering, law, and economics, and inspired by critical science and technology studies and software studies, I will argue that this approach is valuable because of four orientations: the pragmatic, the genealogical, the legal, and the normative. These orientations can guide the critic through the false choices of technophilia or technophobia, uncritical love or endless critique with no way out. To illustrate reverse engineering as a critical method, I will use the examples of Twitter and TalkOpen (a short-lived alternative to Twitter), specifically the ways in which TalkOpen reverse engineered Twitter's interfaces, architectures, and imagined users. Ultimately, I argue that instead of simply giving in or getting out, critical social media scholars have a chance to take their theories and put them to the test by constructing (or at least using) new social media systems that challenge the power of centralized, corporate social media.

Reverse engineering and the humanities

There are various definitions of reverse engineering across the literature I am working with here (engineering, law, and economics). Drawing on them, I would argue for this basic conceptualization: *Reverse engineering is a method of producing knowledge by dissociating human-made artifacts. This knowledge is then used to produce new artifacts that simultaneously improve upon the old and yet also bear a relation to the old.* In other words, during reverse engineering, a human confronts an object. The object bears information: how it was assembled, the material used in its production, the choices made to realize it. This information gestures toward—but can never completely reveal—the process of "forward engineering" that implemented the object. The reverse engineer brings tacit knowledge (these days, often produced in him/her by way of training and study) to bear on that object in order to open it up, take it apart, probe it, test it, stress it, break it, peer inside, and learn how it works. In other words, the reverse engineer uses many techniques to read the object-as-text. The object thus mediates a relationship between the producer, who used tacit knowledge to produce the object, and the reverse engineer, who uses tacit knowledge to take it apart. Such movements across the engineering processes are also oscillations between the concrete and the abstract, objects and theories: the object mutates, going from conception to concrete instantiation back to conception again.

After reading this object-text, the reverse engineer creates new knowledge and information which can be used to "forward engineer" a new object. The process of reverse engineering helps create new tacit knowledge in the reverse engineer, and very often the process begets new information in the form of documentation and manuals. When this knowledge and information is used to build a new object, that new object bears both the traces of the original object of inquiry and the traces of the reverse engineer-cum-forward engineer's desires and intentions. The new object might work in concert with the old, it might be meant to replace it, or it might be something that offers new affordances that on the surface bear little relation to the old object. However, it is always internally linked to the old.

Reverse engineering is, of course, an essential process in any engineering field. Pedagogically, it is one of the key ways that engineers learn their craft. Economically, it provides a tool for firms to either compete with other firms, maintain their stocks of artifacts (Ingle 1994), or generate monetizable information about their artifacts (especially in the form of patents). Legally, as I will explore below, it provides a limit on laws that grant protection to trade secrets, and thus, for engineers, reverse engineering is a sort of promise: go ahead and build something, but know that others will take it apart.

Given the "new materialist" turn in the humanities, marked by theories such as Actor-Network Theory (ANT), Object-Oriented Ontology (OOO), and assemblage theory, and given the turn to the digital and to computation in the humanities (i.e., the digital humanities), I would argue that reverse engineering is not only valuable to fields like engineering or business; it also provides a wealth of methodological, theoretical, and practical paths the critical humanist can take. There are many ways to critically delve into technoscience. Bruno Latour famously tells us to "follow the actors" (Latour 1987). This is of course a call for ethnography, for the direct observation of the actors who do the associative work to construct technoscience systems and discourses. But, as Susan Leigh Star suggests, we can also conceive of an ethnography of objects

(Star 1999). The technical objects we confront contain within them traces of the associations that brought them into being. They are, to use a term from John Law, "punctualizations" standing in for the networks of materials, politics, and discourses that constantly structure them (Law 1992). Those objects that appear stable, become infrastructural, or even fade into the background, can be fruitfully and critically reverse engineered to trace their inner heterogeneity. In this sense, to return to Latour's aphorism, we can follow the actors by turning to the artifacts they produced, looking for traces of their activities and ideals, and the politics conditioning them.

To build on this, I now turn to the four orientations found in the reverse engineering literature: the pragmatic, the genealogical, the legal, and the normative, connecting these orientations to a possible critical methodology.

The pragmatic orientation

Reverse engineers are pragmatic: they consider the technology they have at hand, not an ideal technological assemblage. They do not simply throw away older or poorly designed technology, but modify, shape, and alter it. They accept the positive side of a technology while working against the bad. As Katherine Ingle puts it, when you are a reverse engineer confronted with a technical object,

> every time you have a better idea you will consider all the positive design aspects before condemning an entire product. And for every time you have had a bitter experience with a real lemon you will also roar. The roaring will die down when you realize that you have the power and skill to change this ugly duckling of a design into a graceful swan. (Ingle 1994, 2)

In other words, for the reverse engineer, technical and design shortcomings are not excuses to throw away an object, but to make a better one. For example, in terms of software, most of what is used in firms is bought, not built. Moreover, most of the costs of software use come from maintenance. When a firm has software that does not meet the firm's requirements, it does not just make new software. Very often, it modifies the old. This practical approach, of course, entails reverse engineering.

A great deal of this process entails the discovery of "facts" discerned through thick, close, detailed empirical analysis of technical objects. How does the technology work? What is it comprised of? Who built it? What might have been their intentions? What can we do with it? However, this is not to say that reverse engineering is a simple positivism, a search for one right way to construct a technology. Rather, reverse engineering holds that there are many ways to solve a problem. Unlike positivistic science, which in the ideal seeks the one right, verifiable answer to a question, engineering is a field of heterogeneity. There are many multiplicities involved: multiple problems, multiple users, multiple implementations, multiple patterns, and multiple products of multiple reverse engineering approaches. As software engineers Baxter and Mehlich put it, when one reverse engineers software code, "different abstract concepts map to the same code within one application" (Baxter and Mehlich 1997, 105). In other words, code is not only heterogeneous in how it operates across various settings and times, as Adrian Mackenzie (2006) argues; it is also heterogeneous in terms of the abstract, theoretical ideas we might have about its functions, as well as in its theories of the user/subject. In their prescription for reverse engineering, Baxter and Mehlich (1997) argue for the production of an abstract specification from a concrete system, but they recognize that such abstractions never map directly back onto the original designer's intentions. There are too many permutations, oscillations, algorithms, optimizations, paths through lines of code, subjective design decisions, use cases, subjective requirements, and arbitrary technical choices involved at every stage of the engineering process to ever hope for a complete description of a software system. Unlike positivistic science, however, reverse engineers by and large recognize this, accept this, and simply go for what works (by whatever standard of judgment they decide upon).[1]

Reverse engineering provides this pragmatic approach to the techno-scape we confront: look to the technology you have in front of you. Learn it. Work with it. Tinker. Alter it. Shape it. Imagine possibilities, but do not hold to some ideal best way. Thus, reverse engineering avoids overly idealist approaches to socio-technical problems. It helps us avoid moralizing discourses about technologies, as in "we need a wholly new form of technology to solve problems X, Y, and Z," as if the latest version of the technology will magically erase history, habit, and error. Such hope for novel, "revolutionary" technologies is rendered naïve by the reverse engineering perspective. I will explore this further below.

---

[1]   To be sure, this pragmatism only goes so far. In that same Baxter and Mehlich essay, they share a lamentation: if only forward engineers would document every design and implementation decision in a machine-readable, consistent fashion, we would never need reverse engineering! Given both the existence of proprietary software and the multiplicities of interpretation of designs and code—just to name two problems—their solution seems quite far-fetched, to say the least (Baxter and Mehlich 1997, 106).

The genealogical orientation

Reverse engineers also consider the historical development of a technology. As its name implies, reverse engineering is forward engineering in reverse. The hegemonic engineering process involves starting with an abstract architecture, decomposing it into components, and then implementing each component in whatever material it will be made out of, including code. This takes time, and moreover involves many subjective decisions, heuristics, accidents, coincidences, and acts of labor. This process is one that can be comprehended temporally—even historically—and one way to do this is to start with the artifact and reverse the process.

As Baxter and Mehlich state, "Hidden in this creative construction of the program from the specification are a set of obvious as well as non-obvious design decisions about how to encode certain parts of the specification in an efficient way using available implementation mechanisms to achieve performance criteria (the why of the design decisions)" (Baxter and Mehlich 1997, 105). The artifact, in other words, contains within it traces of the design decisions made to bring it about. For reverse engineers, the designer's intentions, conceptions of the user, and skills can be traced in and through the artifact. To do this, reverse engineers take an existing technology and trace its genealogy backward, looking at a whole host of para-artifacts and practices to uncover how the technology was developed: documentation (Lutsky 1995), white papers, press releases, organizations (their structures, histories, and strategies) (Aiken, Muntz, and Richards 1994), theories of the user, previous versions, databases (Hainaut et al. 1996), vanquished competitors, handwritten specifications (Leite and Cerqueira 1995), older technologies and techniques, and of course lines of code. This is downright Nietzschean in its insistence upon actual documents and utterances and a search for historical conditions that gave rise to the current object. The goal is to work backward toward something approximating (but likely never exactly reflecting) the intentions of the designer, which requires a historical/ genealogical sensibility.

When this happens, the artifact's heritage is traced. Because reverse engineering reverses the hegemonic engineering approach—that is, begin with an abstract architecture and then implement it in a concrete artifact—an intermediate result of reverse engineering is the uncovering of "thought before thought," of the abstractions that shape future actions. This is to say that reverse engineering reconstructs the abstract ideas the original designers *may* have held in the construction of the artifact. In a "noopolitical" sense, reverse engineering is a process of uncovering the thoughts that incite, induce, or constrain future actions (Foucault 2003, 138) by way of what Foucault calls the "body-object articulation," the productive linkage between an artifact and a body (Foucault 1979, 152). In Lazzarato's (2006) theory of noopower, "thought before thought" is a process by which one mind (say, the mind of a designer) may influence the thoughts of another (say, the mind of an end user). Reverse engineering traces this backward from the object, speculating as to the contours of power desired by the original designer. This is, in an admittedly grandiose sense, a genealogy of software artifacts as instruments capable of shaping our thoughts.

Reverse engineering is useful not only because it traces the contours of power, but also because this practice provides an antidote to technological hype, which consistently holds that new things are in radical breaks with the past. In contrast to the hype, reverse engineering understands technology to have a history that is contingent, a history steeped in power relations, discernible in part through genealogical inquiry. And because history and power are the products of social struggle, any technology is open to changing and reshaping.

The legal orientation

We live in what Lawrence Lessig (2004, xiv) has aptly called a "permission culture." That is, when we are confronted with many of the technologies and texts in our lives, we are hesitant to do more with them than simply consume them on the producer's terms (Gillespie 2007). We fear lawsuits or criminal prosecution if we remix texts, quote ideas, copy and distribute items, or put a technology to uses other than those intended by their creators. In the case of software, the lengthy Terms of Service and End-User License agreements we click through are full of prohibitions, stipulations, and thinly veiled legal threats. Thus, despite having a bewildering array of flexible, networked software systems at our command, we hesitate to probe, alter, or use software in ways that the original producers did not intend.

Here we can turn to the legal aspects of reverse engineering. Reverse engineering has a tradition of legal protections in contexts such as the United States and the European Union (Samuelson and Scotchmer 2002). In traditional manufacturing, US courts have held that the sale of an object is akin to its publication, and thus the legal owner of any object is free to take it apart, study it, and even produce a copy of it for sale. This situation is a bit more complex with software, because software is simultaneously ideational (in the sense that it is a materialization in code of the idea of its creator) and functional (Mackenzie 2006). On the ideational side, software is protected by copyright; I cannot copy lines of code from a copyrighted program into a new program. But on the functional side, unless it has been protected by a patent, we are free to replicate the functionality of existing software. And in order to do that, we are in fact allowed to open up, probe, test, and disassemble software—even to make copies of it in the process.[2]

In this sense, the traditional legal protections afforded to reverse engineering are similar to the fair use exception in copyright law in many countries. The fair use exception allows people to quote, copy, remix, and reprint texts for the purposes of education, critique, and transformation. Despite what they may desire, the originators of an object of intellectual property (IP) simply do not have absolute control over the uses of that IP. The fair use limitation sees to that. Likewise, reverse engineering is a way to prevent firms from monopolizing a technology (Samuelson 2002; Samuelson and Scotchmer 2002). Any unpatented technology can be taken apart and replicated by others; without this exception, a simple trade secret would be akin to a limitless monopoly. Courts have seen both fair use and reverse engineering as means to encourage new ideas and to limit the power of firms that originate ideas.

Moreover, like fair use, reverse engineering is an exception that only works when people use it. Established firms have consistently lobbied legislators to ban the use of reverse engineering (Samuelson and Scotchmer 2002). The Digital Millennium Copyright Act (DMCA) is one such troubling example. The only way to maintain the reverse engineering exception is to keep using it (and, in some cases, keep fighting for it in the courts) just as fair use activists have done. To be sure, software firms such as Microsoft, Apple, Oracle, Google, and Facebook have become incredibly economically and politically powerful, which means they have high-octane lawyers who will use intellectual property laws to prevent critical access to their systems. One such technique is the use of terms of service that explicitly prohibit reverse engineering. However, the enforceability

---

[2] Two important cases that have established this in the United States context are *Sega Enterprises Ltd. v. Accolade, Inc.*, 1992, and *Sony Computer Entertainment v. Connectix Corp.*, 2000.

of such license terms is in question: courts tend to look askance at firms that use them to prohibit reverse engineering for the purposes of building interoperable or competing systems. Additionally (and I find this very intriguing), there are explicit exceptions in the DMCA for reverse engineering of any digitally protected software that invades one's privacy.[3]

Finally, in a rhetorical sense, because reverse engineering has greater acceptance in courts than terms such as "hacking" or "copying," the term could provide rhetorical power to the critic. I realize that "hacking" is a fashionable term; I also know full well that hacking does not mean malicious intrusion into networks to steal data. However, this negative connotation is unfortunately popular. By adopting "reverse engineering," a technology critic can fend off some of the negative associations of terms like hacking while drawing on the legal heritage I discuss above.

The normative orientation

Finally, reverse engineers do not simply study existing technologies; they do their work in order to build new systems. Thus, they have a normative position, albeit often an immediate and rationalized one: usually they want to create a competing version of a product in order to sell it, create software that can interoperate with an existing platform or service, or gain the knowledge needed to maintain a system themselves rather than rely on the original producer for maintenance. As interested as they are in discerning the empirical properties of a technology (as I explored above in my discussion of the pragmatic orientation), reverse engineers also seek to change technological systems to meet their needs.

We can take this further and suggest a *critical* form of reverse engineering dedicated to political/economic and media justice. Whereas critical engagements of social media often stop at critique, the reverse engineering approach urges us to keep going. It calls for supporting and even becoming activists and technologists who are seeking to create software alternatives. Reverse engineering allows us to trace the path between alternatives and their less equitable predecessors, to

---

[3] See Samuelson and Scotchmer (2002). Imagine if, especially after the popular revelations about government surveillance and the collusion of major social media firms with the state in the summer of 2013, one could use this exception in the DMCA to reverse engineer social media systems like Google or Facebook! They are in many estimations quintessential privacy-invading software systems.

see how the new alternatives take positive aspects of the old while avoiding the negative. Again, as I argue above in the discussion of the pragmatic orientation, reverse engineering is not about idealized technologies, but rather taking the technology we have, decomposing it, discerning abstractions from it, and using this knowledge to make something better.

This maps onto Marx's observation in the *Eighteenth Brumaire* that "men [sic] make their own history, but they do not make it as they please; they do not make it under self-selected circumstances, but under circumstances existing already, given and transmitted from the past. The tradition of all dead generations weighs like a nightmare on the brains of the living" (Marx 2008, 15). As Andrew Feenberg (1986) writes, a philosophy of praxis can be found in the tension between the concrete circumstances of the present and the abstract, historically developed conceptualizations used to comprehend, idealize, and shape it. Rather than start with an ideal and bemoaning a world that does not live up to it, critical theory seeks out contradictions within the objects it encounters. These fissures provide us with tangible ways forward, new possibilities that are not simply abstract, timeless ethical ideals. Drawing on this, we can imagine a critical reverse engineering: start with the concrete technological system, derive abstractions from it, and use those abstractions to plot and create a better system.

This may seem to exaggerate the ethical dimension of reverse engineering, but I propose that critical humanistic inquiry can learn a lot from this practice. In the next section, I explore this further with the case of TalkOpen, a short-lived Twitter alternative.

Reverse engineering twitter: The case of TalkOpen

Building off of Lessig's point that we live in a culture of permission, I would argue that in the case of social media we live in a culture that denies us permission to push past the interface, to see how such social media systems are structured. Yet, as Ganaele Langlois (2013) rightly argues, social media software provides us with infrastructures to live our lives; their structures have a major influence on our online interactions. Therefore, despite the anxiety we might feel when we push past the interface, we must reverse engineer social media systems in order to see how we are producing ourselves—and how our selves are produced—within them.

One such effort along these lines was a site called TalkOpen. TalkOpen no longer exists, except as a kind of black hole: you cannot see it, but you know it exists because of the gravitational pull of links, tweets,[4] Facebook posts (OpESR 2012), Pastebin chat dumps ("TalkOpen.info & Anon Communications" 2012; "TRG – th3j35t3r & talkopen.info" 2012), Imgur screenshots (@JackalAnon 2013a, b), Internet Archive caches ("Talk Open – Welcome to The Talk Open Community" 2012), and a brief mention in an information security blog (Schwartz 2012) it left behind. These Web traces tell us that there was once something more to talkopen.info than what we see now: "This website is for sale!"[5]

From roughly March 31 until early June 2012, talkopen.info was a microblogging site specifically built as an alternative to Twitter. In that span of two months, TalkOpen had about 250 people sign up. Almost all of the members had usernames like Darknet, Cpher, DoxxyDox, and AnonHooker, and their posts were about topics like Anonymous, the Occupy movement, information security, and hacking. Although the user base was small, it was quite active, with new posts happening every hour.

Two months on the Internet? A user base of 250? New posts by the hour? Admittedly, these are not impressive numbers. And moreover, because the site did not have a large user base, there are only a few screenshots of it, and no accounts of its use beyond what I offer here. However, the case of TalkOpen provides a window into the methodology of reverse engineering I have been describing in this paper, and moreover I think there is value in preserving the memory of a failed technology in order to avoid reifying successful ones as the only or best possible ones. Moreover, by critically interrogating a project that reverse engineered Twitter, we also learn more about Twitter itself. Thus, I hope you will indulge me as I work with such "small data."

As TalkOpen founder XCpherX noted in an interview with me, offering a "Twitter alternative is the focus of the site."[6] What does it mean to be a Twitter alternative? I will explore this through the four orientations of reverse engineering.

---

[4] For a collection of tweets about TalkOpen, contact the author.
[5] This is as of April 22, 2014. Previously, talkopen.info was comprised of a screen that said, "This account has been suspended."
[6] This interview was conducted via TalkOpen. Initially I intended to provide a link to this conversation, but now of course that link is lost. All quotes from XCpherX included in this essay come from that interview.

Pragmatic

TalkOpen was a pragmatic response to the problems of social media, problems I explore below. Rather than crafting a wholly new online communication system, it drew on something quite familiar: the conventions of Twitter. We would recognize the site as a "microblogging" site, which contains many conventions:

- a character limit on posts
- an interface that emphasizes the new (Gehl 2011)
- a client-server architecture
- individual-oriented account structures (i.e., the fields required for signup are biased toward an individual, not a group or other social entity)
- the follower-followed relationship
- structured profile layouts (your profile image is 50 × 50 pixels; your username is limited to a certain number of characters, etc.)
- navigational layout with links such as Home, Members, Sign Out, and Settings
- and the use of hashtags and @ signs in tagging and messaging.

These conventions could appear "intuitive," but if we act like John Law's (2002) "naïve reader" (as this character appears in the book *Aircraft Stories*) we can start to see how this heterogeneous assemblage of objects and processes must be constantly organized in order to cohere. None of it is intuitive; for users to work with it, there needs to be a large amount of pedagogical training that happens via the interface. Thus, for any would-be social media alternative, there is a problem: do we create an assemblage of elements so new that users will not know how to use it? Or do we simply draw on the conventions forged by previous ones, even if those conventions represent the very problems we are seeking to overcome with a new system? TalkOpen opted for the latter. Thus, even though TalkOpen was a Twitter alternative, it did not abandon the old form. As XCpherX explained to me, "Im afraid that [the Twitter elements] may be taken away if we fiddle with it too much so to speak . . . just have to be careful what we do/remove/add."

Moreover, TalkOpen was linked to Twitter from the outset, allowing TalkOpen users to post to both TalkOpen and Twitter simultaneously via Really Simple Syndication (RSS) and the Twitter API. Thus, although TalkOpen was a Twitter alternative, XCpherX made many pragmatic decisions to maintain a link to Twitter. This allowed users to move to TalkOpen without feeling as if they were abandoning Twitter altogether. Indeed, many of the posts TalkOpen users made appeared in both services.

Genealogical

TalkOpen was articulated into a larger historical moment—its potential place in the Occupy movement and in the network politics of the hacker group Anonymous. As such, TalkOpen might have been animated by the Twitter that was: the Twitter that was large enough to have a critical mass of users involved in Anonymous or Occupy, yet small enough to avoid the attentions of states. In other words, TalkOpen might have been redolent of Twitter before it was "friended" by the state, to use Jack Bratich's idea (2011, 629). Moreover, this was a Twitter far removed from an Initial Public Offering (IPO) of stock. If there is any moment in the history of a social media site that reveals the site for what it truly is—a system to gather data on users and sell it for profit—the IPO has to be it.

In other words, TalkOpen might have been intended to be the pre-January 26, 2012 Twitter, the Twitter of #jan25 and #egypt, the Twitter that in many popular accounts fomented revolutions: the pre-Wall Street orgy Twitter. In a famous blog post, Biz Stone (2011) wrote "The Tweets Must Flow," in which he stated: "Some Tweets may facilitate positive change in a repressed country, some make us laugh, some make us think, some downright anger a vast majority of users. We do not always agree with the things people choose to tweet, but we keep the information flowing irrespective of any view we may have about the content."

Wrapped in the language of free speech, Stone's post was seen as a promise to never censor expression in Twitter. However, one year later, on January 26, 2012, Twitter announced its intention to block certain tweets and Twitter accounts by country ("Tweets Still Must Flow" 2012). It turned out that, in order to grow into international markets, the "Tweets Must Flow" in certain contexts only. Alongside this announcement, there was a growing perception among users—right or wrong—that topics like WikiLeaks, Occupy Wall Street, or Anonymous were being algorithmically excluded from Twitter's Trending Topics list (Johnstone 2010a, b). In other words, this was a concern that certain tweets might not flow as well as others. Users protesting these changes used the hashtag #twittercensorship starting in late January 2012.

This was the moment in which TalkOpen reverse engineered Twitter to recreate the older Twitter, the Twitter of "The Tweets Must Flow." We can see this easily when we compare Twitter's Terms of Service[7] to TalkOpen's Terms of Service statement, which in its entirety read:

> By entering this site you take full responsibility for whatever you say or do and acknowledge that TalkOpen.info neither in whole or part is responsible for your actions. With that being said, TalkOpen will NOT sell your information to third parties or give up anyones [sic] information to law enforcement unless it is in regards to murder or cp [child pornography]. You have our word. Take it or leave it:)[8]

Here, TalkOpen's promise is that the users—not the site—would be responsible for their statements. In that sense, although in very different words, TalkOpen repeated Biz Stone's 2011 promise to keep the statements flowing even if the site owners disagreed. Twitter users who defected to TalkOpen picked up on this and began to recruit users to TalkOpen in early 2012. They did so by articulating the Twitter hashtag #twittercensorship with others, including #OpMigrate and variations on #anonymous, to promote the site to any users concerned that after January 26 Twitter was losing its way as a site of free expression.

In this sense, TalkOpen reverse engineered Twitter by comparing its more recent version to older iterations, studying news reports and other para-documentation on the service, and using these insights to build a different, yet redolent, microblogging service.

Legal

TalkOpen was built on StatusNet, which is an open-source alternative to Twitter with roots dating back to the late 2000s. StatusNet reverse engineered ideas such as microblogging to create a Twitter alternative with the added functionality of federation across multiple servers via a social networking protocol (now called OStatus). Using an open protocol and open-source software would allow for a more distributed network architecture than the centralized Twitter system. As

---

[7] Available at https://twitter.com/tos.
[8] This was the Terms of Service statement as it appeared in May, 2012. As far as I am aware, it was not altered during the lifetime of the site. The emoticon was always included.

such, StatusNet is part of a long line of software projects that reverse engineer first-comers to expand interoperability and provide new platforms for users.[9]

In a sense, a major part of StatusNet's reverse engineering of Twitter is to graft the Free and Open Source Software (FOSS) model onto existing social media systems. This is true of other social media alternatives such as GNU social and to a lesser extent Diaspora. Being built on top of StatusNet meant TalkOpen could rely on the long and successful history of legal engineering that is the GNU suite of licenses. As Gabriella Coleman (2009, 424) explains, such licenses use "copyright law, a [US] Constitutional mandate, to undermine the logic of copyright law. The [GNU General Public License] is built on copyright, but disables the restrictions of copyright to allow for modification, distribution, and access; it is also self-perpetuating because it requires others to adopt the same license if they modify copylefted software."

But this use of FOSS copyleft does not exhaust the legal story. In order for a software system to replicate the functionality of another, the history of protections of reverse engineering has to be in place. Part of FOSS production is what Coleman (2009, 425) calls a culture of "legal exegesis" and "legal training" that helps FOSS developers navigate the murky waters of intellectual property law. Such exegesis and training results in the legal jujitsu of copyleft, which is precisely written to use copyright against itself.

This has implications for reverse engineering. Although the emphasis on FOSS since the earliest days of Richard Stallman's work has been on free speech, a corollary emphasis has been placed on the right to open up and alter the software one uses: in the FOSS ethos, one has the right to reverse engineer a software. Moreover, even if the Digital Millennium Copyright Act (DMCA) is often presented as merely a copyright law, its restrictions on reverse engineering coupled with the fact that FOSS activists universally despise it means that FOSS developers must engage with reverse engineering as a legal category of action to resist the DMCA. Thus, being built on StatusNet meant that TalkOpen drew on these legal tactics to reverse engineer Twitter. It enjoyed the protection of being a part of a larger project within a legal context where reverse engineering is protected and with a long legal history of copyleft licensing. These legal protections are "built-in" when we start social media alternatives using copylefted platforms like StatusNet, Diaspora, or Crabgrass.

---

[9]   Important instances of reverse engineering of novel systems include Accolade's reverse engineering of the Sega Genesis and Connectix's reverse engineering of Sony's Playstation system (*Sega Enterprises Ltd. v. Accolade, Inc.*, 1992, *Sony Computer Entertainment v. Connectix Corp.*, 2000).

However, TalkOpen partially failed to build on top of this legal history. While well-engineered legal documents like GNU licenses can protect a project, the far more blunt TalkOpen license (quoted in its entirety above) simply does not play the legal language game. Bad grammar, unclear abbreviations (e.g. "cp"), an emoticon, and a strange transition ("All that said") rendered TalkOpen's Terms of Service somewhat comical. Here, instead of reverse engineering social media terms of service in the same way that copyleft reverse engineers copyright, the TalkOpen Terms of Service appeared to be a flat-out repudiation of legalese, likely—though I cannot be certain—setting TalkOpen up for dissociation if it were to come into contact with the world of lawsuits, National Security Letters, and prosecutions.

Normative

Why build a Twitter alternative unless one has a goal in mind? The goal might be just to make another competitor in the business of inciting, digitizing, and valorizing user emotional labor (see, for example, Pinterest). Or it might be to build a new layer of abstraction on top of the "platform" that a site like Twitter provides developers (see, for example, Topsy.com). But in the case of TalkOpen, it was more about #TwitterCensorship and Anonymous network politics. The hashtag #OpMigrate has a normative and pedagogical sense: make the shift to TalkOpen. There, you can do all the same things you would in Twitter (because TalkOpen is pragmatic and built on that model) but you get new freedoms. In this sense, TalkOpen was another in a long list of projects meant to be alternatives to mainstream social media: Diaspora, GNU social, FreedomBox, Lorea, and Crabgrass, to name a few. As I argue elsewhere (Gehl 2013a, 2014), the technologists and activists building these projects recognize many of the problems that social media critics have pointed out: ubiquitous surveillance (Andrejevic 2007); the modulation of affect, emotion, and communication for the purposes of linking interaction to consumption (Elmer 2004; Langlois 2011); the centralization of the Web (Zittrain 2008); the templated nature of the interfaces (Arola 2010); the exploitation of user creativity for massive profits (Terranova 2000); and the lack of democratic control over the social media systems (Gehl 2013b). To build an alternative that does not have these problems is indeed a worthy goal.

And yet, as I explore above in the section Pragmatic", TalkOpen does not simply reinvent social media, totally disregarding the design conventions of previous systems; this would be an impossible goal, and moreover it would ignore the progressive aspects of social media. TalkOpen came from a recognition that much good can come out of even the most centralized social media system. Although I would never reduce Occupy Wall Street or the Arab Spring to Twitter or Facebook revolutions, research has shown that social media played an important part in organizing movements and shaping public perceptions about them (Morris 2013). Reverse engineering's normative move is to draw on those positive elements, maintain design conventions that people recognize and are comfortable with, and avoid the problems of centralized social media. This is what TalkOpen attempted to do, albeit unsuccessfully.

What went wrong with TalkOpen?

But TalkOpen failed, of course. What went wrong?

As I argue elsewhere (Gehl 2014), one of the great animating ideas of the social media alternative builders is decentralization and distribution. These network architectures are based on the quasi-mythical founding principle of the Internet: redundancy in network paths. That is, rather than having all communications flow through a central hub, the goal is to have them flow through multiple paths and nodes. This reduces the likelihood that any one node becomes a weak spot in the network. Mainstream social media sites, such as Twitter, Facebook, and Google, are not distributed; they are highly centralized, using a client-server architecture. As we have seen in recent revelations about government institutions such as the National Security Agency (US), the Government Communications Headquarters (UK), and the Communications Security Establishment (Canada), such centralized databases of user communications are tempting targets for state surveillance. And, of course, the sites themselves exploit their centrality in the day-to-day communications of billions to collect data on their users and sell them to the highest bidders. Thus, to build an alternative to mainstream social media, one commonly stated goal is to create distributed (or federated) systems, allowing users to host their own node of a social media system on their own computers and link these nodes across the Internet.

And yet, this is exceedingly difficult work. Major software engineering problems in the construction of building distributed social media sites include authenticating users, allowing users to find each other across installations, and encrypting communication to prevent "man in the middle" attacks. Moreover, because mainstream social media is "easy to use" (through many years of training users in their particular interfaces), alternatives would have to do all of the above *and* make the system as "intuitive" as the mainstream sites. This is a tall order for any would-be social media reverse engineer. Thus, it is unsurprising that social media alternatives often end up replicating the client-server architecture. TalkOpen did just this, thus making the site vulnerable to determined attackers. Indeed, because TalkOpen was built for members of hacker groups Anonymous and LulzSec, it attracted the attention of the "patriotic hacker" The Jester, who claimed in an Internet Relay Chat to have taken down talkopen.info on May 31, 2012 ("TRG – th3j35t3r & talkopen.info" 2012). I cannot say for certain if this is true, but the timing is right. TalkOpen might have been too centralized to survive a determined attack by The Jester.

Setting aside the question of centralization, I also wonder if TalkOpen failed to become *enough* of a Twitter alternative. In other words, in its attempt to reverse engineer Twitter, TalkOpen might have kept too many Twitter conventions. Perhaps it failed to account for the highly individualized, personal branding and micro- or macro-celebrity features of Twitter. The rise of Twitter in the popular imagination was marked by the oddity of Ashton Kutcher being a highly followed celebrity. Because TalkOpen reverse engineered Twitter, and because Twitter's core organizing principle is the relationship between the individual follower and followed, perhaps this organizing primitive is not compatible with the politics of TalkOpen's users. To a degree—though certainly not completely—individual-to-individual social media grates against the networked politics of Anonymous and Occupy. We have of course seen "celebrities" heralded by the anons: Julian Assange, Chelsea Manning, Aaron Schwartz, and now Edward Snowden. But the most compelling aspects of Anonymous and Occupy are the politics of networks and aggregations: *we* are the 99 percent. Expect *us*. The iconography of Anonymous includes anons wearing Guy Fawkes masks or suits with no heads. This is not a celebration of individuality but rather a statement about interchangeability and hiding in plain site.

Perhaps TalkOpen's replication of the individualizing structure of Twitter was not the solution to the riddle of producing a social media alternative that more fully meets the organizing principles and politics of Anonymous. Perhaps, then, other social media alternatives—that is, other attempts to reverse engineering mainstream social media—can learn from the culture and architecture of TalkOpen to produce something more viable.

Conclusion: Critical reverse engineering as a bridge between engineering and humanities

In sum, as I hope I have shown here, the methodology of reverse engineering could provide social media critics with a bridge between the critique of contemporary, proprietary social media and the production of better, more democratic media systems. Reverse engineering does more than either celebrating Twitter, Facebook, or Google, or refusing to take part in them. It also does more than simply criticize social media systems. Instead, it provides a method to both disentangle all of the threads that go into any specific social media system *and* build criteria for the production of better systems. While the normative goals of traditional reverse engineering tend to be instrumental and usually tied to industrial ends, critical reverse engineering can involve normative goals that tie into the goals of democracy and media justice. Moreover, the methodology is only complete when the critic becomes a maker and attempts to build a new system that is related to the old while striving to ameliorate the problems of the old. All of this is achieved through a mix of pragmatic, genealogical, legal, and normative orientations that all appear in the reverse engineering literature. This chapter, of course, is not a description of a system I myself built; rather it describes TalkOpen, which I participated in but did not help construct. Indeed, I do not claim to have the technical ability to easily construct a social media alternative on my own. However, reverse engineering is not often a solitary activity. It involves multiple steps, from identifying an artifact to reverse engineer, decomposing it into parts, researching its history across different discursive domains (such as popular, business, legal, and academic), creating new abstractions from the old system, and then implementing those abstractions in a new system. As such, it is well suited to collaboration. Critical reverse engineering thus has the potential to be a practice that brings together humanists and engineers. For example, critical scholars of social media who have done the work of dissociating Twitter, Facebook, Pinterest, etc., might consider partnering with technologists who are building nascent social media alternatives. This might mean helping with design, broad-site goals including social and cultural elements (for example, opposing ubiquitous surveillance or consumerism, or attempting to prevent sexism or racism from taking root in the site's culture), or specific elements of user-to-user or user-software interaction. While none of these practices is explicitly tied to coding, they all can be found in the best traditions of humanities scholarship. Reverse engineering, understood in this way, becomes a potential "boundary object" (Barley, Leonardi, and Bailey 2012; Turner 2008) between engineers and humanists, allowing these fields to bridge discursive and conceptual gaps to collaborate.

Based on the case of TalkOpen elaborated here, were I to work with technologists creating a social media alternative, I would suggest several broad, tentative goals for successful critical reverse engineering of social media. Any new social media system would bear traces of the old, but would be built for social justice. It might be compatible with the old (in the traditions of software reverse engineering) and yet add new layers of functionality that are intended to foster social justice. It would prevent the problems of contemporary social media (i.e., surveillance, reduction of interaction to consumer choices, and the valorization of free labor). It could include an interface that draws on existing design conventions but would also provide a pedagogy for deeper understanding of social media systems, data, privacy, and value production. The new system could expand the meaning of "the social" by building on the older social metaphors (friend, follower, etc.) or creating new ones. It could provide a level of abstraction above the network layer—thus hiding implementations of decentralization and encryption from end users—while providing access to the inner workings of the social media system, allowing users to not only inspect the code but also alter it to improve the system.

TalkOpen failed to do these things, but it provided a useful platform for thinking broadly about the potentials of reverse engineering for social media.

References

Aiken, P., A. Muntz, and R. Richards. 1994. "DoD Legacy Systems: Reverse Engineering Data Requirements." *Communications of the ACM* 37(5): 26–41.

Andrejevic, Mark. 2007. *iSpy: Surveillance and Power in the Interactive Era*. Lawrence: University Press of Kansas.

Arola, Kristin L. 2010. "The Design of Web 2.0: The Rise of the Template, The Fall of Design." *Computers and Composition* 27(1): 4–14.

Barley, W. C., P. M. Leonardi, and D. E. Bailey. 2012. "Engineering Objects for Collaboration: Strategies of Ambiguity and Clarity at Knowledge Boundaries." *Human Communication Research* 38(3): 280–308.

Baxter, Ira, and Michael Mehlich. 1997. "Reverse Engineering Is Reverse Forward Engineering." In Ira Baxter, Alex Quilici, and Chris Verhoef, eds. *Proceedings of the Fourth Working Conference on Reverse Engineering, October 6-8, 1997, Amsterdam, the Netherlands.* Los Alamitos, CA, USA: IEEE Computer Society Press.

Bratich, Jack. 2011. "User-Generated Discontent." *Cultural Studies* 25 (September): 621–40. doi:10.1080/09502386.2011.600552.

Coleman, Gabriella. 2009. "Code is Speech: Legal Tinkering, Expertise, and Protest among Free and Open Source Software Developers." *Cultural Anthropology* 24 (August): 420–54. doi:10.1111/j.1548-1360.2009.01036.x.

Elmer, Greg. 2004. *Profiling Machines: Mapping the Personal Information Economy.* Cambridge, MA: MIT Press.

Feenberg, Andrew. 1986. *Lukács, Marx, and the Sources of Critical Theory.* New York: Oxford University Press.

Foucault, Michel. 1979. *Discipline and Punish.* New York: Vintage.

Foucault, Michel. 2003. "The Subject and Power." In Paul Rabinow and Nikolas S. Rose, eds. *The Essential Foucault: Selections from Essential Works of Foucault, 1954-1984.* New York: New Press, 126–44.

Gehl, Robert. 2011. "The Archive and the Processor: The Internal Logic of Web 2.0." *New Media & Society* 13(8): 1228–44.

Gehl, Robert. 2013a. "'Why I Left Facebook': Stubbornly Refusing to Not Exist Even After Opting Out of Mark Zuckerberg's Social Graph." In Geert Lovink and Miriam Rausch, eds. *Unlike Us Reader: Social Media Monopolies and Their Alternatives.* Amsterdam: Institute of Network Cultures, 220–38.

Gehl, Robert. 2013b. "What's on Your Mind? Social Media Monopolies and Noopower." *First Monday* 18(3/4). http://www.uic.edu/htbin/cgiwrap/bin/ojs/index.php/fm/article/view/4618/3421.

Gehl, Robert. 2014. *Reverse Engineering Social Media: Software, Culture, and Political Economy in New Media Capitalism.* Philadelphia, PA: Temple University Press.

Gillespie, Tarleton. 2007. *Wired Shut.* Cambridge, MA: MIT Press.

Hainaut, J. L., V. Englebert, J. Henrard, J. M. Hick, and D. Roland. 1996. "Database Reverse Engineering: From Requirements to CARE Tools." *Journal of Automated Software Engineering* 3(1): 9–45.

Ingle, Kathryn A. 1994. *Reverse Engineering.* New York: McGraw-Hill.

@JackalAnon. 2013a. *mA5dL.png (PNG Image, 984 × 516 Pixels).* Accessed September 4, 2013. http://i.imgur.com/mA5dL.png.

@JackalAnon. 2013b. *1Suu1.png (PNG Image, 963 × 621 Pixels) – Scaled (94%).* Accessed September 4, 2013. http://i.imgur.com/1Suu1.png.

Johnstone, Angus. 2010a. "Why Isn't #Wikileaks Trending on Twitter, and Should We Care?" Blog. *Student Activism*. November 28. http://studentactivism.net/2010/11/28/wikileaks/.

Johnstone, Angus. 2010b. "New Questions About Why #Wikileaks Isn't Trending On Twitter." Blog. *Student Activism*. December 5. http://studentactivism.net/2010/12/05/twitter-wikileaks-trending-2/.

Langlois, Ganaele. 2011. "Meaning, Semiotechnologies and Participatory Media." *Culture Machine* 12 (The Digital Humanities: Beyond Computing): 1–27.

Langlois, Ganaele. 2013. "Social Media, or towards a Political Economy of Psychic Life." In Geert Lovink and Miriam Rausch, eds. *Unlike Us Reader: Social Media Monopolies and Their Alternatives*. Amsterdam: Institute of Network Cultures.

Latour, Bruno. 1987. *Science in Action: How to Follow Scientists and Engineers through Society*. Cambridge, MA: Harvard University Press.

Law, John. 1992. "Notes on the Theory of the Actor-Network: Ordering, Strategy, and Heterogeneity." *Systemic Practice and Action Research* 5(4): 379–93. doi:10.1007/BF01059830.

Law, John. 2002. *Aircraft Stories: Decentering the Object in Technoscience*. Durham: Duke University Press.

Lazzarato, Maurizio. 2006. "The Concepts of Life and the Living in the Societies of Control." In Martin Fuglsang and Bent Meier Sørensen, eds. *Deleuze and the Social*. Edinburgh: Edinburgh University Press.

Leite, Julio Cesar Sampaio do Prado, and Paulo Monteiro Cerqueira. 1995. "Recovering Business Rules from Structured Analysis Specifications." In Linda Wills, Philip Newcomb, and Elliot Chikofsky, eds. *Reverse Engineering: 2nd Working Conference*. Los Alamitos, CA, USA: IEEE Computer Society Press.

Lessig, Lawrence. 2004. *Free Culture: How Big Media Uses Technology and the Law to Lock down Culture and Control Creativity*. New York: Penguin Press.

Lutsky, Patricia. 1995. "Automated Testing by Reverse Engineering of Software Documentation." In Linda Wills, Philip Newcomb, and Elliot Chikofsky, eds. *Reverse Engineering: 2nd Working Conference*. Los Alamitos, CA, USA: IEEE Computer Society Press.

Mackenzie, Adrian. 2006. *Cutting Code: Software and Sociality*. New York: Peter Lang.

Marx, Karl. 2008. *The 18th Brumaire of Louis Bonaparte*. New York: Wildside Press LLC.

Morris, Laura. 2013. "Did the Kill-Switch Really Kill the Internet?" Presentation at the Frontiers of New Media, University of Utah, September 21. http://www.frontiersofnewmedia.org/schedule/.

OpESR. 2012. "Http://talkopen.info/doxers Group for Doxers." *Facebook*. https://www.facebook.com/permalink.php?id=132449120164059&story_fbid=204518512990354.

Samuelson, Pamela. 2002. "Reverse Engineering Under Siege." *Communications of the ACM* 45(10): 15–20.

Samuelson, Pamela and Suzanne Scotchmer. 2002. "The Law and Economics of Reverse Engineering." *The Yale Law Journal* 111(7). doi:10.2307/797533.

Schwartz, Matthew J. 2012. "Anonymous Builds New Haven For Stolen Data." *Information Week*. http://www.informationweek.com/news/security/vulnerabilities/232900590.

Sega Enterprises Ltd. v. Accolade, Inc. 1992, 977 F. 2d 1510. Court of Appeals, 9th Circuit.

Sony Computer Entertainment v. Connectix Corp. 2000, 203 F. 3d 596. Court of Appeals, 9th Circuit.

Star, S. L. 1999. "The Ethnography of Infrastructure." *American Behavioral Scientist* 43(3): 377–91.

Stone, Biz. 2011. "The Tweets Must Flow." *Twitter Blogs*. January 28. https://blog.twitter.com/2011/tweets-must-flow.

"TalkOpen.info & Anon Communications: A Simple Method for safER (not Safe) Social." 2012. *Pastebin*. http://pastebin.com/72aHMGb9.

"Talk Open – Welcome to The Talk Open Community." 2012. *Archive.org*. http://web.archive.org/web/20120403045749/http://talkopen.info/.

Terranova, Tiziana. 2000. "Free Labor: Producing Culture for the Digital Economy." *Social Text* 18(2): 33–58.

"TRG – th3j35t3r & Talkopen.info." 2012. *Pastebin*. http://pastebin.com/K9weNjUD.

Turner, Fred. 2008. *From Counterculture to Cyberculture: Stewart Brand, the Whole Earth Network, and the Rise of Digital Utopianism*. Chicago, IL: University Of Chicago Press.

"Tweets Still Must Flow." 2012. *Twitter Blogs*. January 26. https://blog.twitter.com/2012/tweets-still-must-flow.

Zittrain, Jonathan. 2008. *The Future of the Internet and How to Stop It*. New Haven: Yale University Press.

Part Three

Alt-Data

9

Mapping Movements—Social Movement Research and Big Data: Critiques and Alternatives

Sky Croeser and Tim Highfield

Introduction

The integration of social media and other online and mobile platforms and technologies into social movements around the globe has received significant academic attention, particularly to the role these platforms play in helping revolutions succeed and shaping information flows during protests. Movements such as Occupy and the Arab Spring, both of which saw widespread social media activity, have been the subjects of numerous studies in different fields that have taken advantage of abundantly available social media data (Conover, Davis et al. 2013; Costanza-Chock 2012; Gaby and Caren 2012; Papacharissi and Oliveira 2012; Starbird and Palen 2012). Automated processes and tools for capturing and processing such activity have meant that large social media data sets, of tweets in particular, are increasingly common sources for research into social movements and their activities and coverage online.

However, with the growing use of big data, social media – oriented approaches in the study of social movements raise new analytical and ethical challenges. There are important differences between big data research methodologies and previous approaches to social movement research, including a radically altered relationship between researchers and movement participants. Social media data capture and analysis around these topics can be carried out without having to be physically near or involved in the movements in question, which raises concerns about how to evaluate potential risks to participants, reciprocity, the accessibility of research to activists, including for comment and criticism, and how researchers engage with movement participants as knowledge producers. Analytically, the use of big data methods for social movement research requires a careful attention to the biases in available data. Biases and gaps in the data may be introduced in many ways, including: the strategic avoidance of social media or self-censorship by activists; the limitations of platform architecture and content policies; practices such as subtweeting and screen capping which deliberately obscure links between accounts; the use of images and other non-text forms not captured by big data tools; the openness of different social media platforms to data capture; and the limitations of data capture tools themselves.

In response to these challenges and concerns, we advocate the use of a mixed-methods approach that combines participant observation, in-depth interviews, and big data methods. This approach offers a framework for balancing the benefits of new quantitative methods with a need to prioritize an ethical approach to social movement research, as well as correcting some of the biases introduced by big data methods. This approach has been developed through the Mapping Movements project, which has examined movements and events in North America, Africa, and Europe. This chapter draws most prominently on the first published case study of the project, looking at the use of Twitter within the Occupy Oakland movement (Croeser and Highfield 2014). This research demonstrates that a mixed-methods approach allows a better understanding of the contexts of social movements and their uses of social media. Considering both the online and the physical aspects of social movements enables a nuanced analysis of social media use by activists, looking beyond the object of study (the social medium of choice) at a quantitative level, to examine the intersections between these aspects of social movements. Crucially, our work demonstrates how blended methods can combine the strengths of different research approaches to collectively overcome the limitations of big, social media data, providing detail and explanation for activity found in—and hidden from—these data sets, addressing some of the gaps in big data research. In this chapter, we outline some of the most pressing ethical and analytical issues for big data research on social movements that are broadly relevant, and to offer potential avenues for approaching (if only partial) solutions; to do so, we draw on experiences and findings from our Occupy Oakland case study.

Big data and social movements

The term "big data" did not originate in communications or political studies, but has increasingly been applied to the analysis of large data sets in these and many other disciplines. It is now strongly associated with social media analysis, in particular (boyd and Crawford 2012), as data sets continue to grow alongside the increasing access to, and availability of, tools for capturing, storing, and processing more data. This also reflects trends around the use of social media, of course, as platforms such as Facebook, Twitter, YouTube, or Instagram saw more users register and thus more data contributed. Even if user numbers plateau or start to decrease, the integration of these platforms into everyday life (by individuals, organizations, and companies alike) means that the amount of data and uses of social media remains vast. Social media are used for information sharing, for activism and collective action, for fandom and media audiences, for keeping in touch with family and friends, and many other purposes by the same users, on the same platforms.

The multiple, publicly visible uses of a common platform such as Twitter have benefited studies of social media. The development of semi-standardized practices and tools for data capture, in particular those making use of APIs, has led to approaches that work across contexts; consistent structural elements of Twitter, such as hashtags, can be tracked in the same way regardless of whether they reflect politics, sports, or any other topic. This means that much Twitter research is methodologically replicable and research designs can be reused for different topics, even if the exact projects and data sets are not reproducible due to the site's terms of use and access to different APIs.

These trends also show that obtaining and analyzing big data around social movements from social media are not limited to major research projects with connections to data providers, high performance computing, and extensive technical literary. Even if Twitter's changing terms of use mean that tools used previously are now unavailable, and that researchers are unable to share data sets, it remains the case that a wide corpus of tweets is being archived by projects around the globe, covering a wealth of contexts and provocations as well as manual and automated processes (Zimmer and Proferes 2014). It is also unsurprising, in the specific case of social movement research, that major events of international interest have acted as flashpoints in the field, representing a confluence of these trends: movements such as the Arab Spring uprisings in the Middle East and Northern Africa, from 2011 onwards, and the Occupy movement demonstrate events wherein social media were seen as key components of the movements, enabling communication from within and receiving extensive coverage from outside the movement. Indeed, both examples have been the subject of numerous big data studies into various aspects of their social media coverage, respectively.

In addition to analysis of smaller collections of tweets and other online activity (as well as ethnographic data), studies into the Arab Spring and Twitter have made use of large-scale data sets featuring thousands and millions of tweets. For instance, Deen Freelon's (2011) exploratory analysis of 5.88 million Arab Spring–related tweets (a corpus featuring seven hashtags, including #egypt, #libya, #sidibouzid, and #feb14) provided initial information around tweeting patterns for each of these movements, including daily activity and user locations. Lotan et al. (2011) analyzed information flows during both the Tunisian and Egyptian uprisings, drawing on data sets of 168,663 tweets (Tunisia) and 230,270 tweets (Egypt). 103,489 #sidibouzid tweets formed the corpus for Poell and Darmoni's (2012) exploration of users, tweeting language, and interaction networks during the Tunisian revolution, while Papacharissi and Oliveira (2012) analyzed 1.5 million Egypt tweets for their study of news patterns, sharing, and affect on Twitter. Finally, Bruns, Highfield, and Burgess's (2013) long-term analysis of language groups and networks featured 7.48 million #egypt tweets and 5.27 million #libya tweets. While all of these studies answered different questions, and covered different time periods, the data sets contain crossover in terms of content, yet for the most part required independent collection (researchers could access shared data sets captured using 140kit and TwapperKeeper.com until late March 2011).

For the Occupy movement, a similar picture emerges, particularly with long-term tracking of tweets around individual Occupy sites. Conover, Ferrara et al. (2013) drew on a data set of 1.82 million tweets (containing the #ows hashtag and #occupy* for other Occupy hashtags) in studying Occupy Wall Street online over time. The initial, prefiltered data set for Thorson et al. (2013) contained 4.87 million tweets, which was also used to support analysis of Occupy-related material on YouTube. Agarwal et al. (2014) studied over 60 million tweets, primarily from Occupy Wall Street, Occupy Oakland, and Occupy Seattle, to explore the role played by Twitter within these movements. Our previous research on Occupy Oakland, while not designed as a purely quantitative, big data – driven study, still gathered a corpus of 43,978 tweets from snapshots of activity (Croeser and Highfield 2014), highlighting that there is a vast amount of information available to researchers regardless of their research aims and design. This is not to say that big data – style approaches are the only ways to explore Occupy, the Arab Spring, or other movements: Benjamin Gleason's (2013) study of informal learning about Occupy Wall Street featured two data sets containing a combined total of 294 tweets, and not all of these studies are limited to Twitter analysis alone. However, this research does establish that the capture and analysis of large-scale social media data sets, subsequently filtered down and with inevitable but not entirely comparable crossover between projects, is not uncommon in the field. This applies to other events and contexts too; for example, Procter, Vis, and Voss (2013) studied social media during the UK riots of 2011, with a corpus of 2.6 million tweets.

The benefits of such big social data research are obvious: the wealth of information provided in such extensive data sets allows for a rich analysis of social movements, from many angles. These include tracking patterns of activity, interaction networks, content shared, languages used, information flows, links to other platforms and supplementary media, tools and technologies used, locations of users, and structural and organizational uses and functions of these platforms. This is especially useful when approaches to using social media within movements develop over time, and when other functions are not immediately apparent—or were unknown to the researcher prior to the analysis—but which are revealed within the data. Furthermore, such data sets provide strong foundations for further, grounded research into the movement overall; methods such as interviews, surveys, and participant observation of the physical and digital aspects of social movements can bring out participants' concerns through, and about, social media, and both complement and outline gaps in the social media data (see, for instance, Gerbaudo 2012; Tufekci and Wilson 2012).

As Paolo Gerbaudo (2012) warns, though, there is also a risk of fetishizing social media, treating platforms such as Twitter *as* the collective action through assigning them "mystical qualities" (8) which serve to overshadow and ignore who is using them, as well as how and why. This may be especially the case when the collective action is being studied only through a social media lens: the analysis only of tweets acquired at a distance from the movement and its political and social contexts. In such cases, over-ascribing importance to social media may be more likely than in studies drawing on mixed data sources and methods. As always, it is crucial to note that social media activity (and especially activity on a single platform) alone is not fully representative of the social movement in question. Furthermore, there are many limits and aspects of big data sets that need to be taken into account, regardless of the subject of the research (boyd and Crawford 2012); these are addressed later in this chapter, and have important implications for the ethics of big data research into social movements.

The ethics of social movement research

Gillan and Pickerill's (2012) article introducing a special issue of *Social Movement Studies* provides a useful overview of key themes and important problems in the ethics of research on social movements that must also underpin any discussion of big data methods in the field. They note that social movement research has particular challenges beyond those faced in other social sciences research, including the intensely politicized nature of the issues addressed (and researchers' own positions on those issues) and the potential vulnerability of social movement participants (133). Whereas the university ethics approval process for social movement research usually requires a one-off application, which may or may not require a further report or follow-up, Gillan and Pickerill (ibid., 135) emphasize that ethics are, instead, a "dynamic, complex and on-going dilemma." The process of using big data techniques in social movement research adds to the existing complexities and requires revisiting and revising existing ethical models for social movement research.

One of the primary concerns for any researcher must be protecting participants from potential harms that might arise from their involvement. Sandra Smeltzer (2012) emphasizes that the issues involved in studying at-risk activists in social movements are considerable. She notes that even relatively privileged participants may be put at risk by involvement in research, as is the case with urban-based, educated, and financially secure activists she interviews in Malaysia (2012, 257), as well as recognizing how easy it is to slip into worrying more about "good data" than about the safety of interviewees (260). Much of the recent big data research on social movements has looked at either events associated with the Arab Spring or the Occupy movement. None of the countries where these movements are based can be considered entirely safe for activists. Tufekci and Wilson (2012), studying social media use by Egyptian protestors, conducted interviews in public spaces in order "to enhance safety and security" for respondents (367). Halavais and Garrido (2014) also note the concerns around users implicated in illegal activities during protests and noted in public data sets, choosing not to directly mention usernames contributing to a G20-related data set of tweets (124). For much research into Twitter, though, across a range of subjects, the collection and presentation of publicly accessible data has been met with inconsistent approaches. Zimmer and Proferes (2014) found that in 382 publications about Twitter, only four percent of them made explicit mention of "ethical issues or considerations" about the research design and methodology, including anonymizing participant details (9). While the implications of revealing user information vary across projects, the decision to anonymize or not for studies of activist networks on Twitter has clear ethical importance for security.

A second concern often raised around social movement research is the need for reciprocity. As social movement research shifted away from seeing activists as largely irrational during the 1960s and 1970s, there was a growing concern that research—particularly research which focused on relatively disadvantaged communities—should provide something to these communities in return (Flacks 2005, 6–7). In part, this is seen as a necessary repayment for the time and effort that activists give up to researchers in the form of interviews or other interactions (Smeltzer 2012, 260). Beyond this, however, reciprocity is also seen as part of a deeper underlying political commitment and positioning. Richard Flacks (2005, 8) asks of the huge amount of work on social movements: "*What is all this analysis for?* In what way does the validation, elaboration, and refinement of concepts provide usable knowledge for those seeking social change?" Meanwhile, Gillan and Pickerill discuss the trend toward "activist-scholars" associated with arguments about "the potential for academics to make a real and positive impact on movements they are studying" (2012, 135). They argue (ibid., 136–37), however, that this should not be seen as a cure-all for ethical concerns in social movement research. Activist-scholars are not exempt from objectifying the movements they study, or from benefiting from this positioning within academia, nor is it guaranteed that they will provide genuine aid to the movements they are studying. The principle of reciprocity also becomes problematic when studying "ugly" movements, as Gillan and Pickerill term them, which researchers have no desire to support, such as neo-nazi movements (ibid., 136). Reciprocity remains an important ethical concern in social movement research, but there is no easy model for ensuring that researchers have adequately "repaid" activists for their time and openness.

One answer that some researchers provide to the dilemma of reciprocity is to focus on the production of relevant and valuable knowledge. Gillan and Pickerill argue that while "it may be impossible to 'pay back' a research participant for their efforts in any direct way that does not somehow compromise the research, . . . the utility of the results of research will offer some benefit at a broader, societal level" (2012, 137). Producing research from a position sympathetic to activists' perspectives, or research guided by activists' interests, will have limited utility if it is not based in rigorous research methods and a thorough analysis. At best, such research might function as propaganda. At worst, it may mislead activists as to the value of particular tactics and strategies or the broader context in which they are working, and may in doing so undermine movements' efforts or even individuals' safety.

Many scholars of social movements argue that allowing research to be guided, or at least informed, by activist communities will help in the production of more nuanced and developed analysis. The idea of activists as "knowledge-producers in their own right," partners in the analysis rather than purely objects of study (Chesters 2012, 145), is an important consideration for the production of relevant and useful research. Graeme Chesters argues that there is an ethical obligation to engage with activists' own analyses, to see them not only as producing knowledge around the issues which movements most directly address, but also around more fundamental questions of political agency and alternative political imaginaries (147). This requires an ongoing and serious engagement with the epistemological and ontological underpinnings of social movements as well as around more surface-level issues, such as day-to-day tactics.

Related to concerns around reciprocity and the production of relevant knowledge is the injunction that knowledge produced about social movements be accessible to activists—that academics should both be engaging with activists' analyses and offering back valuable knowledge. Publishing research on social movements that has relied on activists' openness to researchers in proprietary journals is a form of enclosure, taking knowledge previously shared by activist communities, codifying it, and publishing it in a space that constrains access. This means activists can often neither afford to read it nor can they easily reply to academics' analysis of their movement. Even when research is published in open-access journals or as copyleft books or reports, and is therefore physically accessible, concerns are often raised about the use of academic jargon and obscure language (Dawson and Sinwell 2012, 186). However, Shukaitis and Graeber (2007, 13) caution against the assumption that "accessible" academic writing must be simplistic, noting that some of the authors who are most widely read in activist communities would usually be considered difficult reading.

A less-frequently articulated aspect of ethical social movement research, which is particularly relevant to our work, is the need to consider a spatial politics of responsibility, an "assertion of our identity and visible insertion of ourselves into our research [that] can help us better understand how our sense of responsibility to our research subjects stretches and changes over time" (Gillan and Pickerill 2012, 139). The desire to take an ethical approach to social movement research is often framed in terms of an engagement with physical or intellectual co-presence or, conversely, distance between researchers and activists (ibid., 140). Shukaitis and Graeber (2007, 11), for example, frame their research in terms of a literal, intellectual, and physical closeness: "we ask questions, not from the perspective of the theorist removed and separate from organizing, but rather from within and as part of the multiple and overlapping cycles and circuits of struggle." Dawson and Sinwell (2012, 165), following Jeffrey S. Juris (2007), similarly see physical presence (and the risks associated, such as the risk of arrest or police violence) and the emotional experience of direct action, as an important aspect of social movement research. Researchers therefore need to carefully consider the distance, literal and metaphorical, between their positions and those of the activists with whom they work.

In many ways, big data approaches intensify existing concerns about social movement research and add to the challenge of ethical research practices. Most big data research methods radically change the spatial politics of responsibility, which has flow-on effects for other aspects of the research framework. Physical co-presence with activists is no longer required, nor is permission from or ongoing engagement with activist communities. Discussion with activists is minimized, and in many cases activists may not even know that they are the focus of research. Dawson and Sinwell (2012, 181) cite Ashwin Desai's comparison of academic research not built on dialogue or relevance to social movements to spying: this comparison seems all the more apt when it comes to many big data research methods. We therefore need to think carefully about how existing concerns about the ethics of social movement research are intensified or modified by the use of big data methods.

While at first glance it may seem like using material from publicly accessible social media accounts or services like YouTube creates no additional risks for activists, it is worth noting that recontextualizing and analyzing even public material can have serious consequences. For example, journalists covering a

2014 story about sexual assault were criticized for their use of public tweets in a way that decontextualized a rape survivor's experience and gave her a visibility (through their readership) that her own Twitter account had not had (Stoeffel 2014). As well as issues of contextualization and social privacy, big data analysis has the potential to open activists up to increased surveillance or other risks by, for example, pinpointing key accounts within a movement or mapping connections that might otherwise be invisible. This is particularly important in light of increasing evidence that police and other government agencies are conducting surveillance of activists on social media, including in democratic states (BondGraham and Winston 2013; Palmer 2013; Privacy SOS 2013). Academics therefore have an ethical obligation to remain aware of the ways in which big data research results—or even analytical processes and research methodologies—may be used by state or non-state organizations, and the dangers this might pose to activists.

Reciprocity also becomes more complex. On the one hand, researchers drawing only on large-scale analyses of publicly available data arguably have a lessened obligation to "pay back" activists for their time. On the other hand, the increased distance (both literal and intellectual) between researchers and the social movements they are writing about makes it more difficult to build the kinds of engagement with activists that many researchers (Chesters 2012; Dawson and Sinwell 2012; Lewis 2012) argue is a necessary basis for producing research relevant to activist communities. On a smaller scale, Sandra Smeltzer's (2012, 262) discussion of examples of "token reciprocity" are embedded in everyday interactions, while more extensive "back office" support (such as conducting research or proofreading) becomes much more unlikely without dialogue that highlights activists' needs and the potential for collaboration to researchers.

Related to this, there is a danger of reinforcing the division between researchers and movements. Shukaitis and Graeber (2007, 11), in calling for "militant research," caution that "for the removed theorist, movements themselves are mere abstractions, pieces of data to be categorized, analyzed, and fixed." Arguably, this abstraction becomes more likely when researchers are dealing with activists not face-to-face, or even online, as individuals, but rather as thousands (or millions) of disembodied data points. Big data research may also reinforce the structure of activists as objects of study and researchers as "scientists" peering in from afar at "found," preexisting data which they have not actively constructed. Alexander Halavais (2013) notes that unobtrusive measures (such as gathering public data online) are often framed as more objective, obscuring the position of the researcher in framing research.

These inequalities between the researcher-as-subject and movement-as-object intensify the gap between what scholars gain from their research and what they give back to activist communities (either directly or indirectly). Big data adds to the potential for the increasingly rapid commodification of activists' data, as the slow process of interviewing and participant observation or action research is replaced by quickly analyzing and publishing data to meet the publish-or-perish requirements of modern academia. Without the requirement to engage with activist communities, to be continually (or even occasionally) present and to justify research in both formal and informal communications with activists, it may be easier for academics to find themselves primarily meeting the needs of their institutional context and putting publishing before ethics.

Big data research also has the potential to decrease the ability of activists to engage in collaborative analysis and engagement. While Alexander Halavais (2013) argues that big data research may actually open up possibilities for engagement, in most cases, public participation is limited to small-scale tasks rather than larger questions around research and framing, and it is dubious that social movement research would be open to these possibilities. There are also barriers to access to big data and social media research: data capture processes require researchers to register applications with platform APIs, and large-scale, ongoing captures need server infrastructure and always-on functionality beyond the capabilities of free desktop software. For platforms such as Twitter, free access is also limited to a subset of the total activity; in order to access all tweets around a topic or during a certain period, there is a cost involved that might further reduce the ability of activists to take part in this research. Furthermore, even when the data have been collected, the restrictions of platforms' terms of use limit sharing data sets with others.

New biases in data collection and analysis

There are numerous analytical limitations and blind spots surrounding social media data sources. While big social media data sets provide valuable and rich resources for analyzing online activity across a wealth of contexts, for subjects such as social movements in particular they should not be treated as necessarily representative of the movement. Despite the vast amounts of data at hand for studying the Occupy movement on Twitter, for instance, it is crucial to note that Twitter activity is not the whole movement, regardless of any "official" branding through appropriate hashtags. There are numerous blind spots and assumptions within these large data sets, which limit the scope of findings drawn from their analysis. Understanding and accounting for these absences, including integrating additional methods to attempt to overcome such limits, is an important challenge for social media research, including studies of social movements. Such challenges do not make these data sets unsuitable for study, but they do place limits on the extent to which research can draw on these data sources alone, especially with regard to subjects with notable physical and digital forms, such as social movements. For this reason, we argue that it is important to both acknowledge these limits, and to develop new approaches that combine methodologies and information sources without relying solely on big social media data.

Studying protest movements and activists through their social media activity is, as has been noted earlier, an approach promoted by the integration of hashtags as organizational elements of movements, and by the extensive coverage of events such as the Arab Spring on Twitter. However, considering only the online activity introduces several prominent gaps with regard to the movement as a whole. While the public and semi-public nature of much social media communication, especially on Twitter, makes these platforms ideal for spreading information quickly, these same aspects may cause activists to avoid contributing themselves. As we found in our previous research on Occupy Oakland (Croeser and Highfield 2014), activists central to the movements may work only offline, keeping off social media by choice or necessity; whatever role they play in the physical movement, though, they are also not directly represented in the surrounding social media data. Furthermore, if prominent voices are not contributing to online discussions, other participants may attempt to fill the void. This can have the effect of making activists who are especially vocal on Twitter appear as key figures within the movement when considering only this aspect.

Choosing how to participate on social media, including deliberately not contributing, can be an act of self-censorship, particularly given privacy concerns around individual social media platforms and around government agencies tracking and logging online activity, as we confirmed in our research on Occupy Oakland (Croeser and Highfield 2014) and unpublished interviews with antifascist activists in Athens, Greece. Although the physical sites of social movements are not free from surveillance, some activists choose to participate only through offline means, limiting the amount of information they share and the avenues for surveillance. For those activists who do contribute to social media, self-censorship is practised in other ways: the same concerns remain, and so other means of circumventing them are employed. This can mean that information is made available in more cryptic ways or through private channels, in order to combat threats of surveillance. Users may also actively curb their own contributions, not only to reduce the amount of information they post, but also to avoid accounts being closed down. Since social media platforms are owned by private companies, users are at the mercy of these companies when it comes to continued access to their services, and accounts may be closed down without warning for violating terms of service. Reports from our case studies also suggest there is a perception that government and police surveillance of social media can also lead to pressure on these companies for masking information—hiding movements from trending topics, for instance—or deleting accounts.

Self-censorship as a practice is also shaped by the social media platforms used. With Twitter, for example, the 140-character limit for tweets already imposes arbitrary constraints on communication, as users edit and force their messages into the allowed character range, part of wider social media logics developed in response to what is allowed and not allowed on individual platforms (Langlois and Elmer 2013). However, there are also further practices, not limited to social movements, which can obscure aspects of the communication from researchers without contextual information. As Zeynep Tufekci (2014) outlines, practices such as subtweeting, screen capping, and hate linking all represent Twitter communication in response to others, yet the connections created (or deliberately not directly formed) are not as obvious in intent or direction as a standard @reply or retweet. Subtweeting, for instance, comments on other users without mentioning them—an act that may still be obvious in its subject, given the right context (such as a deep involvement in a particular movement), but that might be meaningless to researchers after the fact, especially when drawing on partial data sets. Similarly, screen capping repeats the contributions of other users in image form, using screenshots, rather than textual quotes; these can be used to showcase comments that have since been deleted or that may contain confronting content again without providing a direct link between users— indeed, for a tweet likely to be deleted, screen capping is a more permanent solution than retweeting, since it provides a record of the original comment. However, much Twitter analysis is focused on textual content, or quantifying messages, and these processes may overlook the non-textual elements of ongoing Twitter discussions.

Personal absence from social media and self-censorship are deliberate choices made by activists that affect the data available on associated social movements. Other blind spots, though, are determined by researchers. As noted earlier, there is a growing corpus of studies of Twitter and social movements, covering numerous aspects of the Arab Spring, several branches of the Occupy movement, as well as other local and international protests. However, in the same way that Twitter is not the movement itself, Twitter is also not the sole social medium in use within the movement. Activists may make use of other platforms, both general and niche, posting on Facebook, uploading content to photo-sharing and video-sharing sites, sharing information across numerous profiles. However, the availability of Twitter data, and the public nature of tweets, means that there is perhaps a comparative over-representation of Twitter within research; Twitter is a popular tool, but it is not the only platform. Because obtaining data from Facebook is accompanied by more extensive ethical and methodological concerns, especially when looking beyond public pages, it may be easier for researchers to draw on public communication from Twitter than other platforms (research into Occupy that covers other platforms as well as Twitter includes inter alia Thorson et al. 2013 and Agarwal et al. 2014). The relative openness of these sites may affect how—and if—activists use them, but they also have clear implications for how researchers determine their object of study. With established tools for capturing and analyzing Twitter data, too, researchers can make use of automated and comparable methods for studying movements on Twitter and link in with similar studies. While these studies do provide important insights into social media use, it is critical to remember that they are limited to only one component of the movement in question, and this may not be the most important aspect of the movement's work.

It also needs to be underlined that data gathered from Twitter are not necessarily comprehensive or representative. These limits apply both to the social context for the data and for the methodological and analytical design of the research. As noted above, the 140-character limit for tweets can restrict the amount of explanatory information and affect nuance, especially for researchers analyzing messages after the fact and without deep knowledge of context. Losing context can also occur when focusing on particular archives; studying a single hashtag, for instance, considers tweets containing that hashtag but not any surrounding comments by the same users on the same topics, without the chosen marker, nor any replies to these comments that are also lacking the hashtag. This also reflects a possible sampling bias in such research, focusing on only one aspect of a potentially much more extensive corpus (Procter, Vis, and Voss 2013, 208). Similarly, as Lev Manovich (2012) notes, online communication, whether tweets or other digital contributions, should not be treated as "authentic," as what people present about themselves is "usually carefully curated and systematically managed" (465). Despite tweets being public communication of a sort, analyzing their content without knowing contextual factors shaping these comments is risking misinterpretation or missing meaning and implications. This applies for both the text and any other media in tweets; while processing the textual content of tweets can be easily automated, images, videos, and other media forms are also important components of the communication, which may not receive the same attention and indeed may serve as replacements or equivalents for text.

The limits to data available to researchers—despite the apparent abundance of Twitter data, especially in comparison to other social media platforms—are also not consistent across projects. While research can gather data from the Twitter API, there are several different APIs that offer different levels of access to the full Twitter content stream; gaining access to the full Firehose, though, is a financial outlay that forces many researchers to rely on the Streaming and REST APIs (representational state transfer), which offer access to a subset of tweets (for a comparison of API results, see Morstatter et al. 2013). There are also limits to what data are returned by various capture tools, as what is tracked is not necessarily all of the corresponding data, nor the only or most important signifiers of intent. Trackers such as yourTwapperKeeper.com or the Archivist (both of which we have used in our research) query the API for tweets containing specified search terms (hashtags, keywords, and user names), collecting corresponding comments (including republished versions of them). However, some data about these individual tweets, such as the total numbers of retweets or favorites received, are not gathered (these create methodological complications, since these are dynamic metadata for previously collected tweets). Favoriting, in particular, is a mechanism for Twitter users to respond to comments without contributing new textual content—or a new comment to track—but can be used to gauge reactions to, and awareness of, a tweet.

At the same time, though, such practices are also not necessarily "authentic"; receiving high numbers of retweets and favorites can be a way for a Twitter user to increase their reputation and follower numbers, their influence on social media, especially through third-party analytics services such as Klout. Gaming such metrics has become increasingly apparent on Twitter (Vis 2013; Karpf 2012), where follower numbers, retweets, and favorites are artificially inflated using fake or spam accounts (for retweet and favorite cartels, see Paßmann, Boeschoten, and Schäfer 2013). Such practices are not limited to commercial aims, and other users, including activists, may engage in "inauthentic" approaches to increase visibility for their accounts, content, or causes. These motivations for comments are not always apparent through the content of the tweets themselves, and this is another contextual aspect that can be overlooked. Quantitative analysis of a large data set of tweets provides, among other things, valuable metrics on which comments and users garnered most attention. However, if the tweet quoted the most times is being republished by fake accounts with no followers, such that the message is appearing prominent statistically, but not reaching a new audience, then the numbers alone are not presenting a complete or accurate view of the Twitter activity. As Farida Vis (2013) notes, there are questions to be addressed around the validity of big data from social media, and around visibility: the data gathered can include replies and retweets, but this does not show how many people read a tweet or follow a link in a comment.

Ultimately, researchers obtain a partial picture of online activity, of which different sections are then interpreted. This may be partially due to the limits of access to data, but also due to the research design, particularly for capture processes run in response to breaking developments or where extensive historical archives are not available; Mahrt and Scharkow (2013) suggest that digital media research can be prone to using "whatever data is available and then [trying] to provide an ex-post justification or even theorization for its use" (25). The vagaries of the research design and capture processes, in addition to the variations across tools and data sets around the same subject, then have implications for the research findings and their applicability to other contexts. Data that is more convenient for researchers' analysis may be far from the data that is most important or relevant for understanding, or contributing analysis to, a social movement.

How the social media platforms present and determine information to be made available to users and researchers alike further impacts upon both the activity and the analysis. The evolving politics of platforms and of the algorithms they use affect the experience of social media, not just Twitter: how Twitter determines "trending" topics, for instance, has changed over time and without clear definition of how the trending algorithm works (Gillespie 2014). Similarly, Facebook's algorithms for filtering and displaying content in individual users' feeds shape activity, since users respond to what they are shown and to where their attention is directed (Bucher 2012). Such processes have a follow-on effect on researchers tracking social media activity, but the conditions determining what a user might or might not see (and the different algorithm results for different users) are unknown for the analysis.

The researcher experience is beholden here to the politics of the platforms in question, for studying activity on corporate social media such as Twitter or Facebook means that the research is limited to what the platforms permit. Puschmann and Burgess (2013) outline the tensions and conflicting interests between Twitter, its users, and analysts both commercial and private in sharing and accessing Twitter data, including questions around ownership regarding user content and data. Although users access and share content on social media for free, and researchers can freely query APIs, the commercial aims of the platforms themselves dictate what can and cannot be done here. These tensions between public communication—on *social* media—and commercial interests are not limited to Twitter, and Tarleton Gillespie (2010) highlights the dilemmas faced by platforms at large in balancing business models, users and their rights, and the operation of their sites and services.

These tensions also apply for related research: since Twitter studies examine public communication on a private, commercial site, researchers are also dependent on what Twitter decides to do with its platform, APIs, and terms of use. Free access to data is already limited as there are commercial deals to honor and protect with companies that analyze and resell social media data (Manovich 2012), but the terms of use could change overnight to drastically change the capabilities of researchers to collect and share data. Platforms could also change their architecture without warning—altering algorithms or phasing out elements such as hashtags, for instance—which would further impact related research, as studies get "scooped" by the objects of their analysis (Rogers 2009). For big data research into social movements and social media, this means that the choice of platforms used by movements, and what they do in these spaces, may change in response to unforeseen corporate actions. Similarly, such decisions may also impact upon the scope and subject of the research itself, including access to data and the viability of its methodology: for social movement research, this then not only affects what is being gathered about the movement, but also how it is being analyzed and represented in research.

Of course, change over time is to be expected regardless of the platforms; as David Karpf (2012) states, the "Internet is in a state of *ongoing* transformation" (9), and the populations of platforms, and their uses, are always changing. Our understanding of Twitter evolves year-to-year, based on how different users employ the site, how Twitter itself changes its architecture and functions, and indeed based on what other sites may arise or become popular in the meantime (see, for instance, Facebook's support for hashtags in 2013, following their widespread use on Instagram and Twitter). Within the context of big social media data and social movements, the scope of research into the Arab Spring on Twitter was in part determined by Twitter's support for hashtags in Latin script but not in Arabic script—making English or other Latin hashtags the default option for centralizing markers across multiple language groups. For online research, then, on social movements or other contexts, there remains a limit to the online subject being studied. In addition to any regional variations in uses of Twitter, for instance, the extent and impact of its adoption and adaptation will also change between studies (Karpf 2012). This has obvious repercussions for discussing online platforms and for the methodologies employed to study hosted activities.

Such evolution also affects the replicability of studies, which is already a gray area for online research, especially regarding Twitter. The development of tools such as TwapperKeeper and its open-source successor yourTwapperKeeper allows researchers easier access to acquiring Twitter data without having to code their own archiving processes, and provides the opportunity for innumerable projects to track the same keywords or hashtags independently. However, Twitter's terms of use also explicitly restrict the sharing of the gathered data with others; without individually gathering a comparable data set, for most researchers it is near impossible to replicate other studies in evaluating their accuracy and value. The exceptions here are researchers with access to complete Twitter archives, through paid on-sellers, and the much-vaunted but still underdeveloped Library of Congress Twitter archive, which also puts a financial barrier around data that have been contributed publicly and freely, limiting access for researchers and activists alike. While the methods used and connections to previous work in the field can act as a means of gauging the accuracy of the interpretations put forth when reviewing these studies, these evaluations are considered responses in place of complete replications. Similarly, rather than allowing a more "open data" – style movement, the restrictions placed on Twitter archives mean that researchers cannot make their data sets available for others to examine and offer additional analyses, asking different questions of, and offering new perspectives on, the gathered data.

These analytical and methodological limits are applicable across social media research; for studies of social movements specifically, it is clear that considering big social media data can only provide so much information without also examining the movement as a whole and its surrounding context. Mahrt and Scharkow (2013) suggest that "Big Data analyses tend only to show *what* users do, but not *why* they do it" (23), giving support to views put forward by boyd and Crawford (2012), Zeynep Tufekci (2014), and Lev Manovich (2012) claiming that research needs to look beyond the data alone and also take into account the context for this activity. For social movements, the social and political contexts are critical for understanding what is taking place online, and indeed comparing what is happening on Twitter with how the movement is physically organized. Mining social media alone, with their access limits, their filters and algorithms determining what information visibility, and the ethical considerations they raise for researchers, is unlikely to provide the information, or even all the cues required, to reconcile the online aspects of a social movement with its wider actions. Blending quantitative overviews with qualitative analysis, with fieldwork, ethnographic research, or observational data is a possible solution to this, and is a means of overcoming the limits and concerns around social media data and platforms.

Mapping big data methodologies for social movement research?

The fundamental underpinning of the methodology adopted for the Mapping Movements project is the combination of quantitative and qualitative approaches, and of complementary offline and online research. Arguments have been made in a wide variety of fields for the benefits of mixed-methods research. Klandermans, Staggenborg, and Tarrow argue in a survey of social movement research methodologies that progress in social movement research has partly been a result of "the intersection of multiple methods" (2002, 315). The first publication in the Mapping Movements project examined Occupy Oakland and Twitter (Croeser and Highfield 2014); this research demonstrated some of the analytical benefits of an approach that combines both qualitative and quantitative analysis of online data, drawing on Twitter activity around the

#oo hashtag, with in-depth interviews and participant observation. These methods allowed us to highlight the contributions of activists who are not highly visible on Twitter, to map some of the ways in which activists engage in self-censorship or otherwise attempt to evade surveillance online, and to build a more nuanced understanding of the relationship between online and offline communication and organization within the Occupy movement. The analytical benefits of this are clear. Combining big data approaches with qualitative research, both online and at movement sites, can also play an important role in navigating the ethical challenges of social movement research.

In the case of Occupy Oakland, our research studied the relationship between the movement, physical place, and social media, including tensions between the perceptions of authenticity in participating physically compared to solely on Twitter. By combining the analysis of online activity with fieldwork, our research was able to consider more than one dominant perspective on the movement (rather than, say, just the framing of Occupy Oakland on Twitter), and also to overcome some of the concerns of research from a distance. Directly communicating with individual participants and the movement at large through hashtagged tweets not only meant that we engaged with how activists themselves viewed social media; this approach also made our presence in both the online and physical spaces visible, and allowed us to make project information and, later, findings available to participants. In addition to allowing us to contextualize the online activity within the movement's physical actions, this approach provides the opportunity for greater reciprocity between researchers and activists: by directly engaging with the movement both physically and online, we attempt to avoid the perception of spying mentioned earlier, by recognizing and involving activists and their analyses in our work.

These connections also aid our ethical responsibility to protect participants. There are inconsistent ethical approaches noted in published social media research, but for social movements in particular there are clear implications for providing identifying information and sensitive material. For our research, we anonymize social media data, taking into account not only activists' own risk assessments but also our responsibilities as researchers: in making our work publicly available, we are aware that different organizations (including state agencies) may be accessing our research. Beyond simply anonymizing data, though, knowing the surrounding context for comments and links between Twitter users means that we can make more informed attempts to avoid presenting information which inadvertently identifies, and might potentially harm, individuals or groups. Quantifying tweets, mentions of other users, and other aspects of social media activity can present a particular picture of a social movement that may not gel with either the wider movement or the participants' experience, and that strips the content of its context and motivations for this activity: tweets serve multiple functions, connections between users might not be positive or reciprocated, and retweets do not mean a message is being endorsed by another user, for instance. By combining the quantitative and qualitative analyses of the online and the physical aspects of a social movement, we can provide not only a more rounded examination of the movement, but also a more nuanced and ethically responsible representation of the object of study.

While the Mapping Movements project has followed standard practices for interviews and participant observation, including providing information sheets on the research and using consent forms, we have also attempted to develop new practices for the online component of our research. We refer specifically to our research on Occupy Oakland here as this is the first case study to reach the publication stage, but our subsequent case studies (on antifascist activism in Greece and on the Tunisian World Social Forum) have followed similar models. A primary consideration here has been to make online data collection visible to activists in a venue that will allow for discussion and, potentially, for activists to voice concern about, or objections to, the research. In order to do this, we created a blog post that outlined the project, including giving an example of the kinds of data mapping we were undertaking (Croeser 2012), and tweeted about this using hashtags likely to be visible to movement participants (#oo and #occupyoakland). The post offered two platforms for activists to give feedback publicly: through blog post comments and on Twitter. It also gave details of the Curtin University Human Research Ethics Committee, opening a route for activists to object to our work without having to be publicly visible or to contact us directly. These steps may not fully answer activists' concerns about becoming the object of research, but they do at least address some of the issues involved in conducting analysis of a movement completely invisibly.

We attempted to build on this initial openness by creating spaces for activists' voices throughout the research process. Extended, semistructured interviews provided opportunities for activists to foreground issues they considered important in the research area. Debriefings after the interviews also created a more informal space in which activists frequently asked pointed questions about the interviewer's politics and understanding of the movement. These discussions helped to frame the research and allowed participants more control over the research process (for example, participants may have withdrawn permission for quotations or refused to provide introductions to movement spaces if these conversations provided unsatisfactory answers). As our analysis developed, we published and tweeted blog posts with abstracts, slides, and audio recordings with preliminary research findings, again inviting comment from activists and others. Before the final publication of "Occupy Oakland and #oo: Uses of Twitter within the Occupy movement" (Croeser and Highfield 2014) we sent the draft text to all interviewees who had indicated an interest, explicitly inviting comment on the analysis as well as around the representation of interviewees' interview material. Another option we considered was to tweet using the #oo and #occupyoakland hashtags and invite comments from any movement participants who wished to. An open invitation such as this may be useful, but care should be taken that any draft offered does not expose interview participants to risks or misrepresentation. A two-stage process allowing for interviewee feedback in one round and more general feedback in the second may be one way to manage this.

As well as creating space for activists' critiques during the analysis, the accessibility of research publications is a fundamental concern. Publishing in open-access journals should be a key component of an ethical research practice, as it ensures at a bare minimum that activists can read analyses of their movement. Other practices, such as posting final or preprint copies of copyrighted publications on researchers' homepages or social media accounts, may assist with this, but they should be treated with caution given the very real possibility that publishers will attempt to constrain such public sharing (Solon 2013). However, open-access by no means guarantees that an ethical commitment to accessibility has been met. Other important steps we attempted to build into the Mapping Movements project included avoiding unnecessary jargon, contacting interview participants to inform them of the final publication, and tweeting about the publication using relevant hashtags. Again, we attempted to create space for critique and feedback by creating a blog post (Croeser 2014) and explicitly soliciting comments on Twitter.

Concluding thoughts and directions forward

There is no single model that can ensure that big data research on social movements will be ethical. As noted above, navigating the complexities of social movement research is challenging at the best of times, and even ideals seen as central to an ethical approach (such as reciprocity) may be unsuitable for some contexts. The methodologies we have followed for case studies subsequent to our research on Occupy Oakland have been modified in several ways in order to meet the needs of our analysis and account for the specificities of the relevant contexts, as well as in response to our reflections on the initial research. Academics need to take into account a wide range of issues including the specific politics of the movement concerned and the researchers' own political stance, power imbalances between movement participants and academics, risks that participants face from both state and non-state actors, and the deeper process of engagement between activists and researchers. Practical considerations around funding limitations and the shifts in academia that have accompanied neoliberalism and austerity are also key factors that cannot be ignored. It may not be possible to put into practice an ethical commitment to long-term participant observation or engagement with a movement, for example, and researchers should consider whether or not these constraints allow a particular case study to be undertaken ethically.

Nevertheless, we hope to have offered a starting point for adapting the existing ethical framework (contested as it is) for social movement research to new big data methods. Perhaps the most vital aspect of this framework is the need to grapple with an altered politics of spatial responsibility, which impacts nearly every aspect of the research framework. Firstly, researchers need to consider strategies that make their data collection visible to movement participants. This has flow-on implications for a range of ethical issues, including activists' assessments of risk (their awareness, for example, that particular hashtags may be tracked by researchers may lead to discussions about other surveillance of their social media use), and activists' abilities to resist and intervene in the research process if they choose. Strategies for making research visible should be informed by preliminary research, and might, for example, include tweeting using hashtags prominent in the movement, or posting information about research on platforms or in formats most in use by activists. Online visibility should, as far as possible, be supplemented by researchers' visible presence within movement spaces.

Secondly, an ethical approach to big data research on social movements requires consideration of how publishing analysis might impact on the movement's goals and on risks to activists. For example, big data research has the potential to highlight key activists or groups within the movement, facilitating repression or harassment by opponents. Beyond these direct risks, however, a focus on a biased sample of movement participants can have serious political consequences for movements: big data analysis focusing on a single social media platform may give the impression that a movement is whiter, more privileged, or in other ways more unrepresentative of the general population than it is, undermining its political claims. It may also undermine the position of key activists or tendencies within a movement by providing disproportionate visibility to activists who are more vocal on social media. Researchers therefore need to be willing to engage in reflection on their own relationship to the broader political process movements are engaged in.

Thirdly, an ethical approach requires careful attention to issues of access. As discussed above, publishing in open-access journals should be a minimum starting point when it comes to meeting the ethical requirements of reciprocity and access. Other aspects of access also need to be addressed. For example, researchers should consider whether or not the data and tools they use would be useful to movement participants, requiring direct engagement with movement participants and, if reasonable, to make analysis more broadly available to activists. Physical presence allows participants fuller access to research processes, which may also include asking questions or raising concerns about online data collection. Researchers will also need to think about the ways in which the use of jargon and the presentation of their results in particular spaces hampers activist access. Each of these considerations will, of course, need to take place in the particular context of the movement being studied.

Attempts to overcome biases in available data must similarly change in response to context and be informed by engagement with movement participants. In the current context, it is reasonable to assume that at least some participants in any social movement will be engaging in strategic avoidance of social media and/or self-censorship online. Researchers need to develop strategies that actively look for these gaps in the data, and find ways to make them visible in their analysis. This is particularly important in order to avoid eliding subtle forms of censorship and repression—including those enacted by social media platforms—which shape movement communications. The most obvious way to seek information on these gaps is to talk to activists directly and ask about their social media practices.

Researchers need to be aware of the embedded politics of the tools they are using, and of how these tools interact with the politics of the platforms themselves to shape research outcomes. This might include, for example, being aware of the benefits and limitations of studying particular platforms, or of tracking some behaviors rather than others. Research that focuses on Twitter may produce a very different picture of a movement to research on YouTube. Similarly, tools may provide different analyses depending on whether or not they capture particular linking practices (such as retweets or reblogs), accumulations of social approval (such as "likes," "favourites," or "plus ones"), and users' attempts to "game" the platform (such as bots and retweeting circles). Many of these factors change rapidly in response to updates made to research tools and to the platforms themselves, as well as through user innovation.

Finally, researchers must consider the biases introduced by a focus on the platforms and tools most readily available and accessible. Attention needs to be paid to platforms playing an important role within movements, whether or not these are open to public access and facilitate collection of data on a mass scale. This may, at times, require making changes to data collection strategies. It will certainly also require more engagement with movements in order to make visible hidden platforms, practices, and networks, particularly for those movements most concerned with evading surveillance. This, in turn, requires serious thought about how to gather data ethically, without creating additional risk for activists while a more complete analysis is being produced.

None of these challenges are easily met, and certainly there is no template available that is applicable across all movements and contexts. Researchers therefore need to build reflexive processes that respond to changing political contexts and technological developments. It is also vital that these processes draw on movement knowledge and are open to critiques from activists. Big data methods have the potential to add significantly to social movement researchers' toolboxes, but they must be used with caution and in combination with other methods, particularly those that involve researchers with movements on the ground.

References

Agarwal, S., M. L. Barthel, C. Rost, A. Borning, W. L. Bennett, and C. N. Johnson. 2014. "Grassroots Organizing in the Digital Age: Considering Values and Technology in Tea Party and Occupy Wall Street." *Information, Communication & Society* 17(3): 326–41. doi:10.1080/1369118X.2013.873068.

Agarwal, S., W. L. Bennett, C. N. Johnson, and S. Walker. 2014. "A Model of Crowd-Enabled Organization: Theory and Methods for Understanding the Role of Twitter in the Occupy Movement." *International Journal of Communication* 8: 646–72. http://ijoc.org/index.php/ijoc/article/view/2068.

boyd, danah and Kate Crawford. 2012. "Critical Questions for Big Data: Provocations for a Cultural, Technological, and Scholarly Phenomenon." *Information, Communication & Society* 15(5): 662–679. doi:10.1080/1369118X.2012.678878.

BondGraham, Darwin and Ali Winston. 2013. "'The Real Purpose of Oakland's Surveillance Center." *East Bay Express*. December 18. Accessed May 12, 2014. http://www.eastbayexpress.com/oakland/the-real-purpose-of-oaklands-surveillance-center/Content?oid=3789230.

Bruns, A., T. Highfield, and J. Burgess. 2013. "The Arab Spring and Social Media Audiences: English and Arabic Twitter Users and Their Networks." *American Behavioral Scientist* 57(7): 871–98. doi:10.1177/0002764213479374.

Bucher, Taina. 2012. "A Technicity of Attention: How Software 'Makes Sense.'" *Culture Machine* 13. http://www.culturemachine.net/index.php/cm/article/view/470/489.

Chesters, Graham. 2012. "Social Movements and the Ethics of Knowledge Production." *Social Movement Studies* 11(2): 145–60. doi:10.1080/14742837.2012.664894.

Conover, M. D., C. Davis, E. Ferrara, K. McKelvey, F. Menczer, and A. Flammini. 2013. "The Geospatial Characteristics of a Social Movement Communication Network." *PLoS ONE* 8(3): e55957. doi:10.1371/journal.pone.0055957.

Conover, M. D., E. Ferrara, F. Menczer, and A. Flammini. 2013. "The Digital Evolution of Occupy Wall Street." *PLoS ONE* 8(5): e64679. doi:10.1371/journal.pone.0064679.

Costanza-Chock, Sasha. 2012. "Mic check! Media Cultures and the Occupy movement." *Social Movement Studies: Journal of Social, Cultural and Political Protest* 11(3/4): 375–85. doi:10.1080/14742837.2012.710746.

Croeser, Sky. 2014. "Occupy Oakland and #oo: Uses of Twitter within the Occupy movement." *skycroeser.net* (March 9, 2014): http://skycroeser.net/2014/03/09/occupy-oakland-and-oo-uses-of-twitter-within-the-occupy-movement.

Croeser, Sky. 2012. "Mapping Movements." *skycroeser.net*. January 25: http://skycroeser.net/2012/01/25/mapping-movements/.

Croeser, Sky and Tim Highfield. 2014. "Occupy Oakland and #oo: Uses of Twitter within the Occupy movement." *First Monday* 19(3). doi:10.5210/fm.v19i3.4827.

Dawson, Marcelle and Luke Sinwell. 2012. "Ethical and Political Challenges of Participatory Action Research in the Academy: Reflections on Social Movements and Knowledge Production in South Africa." *Social Movement Studies* 11(2): 177–91. doi:10.1080/14742837.2012.664900.

Flacks, Richard. 2005. "The Question of Relevance in Social Movement Studies." In D. Croteau, W. Hoynes, and C. Ryan, eds. *Rhyming Hope and History: Activists, Academics, and Social Movement Scholarship*. Minneapolis: University of Minnesota Press, 3–19.

Freelon, Deen. 2011. "The MENA protests on Twitter: Some empirical data." *DFreelon. org.* May 19. http://dfreelon.org/2011/05/19/the-mena-protests-on-twitter-some-empirical-data.

Gaby, Sarah and Neal Caren. 2012. "Occupy Online: How Cute Old Men and Malcolm X Recruited 400,000 US Users to OWS on Facebook." *Social Movement Studies: Journal of Social, Cultural and Political Protest* 11(3/4): 367–74. doi: 10.1080/14742837.2012.708858.

Gerbaudo, Paolo. 2012. *Tweets and the Streets: Social Media and Contemporary Activism.* London: Pluto Press.

Gillan, Kevin and Jenny Pickerill. 2012. "The Difficult and Hopeful Ethics of Research on, and with, Social Movements." *Social Movement Studies* 11(2): 133–43. doi:10.108 0/14742837.2012.664890.

Gillespie, Tarleton. 2010. "The Politics of 'Platforms.'" *New Media & Society* 12(3): 347–64. doi:10.1177/1461444809342738.

Gillespie, Tarleton. 2014. "The Relevance of Algorithms." In T. Gillespie, P. J. Boczkowski, and K. A. Foot, eds. *Media Technologies: Essays on Communication, Materiality, and Society.* Cambridge, MA: The MIT Press, 167–94.

Gleason, Benjamin. 2013. "#Occupy Wall Street: Exploring informal learning about a social movement on Twitter." *American Behavioral Scientist* 57(7): 966–82. doi:10.1177/0002764213479372.

Halavais, Alexander. 2013. "Home Made Big Data? Challenges and Opportunities for Participatory Social Research." *First Monday* 18(10): doi:10.5210/fm.v18i10.4876.

Halavais, Alexander and Maria Garrido. 2014. "Twitter as the people's microphone: Emergence of authorities during protest tweeting." In M. McCaughey, ed. *Cyberactivism on the Participatory Web.* New York: Routledge, 117–39.

Juris, Jeffrey S. 2007. "Practicing Militant Ethnography." In S. Shukaitis, D. Graeber, and E. Biddle, eds. *Constituent Imagination: Militant Investigations: Collective Theorization.* Oakland: AK Press, 164–76.

Karpf, David. 2012. "Social Science Research Methods in Internet Time." *Information, Communication & Society* 15(5): 639–661. doi:10.1080/13691 18X.2012.665468.

Klandermans, B., S. Staggenborg, and S. Tarrow. 2002. "Conclusion: Blending Methods and Building Theories in Social Movement Research." In B. Klandermans and S. Staggenborg, eds. *Methods of Social Movement Research.* Minneapolis: University of Minnesota Press, 314–49.

Langlois, Ganaele and Greg. Elmer. 2013. "The Research Politics of Social Media Platforms." *Culture Machine* 14. http://www.culturemachine.net/index.php/cm/article/view/505/531.

Lewis, Adam Gary. 2012. "Ethics, Activism and the Anti-Colonial: Social Movement Research as Resistance." *Social Movement Studies* 11(2): 227–40. doi:10.1080/147428 37.2012.664903.

Lotan, G., E. Graeff, M. Ananny, D. Gaffney, I. Pearce, and d. boyd. 2011. "The Arab Spring | The revolutions were tweeted: Information flows during the 2011 Tunisian and Egyptian revolutions." *International Journal of Communication* 5: 1375–1405. http://ijoc.org/index.php/ijoc/article/view/1246.

Mahrt, Merja and Michael Scharkow. 2013. "The Value of Big Data in Digital Media Research." *Journal of Broadcasting & Electronic Media* 57(1): 20–33. doi:10.1080/088 38151.2012.761700.

Manovich, Lev. 2012. "Trending: The Promises and the Challenges of Big Social Data." In M. K. Gold, ed. *Debates in the Digital Humanities*. Minneapolis: University of Minnesota Press, 460–75.

Morstatter, F., J. Pfeffer, H. Lui, and K. M. Carley. 2013. "Is the Sample Good Enough? Comparing Data from Twitter's Streaming API with Twitter's Firehose." In *Proceedings of the Seventh International AAAI Conference on Weblogs and Social Media*: AAAI.

Palmer, Charis. 2013. "Police Tap Social Media in Wake of London Attack." *iTnews*. May 23. Accessed May 23, 2013. http://www.itnews.com.au/News/344319,police-tap-social-media-in-wake-of-london-attack.asp.

Papacharissi, Zizi and Maria de Fatima Oliveira. 2012. "Affective News and Networked Publics: The Rhythms of News Storytelling on #Egypt." *Journal of Communication* 62(2): 266–82. doi:10.1111/j.1460-2466.2012.01630.x.

Paßmann, J., T. Boeschoten, and M. T. Schäfer. 2013. "The Gift of the Gab: Retweet Cartels and Gift Economies on Twitter." In K. Weller, A. Bruns, J. Burgess, M. Mahrt, and C. Puschmann, eds. *Twitter and Society*. New York: Peter Lang, 331–44.

Poell, Thomas and Kaouthar Darmoni. 2012. "Twitter as a Multilingual Space: The Articulation of the Tunisian Revolution Through #sidibouzid." *NECSUS: European Journal of Media Studies* 1(1). http://www.necsus-ejms.org/twitter-as-a-multilingual-space-the-articulation-of-the-tunisian-revolution-through-sidibouzid-by-thomas-poell-and-kaouthar-darmoni.

Privacy SOS. 2013. "Twitter anarchists! May Day celebrants! You are being watched." *Privacy SOS*. May 1. Accessed July 11, 2013. http://www.privacysos.org/node/1046.

Procter, R., F. Vis, and A. Voss. 2013. "Reading the Riots on Twitter: Methodological Innovation for the Analysis of Big Data." *International Journal of Social Research Methodology* 16(3): 197–214, doi:10.1080/13645579.2013.774172.

Puschmann, Cornelius and Jean Burgess. 2013. "The Politics of Twitter Data." *HIIG Discussion Paper Series No. 2013-01*: doi/10.2139/ssrn.2206225.

Rogers, Richard. 2009. *The End of the Virtual: Digital Methods*. Amsterdam: Vossiuspers UvA.

Santos, Ana Cristina. 2012. "Disclosed and Willing: Towards a Queer Public Sociology." *Social Movement Studies* 11(2): 241–54. doi:10.1080/14742837.2012.664904.

Shukaitis, Stevphen and David Graeber. 2007. "Introduction." In S. Shukaitis, D. Graeber, and E. Biddle, eds. *Constituent Imagination: Militant Investigations: Collective Theorization*. Oakland: AK Press.

Smeltzer, Sandra. 2012. "Asking Tough Questions: The Ethics of Studying Activism in Democratically Restricted Environments." *Social Movement Studies* 11(2): 255–71. doi:10.1080/14742837.2012.664905.

Solon, Olivia. 2013. "Elsevier Clamps Down on Academics Posting Their Own Papers Online." *Wired UK* December 17. Accessed December 17, 2013. http://www.wired. co.uk/news/archive/2013-12/17/elsevier-versus-open-access.

Starbird, Kate and Leysia Palen. 2012. "(How) Will the Revolution Be Retweeted?: Information Diffusion and the 2011 Egyptian Uprising." In *Proceedings of the ACM 2012 conference on Computer Supported Cooperative Work*. New York, NY: ACM. doi:10.1145/2145204.2145212.

Stoeffel, Kat. 2014. "Twitter, Rape, and Privacy on Social Media." *The Cut*. March 14. Accessed May 12, 2014. http://nymag.com/thecut/2014/03/twitter-rape-and-privacy-on-social-media.html.

Thorson, K., K. Driscoll, B. Ekdale, S. Edgerly, L. G. Thompson, A. Schrock, L. Swartz, E. K. Vraga, and C. Wells. 2013. "YouTube, Twitter and the Occupy Movement: Connecting Content and Circulation Practices." *Information, Communication & Society* 16(3): 421–51. doi:10.1080/1369118X.2012.756051.

Tufekci, Zeynep. 2014. "Big Questions for Social Media Big Data: Representativeness, Validity and Other Methodological Pitfalls." *ICWSM '14: Proceedings of the 8th International AAAI Conference on Weblogs and Social Media*.

Tufekci, Zeynep and Christopher Wilson. 2012. "Social Media and the Decision to Participate in Political Protest: Observations from Tahrir Square." *Journal of Communication* 62(2): 363–79. doi:10.1111/j.1460-2466.2012.01629.x.

Vis, Farida. 2013. "Twitter as a Reporting Tool for Breaking News: Journalists Tweeting the 2011 UK Riots." *Digital Journalism* 1(1): 27–47. doi:10.1080/21670811.2012.741316.

Zimmer, Michael and Nicholas Proferes. 2014. "A Topology of Twitter Research: Disciplines, Methods, and Ethics." *Aslib Journal of Information Management* 66(3): 250–61. doi:10.1108/AJIM-09-2013-0083.

10

Data Activism

Alessandra Renzi and Ganaele Langlois

Introduction

Let us start with a commonplace observation: whoever owns, controls, and has the right to access and analyze data holds tremendous power over individuals and populations. This is true for governments that collect data on their citizens to develop policy and provide or eliminate social services and of social media corporations that gather, analyze, and sell all kinds of user data about consumer preferences and behaviors. And let us continue with a correlative statement: the power of data not only resides in its capacity to produce knowledge, but also in its ability to shape perceived realities. Data maps, graphs, and visualizations commonly circulate in both mass and social media to show us what our world is like, how we will be impacted by environmental or social changes, what kind of communities and individuals surround us, and whether these communities and individuals are friends or foes. Data shapes realities not only by enabling certain representations of the world around us, but also by enticing us to internalize these realities and make them our own. Data clearly has transformative and affective potential: the most powerful data visualizations are intuitive in that they immediately convince us that they make sense, that they are truthful, trustworthy, and empowering. They can, in turn, foster feelings of elation or fear, and they have the power to shape our sense of belonging to diverse communities.

Data, in short, yields tremendous *political* power and we rely more and more on data to understand and navigate the complexities of our individual and collective realities. It comes as no surprise that data therefore has an important role to play in civic life, and that activists are drawing on data as a way to provide means for social transformation. Political organizing and real-time communication through social media are some of the ways in which data is mobilized in activism. Many studies are understandably critical of the impact of social media on activism because of how social media tie autonomous social justice projects to dominant corporate players—that is, YouTube, Twitter, Facebook, and the like—who collect and mine data and exploit free labor (Terranova 2000). Researchers have discussed this tension between autonomy and social control, as well as the risks social media pose to privacy and surveillance (Lovink and Rasch 2013). And yet, fewer have paid attention to how the sociality that emerges in this tension between freedom and capture reshapes activists' and other political actors' individuality and collectivity, redefining modes of solidarity, participation, and knowledge production along shifting notions of community, agency, and engagement.

Our aim in this chapter is to understand some of the new data-based activist practices and the ways in which they challenge and resist existing power relations. We want to hone in specifically on how activism engenders new modes of being and acting together through a direct engagement with data and the means of its mobilization. Thus, we look at the socio-technical field of seemingly cold or "objective" knowledge and facts in order to examine a live and fluid system of negotiations of individual affects, group belongings, and transformation of social bonds and that builds on data and organizing metadata.

Let us give an example of this with the recent case of protests sparked by the killing of unarmed African-American teenager Michael Brown by a white police officer in Ferguson, Missouri. As news of the killing circulated, people mobilized both on the streets and online to discuss and protest institutional racism in the United States. One way in which such mobilizations were reflected online was through the use of hashtags, a particular kind of metadata. On Twitter, hashtags like #handsupdontshoot and #Ferguson connected people across spaces and in some cases fostered unexpected solidarities: during the protests, Palestinians stood by the people of Ferguson and shared advice on how to deal with teargas and militarized police (Aljazeera 2014). The coupling of hashtags #Gaza and #Ferguson in the same tweets was not just symbolic. The ability to pool metadata enabled the circulation of information about the same teargas used in both places. It made a statement about the shared realities of oppressed peoples and created a bond among those affected. This capacity to impact individuals and groups is at the heart of understanding the power of data in the fostering of new activist practices.

Such instances of change cannot be understood as unfolding along the binary of technology, on one side, and collective practices, on the other. Rather, as will become evident when we trace the relations among disparate fields (social, cultural, and technological), processes (communication and action), and actors (activists, artists, and researchers), technology and collective practices are today indissolubly linked. Thus, in order to trace this transformative power of data while attending to both technological and social forces, we rely on the concept of *transindividuation* (Simondon 1989b; Stiegler 2013). Simply put, transindividuation designates the socio-technical context, or milieu, through which transformation unfolds, allowing for individuals to gain new awareness and to bond with groups that also evolve and mutate in reaction to events, other groups, and individuals. Transindividuation is an evolving process of co-constitution between the individual *I* and the collective *We*, and this process is often now produced, mediated, and transformed through data. In this sense, data activism is not separate from other forms of activism. The examples we examine in this chapter show how data activism is part of on-the-ground activism because of the sociality of the practices involved and because of the intimate relations that individuals develop through technological means in general, and data in particular.

This chapter examines some of these processes of individual and collective transformation that are mediated by data and that trigger the emergence of new activist practices. But first, a discussion of social transformation and transindividuation in relation to data is needed. This will be followed by three vignettes of different activist contexts where data mediates affective bonds (Occupy Streams and metadata), creates new forms of shared knowledge (Occupy Data and big data), and new vectors of transformation (Facial Weaponization Suite and biometric data). In the following discussion we argue that, in addition to studying the role of data for political and economic control, we need to pay attention to the different ways in which data is implicated in the circulation of mediated and unmediated psycho-physiological stimuli (affects, perceptions, and emotions) precisely because these stimuli generate self-perceptions, belonging, and collective action.

Transindividuation and data activism: Socio-technical and political considerations

Since the growth and availability of data, especially so-called big data, we have witnessed the emergence of a data paradigm that ties social dynamics to economic and political interests. Data is increasingly used to analyze and understand the behavior of individuals and groups; the knowledge gained is employed to organize social life in all of its aspects, from the intimate (e.g. through targeted advertising on social media that piques desire) to the public (e.g. through policymaking and surveillance). In this context, we see data as socio-technical: it consists of technologically produced sets of informational resources that are mobilized within social, economic, and political processes. Data activism takes place at the crossroads of the technological and communicational logics feeding capitalism. It attempts to wrestle the socio-technical power of data from the hands of dominant groups to promote social and economic justice.

In order to understand how data mobilizes and is mobilized in the context of activism, it is necessary to first discuss the relationship between individual and collective action and data. Often, to explain social change we posit the preexistence of at least one of these two reference points—the individual and the collectivity—as already-formed and distinct entities partaking in collective action through rational choices. We often hear about how actors such as activists *act* within collectivities to promote social change: for instance, groups of citizens dissatisfied with the government response to the 2008 financial crisis decide to occupy public space giving rise to the Occupy movement in many parts of the world. In other cases, someone may mobilize members of their community to launch an advocacy campaign, as was the case with the online petition that called for the prosecution of George Zimmerman, the man released without charges after killing unarmed seventeen-year-old African-American Trayvon Martin. The petition sparked a series of antiracism protests and "hoodies walks" all over the United States. In both examples, it is easy to focus on the preexistence of individuals and collectivities that are mobilized around specific issues; but this glosses over the complexity of how collective action comes to be.

Drawing on the concept of transindividuation, we can look at the relationships that *generate* both individual and collective action and conceive of the individual and collective as the result of a socio-technical genesis. In the case of the Trayvon Martin campaign, it would be reductive to simply claim that the individual who initiated the petition sparked collective action. Rather, specific social and data-related events had to take place before the campaign could gain public attention and mobilize supporters. In fact, as David Karpf explains elsewhere in this volume, members of the online petition company Change.org came across a petition circulating on a mailing list by someone who had read about the killing in the news. Change.org staff decided that the issue had the potential to go viral and contacted Martin's family to start a new petition with them. High profile sponsors, algorithmic calculations, and a professional social media campaign heavily relying on metadata guaranteed that the call to action reached large audiences (and not without financial gain for Change.org). Here, the context in which transindividuation engenders individual supporters, as well as the marching crowds that hit the streets, can be described as one wherein a variety of factors, including data analysis and complex algorithms that extract surplus value from social justice causes (while supporting them), viral information circulation, and the emotions circulating on social media networks converge to establish a new relationship between the one and the many. This is how transindividuation takes place within a socio-technical field where the two poles of individuality and collectivity emerge simultaneously as the *result* of newly established relations (instead of having individuals and collectivities be the preexisting terms of a relation). Importantly, transindividuation is not simply a technological process but one wherein technology, and in our case data, is a vector for the circulation of affective and emotional bonds. If we think of transindividuation as layered, the genesis of individuals and collectivities unfolds at multiple levels, from the micro-sensorial (affects and emotions) to that of action—both individual and collective action. And as the previous Ferguson example demonstrates, data bridges individuals, modulating the relation between the *I* and the *We*—our sense of ourselves both alone and as members of a community.

To illustrate how affective modulation takes place, we can think of how people come together around a protest. There are different ways of participating in protests: as organizers, as affinity groups (e.g. a pink or black bloc); there are those who walk alongside the march "lending bodies," bystanders who cheer or honk, and those who follow through media. These different participants will share an open field of intensive relations where affects ultimately connect them. According to Simondon, both individuals and collectives are fluid entities that are always in a metastable equilibrium, that is, an intensive state where change is triggered by external events that alter their existing equilibrium. These changes can be as small as a sensation or as far reaching as a crisis—they trigger flows of transformation. Indeed, as a context for transindividuation, a protest is the site for the circulation of mediated and unmediated psycho-physiological stimuli that are constantly reorganized into feelings and emotions along a personal-social continuum.

In this context, sensorial and bodily experience—so-called affects—precede and trigger emotions, which then prompt action. It is through affect and emotions that the tension between constituted individuality and the collective is first felt; affect regulates the relation between an individualized being and the pre-individual milieu (the "interiority" of an individual) as it encounters the world; emotion, arising from the difficulty of rendering an affective plurality into a unitary meaning, engenders the collective when structured across many subjects (Simondon 2006, 111–22). One may be motivated to join in a protest, or chant, or confront the police because of feelings that emerge through these relations. Indignation, for example, is a feeling so widespread lately that it has even become the name of an entire social movement in Spain (the *Indignados*). Data often mediates and modulates such processes. Given the intense use of social media during protests, data plays a key role in the mediation of affects that modulate the transindividual field of relations—what Simondon calls the transindividual milieu (Simondon 2006). For instance, the metadata of tweets choreograph protests by moving crowds as they communicate about events, routes, and encounters with the police and media (Gerbaudo 2012). In this sense, data is a vector of affects that itself has a kind of agency.

VersuS' real-time visualization of a protest in Rome on October 15, 2011 provides an animated map of the affects and emotions circulating at different times of the day, with intensity literally peaking as police attack protestors and more people join in the streets (Art is Open Source 2011). The map uses data collected from major social networks like Facebook, Twitter, YouTube, Instagram, Foursquare, and Flickr, and analyzes it through natural language analysis and artificial intelligence that isolates words indicating affects, emotions, and participation. The visualization itself only makes evident the extent of the engagement with social media during this attempt at social change. Still, it helps us consider how the socio-technical space of social media networks and the proximity of bodies with mobile technologies on the streets of Rome function together to create "milieus" where circulating feelings like joy and belonging or outrage and panic reposition individuals within and among groups. We understand this field as a transindividual milieu composed of the affects and emotions circulating in connection with specific technologies (what Simondon calls "technical individuals"), technical ensembles (the discourses and contexts that produce and make sense of technology), individuals, and the collective. In the Rome protest, both individuals and collectivities are reshaped through the mediated process of communicating about and actually engaging in protest in the streets. These experiences are processed differently in each individual because of the unique interiority of the individual processing the stimuli—their "pre-individuality" to use Simondon's term. Nevertheless the emerging relations bring people to act collectively along shared intensities. In this context, the VersuS map can be read as a real-time simulation (rather than visualization) of the intensities that traverse the transindividual milieu and affect those that inhabit it. It is a simulation of the process of *becoming collective as activity*, that is, as a set of practices, perceptions, significations, communications, and so on; it poses the problem of intersubjective relations not at the level of discourse but at the level of affectivity and emotivity that are deeply intertwined with the data enabling and channelling their expression (Simondon 1989, 13).

The implications for thought of the transindividuated subject are very different from those of the preformed individual belonging to an existing community. Focusing on the latter subject, we argue, is not helpful for answering questions about the role of data in the feasibility, scalability, and durability of activist formations because it does not interrogate how movements emerge. Rather, by refusing the individual as the measuring unit of the collective, we can pose the problem of the collective from the perspective of its members as sets of affective, communicative, and embodied relations that are mediated by data, and where the process of becoming can be investigated. What interests us is not how groups retain their identity or structure but how they change (Simondon 2006) and how they do so in relation to data. The concept of transindividuation enables us to look at data in the form of information, metadata, and algorithms as structuring elements of a transindividual milieu wherein the individual and the collective emerge simultaneously through relations shaped by circulating affects. Contemporary forms of data activism act within the transindividual milieu to deconstruct, create, and realign specific articulations of the social and the technical in order to enact change. And, as we will see, these transformations also take place in different kinds of socio-technical environments that are not necessarily connected to social media, like those for the collaborative production of knowledge through big data, or the creative use of data for radical community art projects.

To further frame our case studies, we are guided by Felix Guattari's remark about the post-media era (2012). While Guattari did not live to witness the rise of contemporary forms of digital technologies, he nevertheless saw emerging digital technologies of the 1990s as ushering in a post-mass media era, which he thought would be composed of decentralized networks, affiliations, and associations that would act much in the same way as localized activist movements engage in broader global alliances. New technologies of communication, Guattari argued, could be appropriated in order to deconstruct power formations, to give birth to new creative processes and thus foster new subjectivities and new ways of being and living together in the world. The role of communication technologies was to be the vector through which new creative and resistant relationships could be transmitted. What mattered was not only the appropriation of the media themselves, but the mobilization of alternative media as sites of experimentation with new social relationships. The idea was that communication technologies would increase the possibilities of creating radically new ways of being together that would escape and neutralize dominant and unequal economic and social relations. In Guattari, we already find some key modes of activist transindividuation in his experiments with pirate radio stations in France and Italy, where he was a contributor and supporter. The pirate radios were not just producers and distributers of alternative information. Their experiments with the form and content of radio transmission (experimental shows, phone-in contributions, poetry readings, street parties, etc.) fostered encounters among a variety of groups—the activist and community groups contributing to the programming and running of the project. These encounters engendered decentralized alliances and ways of being together that crafted different social imaginaries.[1]

Much work has already been done examining how Guattari's post-media era is reflected in contemporary forms of activisms, although not so much for data activism. Software activists have been working to create alternative social media platforms allowing for decentralized alliances and protecting users from surveillance through greater anonymity. The greater availability of mobile media recording devices along with fast access to the Internet has provided for alternative forms of expression and new modes of sharing information (e.g. Indymedia). The crafting of social imaginaries along with new subjectivities emerging from

---

[1] Guattari was interested in the kinds of multiple refractions that new techno-social alliances could produce. What he called "co-individuation" among groups and individuals, in other words, could not be understood using linear causality models: it required understanding both macro and micro practices and states of being, from one's psychic experience to broad economic systems. In the same way, transindividuation cannot be understood from a linear perspective: rather, transindividuation involves echoes, resonances, and refractions that spread in no logical fashion. As such, for Guattari, the work of activism was not simply one of targeting a specific area, such as the economy or the environment, but rather of working at the intersection of different ecologies (Guattari 2000): political, social, and economic, of course, but also communicative and subjective through the refashioning of human bonds and modes of collective imagination.

new ways of being together has been at the center of contemporary activist practices. One could think of the *Indignados* from Spain, where the sentiment of outrage at current inequalities and economic policies fuels alternative social, economic, and political responses. What matters there is the creation of new perceptions through the deconstruction of power formations, for instance, the dissociation of higher education from the imperative of economic return on investment. In the same way, the Occupy movement was both a denunciation of current inequalities—the famous "We are the 99%" slogan—and an experiment in new ways of living together through, for instance, general assemblies, consensus-based decision making and human megaphones. Crucially, the concept of transindividuation along with Guattari's theories on the post-media era, open up a discussion about the socio-technical character of the new alliances and practices that emerge, or may be intentionally fostered among activists. The following three vignettes take up this task: they map the composition of new socio-technical activist formations, identifying the kinds of data that engender new relations, exploring how affect and emotions circulate in the transindividual milieu, and describing the flows of individual and collective transformation that mobilize actors.

Occupy Streams: Data and social media platform politics

Our first case study is about the connection of activism and data through social media platforms. Occupy Streams, along with similar platforms, helps us better understand activist practices based on changing notions of solidarity and participation. Such notions, in turn, are shaped through the tension between autonomous and commercial platforms, which channel users' affective and emotional reactions to circulating information about political events. On these platforms, data takes the form of content—textual and increasingly visual, but also metadata like hashtags—and circulates through information objects such as "Like" buttons. We argue that it is important to investigate how these different manifestations of data come together with human agents into a shared socio-technical field where new forms of participation and solidarity emerge.

In general, social media platforms allow for the collection, storing, and distribution of digitized content, from video to comments. Social media platforms are meant to manage this digitized content by classifying and organizing it. This requires the use of metadata, that is, data that provide a piece of information about the contents and context of other data (e.g. the time a video was uploaded). Since metadata facilitates the search and circulation of data, it helps activists reach wider audiences. It also helps to make connections across issues and to circulate information across social and technical environments. As already mentioned, the use of metadata such as hashtags pools content together, enabling the spontaneous emergence of counterpublics around specific events or issues (Warner 2002). Finally, metadata also enables new kinds of archiving and preservation practices that contribute to the creation of an embedded social movements memory. Thus, paying attention to the socio-technical composition of this field where activist practices play out demands that we recognize the ways in which metadata itself has a certain kind of agency. Metadata corrals activism into processes of capital accumulation (e.g. through data mining) but it can also create the conditions for the development of new activist practices (e.g. campaigns around hashtags). Most importantly, it is actively implicated in circulating affects and fostering social relations.

Since its beginnings in the 1990s, autonomous media in general, and Independent Media Centres (IMC or Indymedia) in particular, have changed a lot. In addition to mobile technologies that have made the necessary infrastructure (Internet connections, video cameras, etc.) increasingly accessible, open publishing platforms are more sophisticated, allowing for immediate posting of text, images, and video and hosted discussions. New media platforms can integrate the traditional features from Indymedia with feeds from various social media and live streaming. For example, the platform used during the anti-G20 convergences in Pittsburgh and Toronto, and during the protests against the Vancouver Olympics, automatically published YouTube videos, tweets, text, and a map to locate events as they were happening. Livestreaming, in particular, has become very popular during the wave of protests that followed the financial crisis in Europe and North America. Commercial platforms Livestream and Upstream provide the infrastructure to sites like Global Revolution and Occupy Streams to output and centralize 24-hour coverage of protest camps around the world, while chats and Twitter and Facebook feeds offer an interactive experience for activists and viewers (Costanza-Chock 2012; Juris 2012).

At the formal level, streaming technologies have changed the content as well as practices of radical media from reports and analysis to embedded journalism and live correspondence. The availability and transferability of standardized platforms and media activist toolkits has created a sort of "media centre franchising," where different citizen reporters' websites offer similar interfaces and features like social media buttons, embedded chats channels and livecasts. On these platforms—and across them—the metadata behind the familiar features organizes content in a way that is intelligible to the majority of users. Much of the similarity and uniformity of the interfaces comes from incorporating black-boxed commercial social media modules like Twitter feeds or share buttons into activist projects' websites. Not unlike the franchising of a successful business model or brand, corporate-built, customizable platforms or modules are made available to users who will customize them for their goals. Instead of paying a fee, the activists will make the collected metadata available to the different companies embedding their services in the platform.[2] To add to this franchising analogy: familiarity with the services and brand (for instance, different Occupy streaming channels) more easily engage users, plugging new actors into networks where they feel at ease with the interfaces and comfortably take on the roles of reporters, participants, moderators, and voyeurs at protests and other political events. Here, the habituated gestures of engaging with commercial platforms for social networking—the sharing and endorsing for instance—are embedded directly into political practices simply as a result of their new context.

Thus, despite their problematic ties to corporate actors, new media activist toolkits have expanded the context for transindividuation: in the constant flow of information at rallies and encampments, the unleashing of affects and emotions not only impacts public perception of actions by denouncing violence and portraying experiments in direct democracy, it also redefines participation, allegiance, and group boundaries through the recovery or invention of political and cultural practices. This happens as individuals connect to others through circulating data. For example, reporting within social movements, today, seems to be done more by single individuals than by groups and it tends to connect people who identify as movement reporters on shared platforms, rather than in the physical space of a media center. These mediated relations among activists are an important indicator of the changes to the composition of social formations, which stem from specific social conditions (e.g. a stronger sense of individualism that is promoted by social media) and new political needs

---

[2] This happens by signing the Terms of Service for the use of a platform.

(e.g. to break through overcrowded social media channels). At the same time, the changes fold in established traditions of struggle (e.g. media activism) and may build on practices of co-option that are latent or present in hidden forms at sites of conflict (e.g. the repurposing of commercial platforms).

Looking at activist social media data and metadata and their function as producers of affective and emotional relations (for instance, relations of solidarity) and as vectors of agency, we see these practices of resistance as not limited to the *communicative* action often ascribed to social media public spheres. Rather, they exist alongside and in connection with *direct* action. For instance, the live feed of CUTV during the 2012 Quebec student protests was a fundamental tool to update and draw to the streets students who followed this established university channel and became involved in five months of intense mobilizations against tuition hikes. Studying the deployment and function of CUTV and the circulation of its data offers a map of the emerging affective relations between activists, students, and wider publics that were key in sustaining the protests at a high intensity for an extended period of time. Similarly, the streaming of the Occupy Toronto channel functioned as a monitoring system to quickly mobilize critical mass at the encampment to prevent impending evictions. In addition to being part of phone trees, following this encampment's stream was an activist tactic to guarantee a quick response in case of emergencies, rather than simply a way to keep up with current affairs.

In these examples, the socio-technical milieu for transindividuation that emerges in connection with new manifestations of media activism is composed of human, machines (what Simondon calls technical individuals), technical elements, resources, and *data*, both as metadata and as information in its more traditional sense of content. As part of wider socio-technical milieus, social media platforms themselves consist of a variety of interconnected technical elements that resonate with each other, modulate our relations to technology, and mediate our interaction with others. These streaming platforms extend and connect life at protests and camps to the outside and to other platforms; they are sites where technology plays a vital role because of how we develop relationships with it, and to others through it. Networked social media, both autonomous and corporate, are not only the means or tools to connect individuals but they are active agents that carry with them an associated milieu where the functions of technology are organized, reproduced, and in some cases contested. This aspect too speaks to the agency of technological elements in the socio-technical milieu.

In fact, we might think of platforms themselves as "technical individuals," modern machines that bridge humans and the natural world (Simondon 2006, 262) and also as the site where the machine and its associated milieu simultaneously emerge in a pattern of recurrent causality (Simondon 1989a). The "organs" of the platform—its interface, buttons, chat boxes, algorithms— connect it with other platforms into ensembles that enable reproduction of the platforms' functions but also their transformation. Here, we can think of the ways in which algorithms and buttons, as well as log-in functions, have enabled the development of interconnected platforms as a way to extract value from data. Yet these processes are not only economic but also affective. Since the use of platform's features is by now almost "intuitive," standardized platform elements like the chat boxes, Twitter roll, and related live channels framing the main feed of sites like Occupy Streams can be thought of as highly concretized forces that function in a variety of milieus and can work together in various kinds of machines and technical ensembles (Lamarre in Combes 2013, 104–5). As mentioned, the interface features that travel from commercial technical individuals like YouTube to radical media ones harness feelings of familiarity, participation, and interactivity that tap into a discursive field emerging from and engendering social media as specific technical individuals (this is what Simondon calls the technical ensemble).

This means that standardized streaming platforms, which seemingly leave very little space to do other than create a voyeuristic experience, can yield insights into the continuum between communication and action, individuality and collectivity, because of the way they enter into composition with specific activist formations. The individual's engagement with a platform's different elements—the interaction with the algorithms linking and filtering content, and then creating patterns of meaning from this—is rife with moments of intensive affectivity and emotivity that are dependent on presence (encounters) and action. As mentioned earlier, the individual does not preexist the collective, and since it carries with it a shared field of metastability that makes it always open to change, we can conceive of the collective as a system of relations that is itself transindividual (Combes 2013, 40–43).

Many of the protest live feeds on Occupy Streams no longer broadcast and yet endure in an online afterlife in what resembles a haunted TV studio. Here, the frozen interface is a testimony to the processes of production that took place but also signals the potential for new relations. In particular, the metadata and code of the platform—its information objects—can engender new kinds of relationality that produce transindividuation. The interfaces leave different kinds of archives than previous forms of autonomous media. As opposed to the articles, images, and video of selected events that we found on alternative media sites up until five years ago, the archived streaming of activities, assemblies, and confrontation with police offers raw material for analysis and reflection, not just for scholars but *especially* for activists. The activist art installation *Printemps CUBEcois* by David Widgington is an example of creative use of archival material to remember and reflect on the student protests in Quebec. This public art project installed in the atrium of Concordia University Student Union consists of a large cubic room covered in over 3,000 posters, banners, signs, and stencils collected from various social movements during and after the protests. Inside, TV sets broadcast CUTV footage of the rallies. Widgington's intention as an artist/ activist is to activate a non-nostalgic archive for reaggregation and collective self-reflection (Widgington 2013). The *CUBEcois* seeks to nurture the oppositional consciousness that was strong during the protests, reacquainting activists with past protest performance, in order to prepare for future struggles (Widgington 2013). The archive/installation functions as a site where affect and emotions "re-play" in relation to memory, reorganizing the relation between the *I* and the *We* of the students and relocating individuality and collectivity within a shared history (rather than a shared moment as is the case at protests). This memory is not just looking into the past but is mobilized to situate the students in relation to a potential shared future. As relational artifacts, the banners in connection with the replayed video streams reconnect to the past but also produce anticipation because they can be used again in the streets. In this context, thinking about potential processes of transindividuation alongside Guattari's conceptualization of the post-media era opens a discussion about the potential for those in struggle to reimagine the power of radical media platforms through different practices that take up new forms of archiving, meaning-making, and analysis of the events as they happen and in their aftermath.

Occupy Data: Data visualization and knowledge production

The previous case study focused on data as transformed media material, and on how the platform as a site for data management catalyzes new relations that build on the affectivity and emotions involved in witnessing, producing, or remembering political events. This case study engages with big data as a source of new knowledge. Using the example of Occupy Data we discuss how data activism takes the form of a direct engagement with big data through data correlation and the production of new insights into the past, present, and future. In this context, the process of transindividuation unfolds as data analytics are used to redefine the parameters of the possible through the creation of shared meanings, memories, and expectations. The knowledge yielded by big data (defined here as large sets of facts about an object) is commonly believed to offer a more comprehensive picture of the state of a situation and its future development. In the process of wrestling data from the hands of the dominant groups who control this picture, Occupy Data activists forge new alliances and push the boundaries of the imagination aided by independent data analytics. As a result, new relations are engendered that allow for the organic construction of individual and collective expectations that are not imposed through top-down mythologies.

Bernard Stiegler offers two useful concepts to understand how knowledge resulting from data modulates transindividuality: *retention*—what we retain from the past; and *protention*—what we come to expect of the future (Stiegler, Daniel, and Arnold 2011). In so doing, Stiegler usefully shows that individual and collective past, present, and future are constructed through what affects us, what is remembered, and what comes to be expected. It is within these parameters that decisions are made, be they personal, collective, political, economic, social, and so on. In the big data paradigm, data is increasingly used to manage the consequences of neoliberalism. An example that comes to mind is data mining to extrapolate the consequences of global warming and climate change if no political action is taken. As Wendy Chun (2011) astutely argues, such visualizations serve to reify the future: they convince us that only one kind of reality is possible. Since this goes against the idea of the future as open to possibilities, we have a tension in the data management paradigm. The new knowledge that big data yield always runs the risk of narrowing a horizon of imagination about what could be, and thus further reinforce existing power structures. What is at stake in Occupy Data, then, is the management of the knowledge that serves to create memories and expectations that contribute to shaping self-perception and visions of the world.

Our sites of analysis—Occupy Data and the local Occupy Data New York— work within that tension, engaging in data collection, storage, and analysis to push the boundaries of what can be known or imagined. These Occupy

Data initiatives directly address the question of the production, distribution, and ownership of data. As its name indicates, Occupy Data is an offshoot of the Occupy movement, and focuses particularly on strengthening "initiatives of the Occupy Wall Street Movement through data gathering, analysis, and visualization" (Occupy Data 2012). At the data production level, Occupy Data works to make existing public data sets available to the general public. It also hosts projects that enable users to set up data collection. For instance, the "Data Anywhere Project" from February 2013 states that: "data is available in bits publicly, but aggregated by companies that want to charge for it. Other data may be free in aggregate form, but not available for live query/access. This project aims to solve both problems, one data set at a time" (Occupy Data 2013). Occupy Data also makes data sets available to the public, along with tools and tutorials for data analysis. The site features reports from specific projects, some focused on the effects of the financial crisis (e.g. foreclosure statistics) and environmental disasters (e.g. Hurricane Sandy), others focusing on using data to understand the reach and dynamics of the Occupy movement. Last but not least, Occupy Data initiatives provide tutorials as well as organize events and hackathons where people can gather and work on common projects.

As such, Occupy Data engages with all levels of data management and highlights the different kinds of struggles that operate in the big data paradigm:

- Data collection: Who has the right to collect data and how? Who owns data?
- Data storage and retrieval: Who has the right to access data and under which conditions?
- Data analysis: What are the algorithms used to analyze data, and what kind of logics (commercial, social, for instance) is embedded in them? How does one define what data stands for?
- Data visualization and distribution: How is data represented as human-comprehendible information? How is processed data made accessible?

Each of these stages of data production and circulation presents us with specific forms of struggle around commercialization, secrecy, and ownership of data. As the struggles unfold, individuals come together in a variety of interactions that affect and change them.

Occupy Data argues for openness at all stages of data management by making both data sets and tools available. While corporate research argues for the right not to let participants know that they are subjects of research—e.g. the recent Facebook emotional manipulation experiment (Kramer, Guillory, and Hancock 2014) where a large number of users unknowingly had their newsfeeds manipulated to study mood changes—projects like Occupy Data urgently ask about the goal of such data research. They promote independent data gathering, transparency of research processes, and active participation in designing research projects and their parameters. Here, the collective visioning of reality does not only manifest itself in the final data analysis and visualization, but also and especially while responding to the challenges that this type of data activism faces—for instance, developing a research paradigm that would be different from the neoliberal one or discussing the ethics of data collection, storage, and retrieval.

The data visualizations produced look like many other kinds of mainstream information visualization. Occupy Data mobilizes standard open-source tools for analyzing large data sets through different kinds of semantic and geo-locative visualizations. They favor user-friendliness and readability by organizing and categorizing information in spatial and visual terms: semantic closeness becomes spatial clustering, and thematic links are rendered as actual lines. Data here engages participants and viewers in a redefinition of the past, present, and future, whereby the circulation of affects is structured across a collective that often comes to be a coherent body in the moment it assembles, or in the resulting visualization itself. Facts become visible by being organized as coherent, shared representations that are almost imperceptibly mediated by software for data analysis. Those producing or relating to the representations are able to make sense of themselves and their peers anew through a direct connection that is established and modulated by the technical interface. The parameters of belonging to this collectivity and the boundaries of the groups that compose it are reshaped in the resulting field of visibility: Occupy Data as a symbolic gesture that occupies dominant knowledge production, as well as the actual projects that visualize specific issues. Nowhere is this more apparent than in the case of data analysis and visualization of projects focused on the Occupy movement itself. The Occupy Data NYC page lists that thirteen out of their twenty-three projects are focused on the Occupy movement itself. The projects mostly include visualizations of different aspects of the movements, from mapping police violence during the protests to visualizing the themes and thematic links among participants and groups in the movement. Working from the inside, such visualizations tend to give coherence to a movement that has often been criticized for being decentralized, nonhierarchical, and disparate in terms of political and social demands.

Studying Occupy Data from the perspective of transindividuation draws attention to the uneasy link between activism and the established practices of data management. In particular, we want to briefly consider the issue of how activists using big data perceive the relationships between data and so-called reality. Data management is overall a positivist paradigm: it assumes that by extracting and analyzing facts about objects, a more precise picture of reality can emerge. As Bruno Latour (1993) and other critics of the positivist paradigm in techno-social research would argue, this is a fallacy: data management is about the construction of a specific reality, not the discovery of a preexisting one. That is, the data management paradigm is not an objective measure of a world out there, but a specific construction of it. We have already talked about how the neoliberal paradigm used data management as a way to reify a specific conception of the world and its future development. But the issue is not only about questioning neoliberal assumptions built into the data research process, it is also about questioning how data management itself already offers some kind of reified representation of the world. The problem lies in the claim that such representations are pictures of reality. As Galloway (2012, 80) argues:

> Data, reduced to their purest form of mathematical values, exist first and foremost as number, and, as number, data's primary mode of existence is not a visual one. Thus . . . any visualization of data requires a contingent leap from the mode of the mathematical to the mode of the visual. This . . . means that any visualization of data must invent an artificial set of translation rules that convert abstract number to semiotic sign. Hence . . . any data visualization is first and foremost a visualization of the conversion rules themselves, and only secondarily a visualization of the raw data. . . . And because of this, any data visualization will be first and foremost a theater for the logic of necessity that has been superimposed on the vast sea of contingent relations.

It would be thus a mistake to think that data visualization automatically leads to a faithful representation of reality and that it is that representation which, in turn, enables processes of transindividuation. Rather, data visualization imposes a specific logic of correlation and relation among data points and individuals that creates the conditions for processes of transindividuation that build on events and encounters, but also on the knowledge and discourses that feed the processes of meaning-making. In this sense, it is more useful to see data visualization as an entry point into an emergent field of socio-technical relations composed of temporary and biased representations that foster new alliances and forms of intersubjectivity. Here, studying the practices that reimagine the potential relations to data itself makes new modes of resistance to the data paradigm visible. These modes of resistance openly contest the politics of data knowledge and adopt a more experiential and playful approach to envisioning and visualizing possible realities. The projects discussed in the final case study do so, using creativity to critique and subvert the dominant data paradigm.

Creative data activism

Activists and artists are indeed interrogating the politics of data knowledge and doing so in surprising ways. One such example is Zach Blas' Facial Weaponization Suite, which addresses the paranoia about the inability to recognize faces in a society where face recognition technology is increasingly prevalent. The project consists of a series of community-based workshops where participants make "collective masks" that are modeled from the aggregated facial data of participants, resulting in amorphous masks that do not register as human faces to biometric technologies. The masks produced are then used for public interventions and performances. The project troubles common assumptions about the objectivity of data and, in particular, of biometric data for facial recognition. The latter is unmasked as building on centuries of hetero-normative, racist, ableist, and classist (Magnet 2011) principles that set the standard of normalcy, against which alterity is constructed and monitored. Unmasking takes place by creating what Blas calls "social opacity" (2011). Masks like the Fag Face Mask, created by merging facial data of queer people, question the assumptions and consequences of scientific studies determining sexual orientation through facial recognition techniques. Another, the Black Mask, "explores a tripartite conception of blackness, divided between biometric racism (the inability of biometric technologies to detect dark skin), the favoring of black in militant aesthetics, and black as that which informatically obfuscates" (Blas 2011). Other masks focus on issues of visibility and concealment in feminism, and on migration, xenophobia, and nationalism. As Blas puts it: "These masks intersect with social movements' use of masking as an opaque tool of collective transformation that refuses dominant forms of political representation" (Blas 2011). "Informatic opacity" is one way of resisting the positivist assumptions of data objectivity (Blas 2013). This approach brings data activism in alignment with other acts of escape and opacity that have increasingly marked new cycles of struggle to resist capture and recognition, from Anonymous and black blocs to Pussy Riot and the Zapatistas. Finally, the Facial Weaponization project also gestures toward the development of tech tools for encryption, anonymity, and privacy (Blas 2013).

While Blas' project is described as one that creates "opacity," we can, of course, see data activism like this as also rendering the power relations connected to data less opaque. As a form of data activism, the Facial Weaponization Suite, like many other collaborative design projects, points in the direction of what could be called "co-research-creation." The important aspect of these projects is coproduction as a form of organization, one that is critical enough to know how to harness the technology within sociality or, when necessary, reject it to reclaim our social time and energies. Because of the co-involvement of activists and artists—the two often coexist, even in the same person—the production of knowledge and artifacts mobilizes politicized creative practices—what Guattari would call ethico-aesthetic practices (1995)—that are affective in the very way they foster political organization. Individual and collective transformation takes place first in the encounter and exchange between individual and data, and then as forms of oppression and forms of resistance come to light at the intersection of sociality and technology.

It is not only the masks themselves, and their exhibition out in the world, but also the workshop-based production of these masks that we consider a form of data activism. In fact, the critical discussions and the collaborative process behind the design and production of the different masks are important moments for a radical transformation of the participants' relationship to media representations (Guattari 2000). In the collaborative process of producing the collective mask, we can see the unfolding of processes of transindividuation, first, in the sharing of the experience and engagement with the object, and then, in the actual mask. The mask symbolically and materially cuts the duality between the individual and the group by scrambling and reassembling the data that might otherwise be used to control them. Furthermore, the performances that incorporate the mask establish a relation to wider audiences than the workshop participants; they not only draw out knowledge about biometric data, and how it is collected and used, but also illustrate how transparency and structural discrimination affect the communities that develop the performances. The kind of community emerging as people interact with the mask (or masks) is the *product* of these interactions, rather than a predefined category to describe those involved in the project.

This kind of project resists data as a form of control. As opposed to the more traditional approach toward data management pursuing objective certainty, the Facial Weaponization Suite humorously serves to interrogate and trouble the common data paradigm. What is particularly interesting about the masks is that they show that data can be used to explore potentials rather than construct a specific version of reality. This kind of experimentation into what could be is playful, but in a serious way. The concept of serious play as an important step for activism is about engaging in experimentation with the world, where common assumptions are deconstructed and alternatives tested. In psychotherapy, this process is referred to as transitionality (Winnicott 1953): the space of experimental engagement with the world in order to reposition the individual in relation to others. In that regard, Blas' masks show how the distortion and refashioning of data can be used to question internalized frames of reference and open up new alternatives and new ways of thinking and being together.

Conclusions

This chapter initiated a discussion of the role of data in processes of transindividuation, wherein activists are mobilized as individuals and as members of collectivities. After discussing the relationship between activism, data, and transindividuation, we provided three examples of what we call data activism. The example of Occupy Streams discussed how new media activist practices relying on the circulation of data and metadata sustain and perpetuate affective bonds among those involved in protests. Occupy Data showed how big data analytics create a new, shared vision of the past, present, and future for activists involved in rethinking the role of data-derived knowledge, and in using data to contest dominant visions of reality. Finally, the Facial Weaponization Suite is an example of the creative use of biometric data as a vector of transformation that repositions profiled groups in relation to generalized fears and dominant discourses about transparency. These examples share an indirect and direct critical engagement with the data management paradigm that has become more common in the security and austerity cultures after 9/11 and the 2008 financial crisis: due to a widespread loss of faith in the securitized, free-market paradigm, citizens are increasingly questioning the rationale used to justify neoliberal discourses and policies.

Moreover, the projects discussed illustrate three different cases of the co-emergence of the *I* and the *We*. They emphasize how data facilitates the genesis of these two terms. Here, individuals and collectivities do not predate the relation that data affords; as entities that are in a metastable equilibrium, subject to change, they are engendered or constantly affected by such relations. In this context, projects like Occupy Streams, Occupy Data, and the Facial Weaponization Suite call for new research methods that make sense of the potential for change in a socio-technical field where data has a growing presence. We argued that to grasp this potential it is not enough to study the implication of data in mechanisms of political and economic control, whereby data is used to collect information about citizens/users and to organize civic life and consumption habits. We also need to pay attention to the different ways in which data is implicated in the circulation of mediated and unmediated psycho-physiological stimuli. These stimuli and affects, constantly reorganize the personal-social continuum of feelings and emotions and impact self-perception, belonging, and collective action.

Finally, we emphasized how positivist notions about data analysis' objectivity and reliability guide the study and use of data, especially big data (which sets the policy agendas in neoliberal economies). The modes of data activism we discussed reject this paradigm, directly addressing the question of the production, distribution, and ownership of data and questioning any claims about data's truthful representation of so-called reality. Therefore, research on data and activism should be adapted to the shifting reality of the challenges that the use of data poses for groups seeking to actively effect change. It is particularly important to embrace the complexity and paradoxes that are ignored by positivist approaches to the meaning and function of data. Ultimately, with this initial discussion, we would like to call for future research on data and activism that pays attention to the multilayered ways in which data in all its forms both fosters and restricts new socio-technical compositions.

References

Aljazeera. 2014. "Palestinians share tear gas advice with Ferguson protesters." *The Stream*. August 14, 2014. Accessed September 30, 2014. http://stream.aljazeera.com/story/201408141902-0024060.

Art is Open Source. 2011. VersuS. Accessed October 15, 2014. http://www.artisopensource.net/projects/versus-the-realtime-lives-of-cities.html.

Blas, Zach. 2011. "Facial Weaponization Suite." Accessed September 10, 2014. http://www.zachblas.info/about/.

Blas, Zach. 2013. "Informatic Opacity." *Journal of Aesthetics and Protest* 9. Accessed September 10, 2014. http://www.joaap.org/issue9/zachblas.htm.

Chun, Wendy Hui Kyong. 2011. *Programmed Visions Software and Memory*. Cambridge, MA: MIT Press.

Combes, Muriel. 2013. *Gilbert Simondon and the Philosophy of the Transindividual*. Cambridge, MA: MIT Press.

Costanza-Chock, Sasha. 2012. "Mic Check! Media Cultures and the Occupy Movement." *Social Movement Studies* 11(3/4): 375–85.

Elmer, Greg and Andy Opel. 2014. *Preempting Dissent Policing the Crisis*. Documentary, Canada, 41 min.

Galloway, Alex. 2012. *The Interface Effect*. Cambridge, UK: Polity.

Gerbaudo, Paolo. 2012. *Tweets and the Streets: Social Media and Contemporary Activism*. London: PlutoPress.

Guattari, Felix. 1995. *Chaosmosis: An Ethico-aesthetic Paradigm*. Trans. Paul Bains and Julian Pefanis. Sydney: Power Publications.

Guattari, Felix. 2000. *The Three Ecologies*. London; New Brunswick, NJ: Athlone Press.

Guattari, Felix. 2012. "Towards a post-media era." Accessed September 9, 2014. http://www.metamute.org/editorial/lab/towards-post-media-era.

Juris, Jeffrey S. 2012. "Reflections on #Occupy Everywhere: Social media, public space, and emerging logics of aggregation." *American Ethnologist* 39(2): 259–79.

Kramer, Ad, J. E. Guillory, and J. T. Hancock. 2014. "Experimental evidence of massive-scale emotional contagion through social networks." *Proceedings of the National Academy of Sciences of the United States of America* 111(24): 8788–90.

Latour, Bruno. 1993. *We Have Never Been Modern*. Cambridge, MA: Harvard University Press.

Lovink, Geert and Miriam Rasch. 2013. *Unlike us Reader: Social Media Monopolies and their Alternatives*. Amsterdam: Institute of Network Cultures.

Magnet, Shoshana. 2011. *When Biometrics Fail: Gender, Race, and the Technology of Identity*. Durham: Duke University Press.

Occupy Data. 2012. "About Occupy Data." Accessed October 14, 2014. http://occupy-data.org.

Occupy Data. 2013. "#OccupyData NYC." Accessed October 14, 2014. http://occupydatanyc.org/category/projects/.

Simondon, Gilbert. 1989a. *Du mode d'existence des objets techniques*. Paris: Aubier.

Simondon, Gilbert. 1989b. *L'Individuation psychique et collective*. Paris: Aubier.

Simondon, Gilbert. 2006. *L'individuazione psichica e collettiva*. Trans. Paolo Virno. Roma: DeriveApprodi.

Stiegler, Bernard 2013. *What Makes Life Worth Living: On Pharmacology*. Trans. Daniel Ross. Cambridge, UK: Polity.

Stiegler, B., R. Daniel, and S. Arnold. 2011. *The Decadence of Industrial Democracies*. Cambridge, UK: Polity Press.

Terranova, Tiziana. 2000. "Free Labor: Producing Culture for the Digital Economy." *Social Text* 18: 33–58.

Warner, Michael. 2002. "Publics and Counterpublics." *Public Culture* 14(1): 49–90.

Winnicott, Donald W. 1953. "Transitional Objects and Transitional Phenomena—A Study of the First Not-Me Possession." *International Journal of Psycho-Analysis* 34: 89–97.

Widgington, David. 2013. "Artéfacts d'un Printemps québécois Archive." Accessed October 14, 2014. http://www.printempserable.net.

11

A Contribution to the Political Economy of Personal Archives

Yuk Hui

One of the still unfolding impacts of the computer age is that everyone now must be their own digital archivist.

US Library of Congress, 2013[1]

Introduction

With digitization, archives are now everywhere, from online libraries to personal timelines on social media. These days, the archive is less of a critical concept and more of a socioeconomic category. Indeed, the issues that surround the archive concern techniques of digitization and modes of access in an environment dominated by a few corporate players such as Google. In this new reality of the archive, the relation between the digital and the archive is often presupposed: the digital serves the purpose of archiving, from management to access. In this chapter, I want to bring this presupposition into question. Let us first ask: What really is an archive after digitization? The way we talk about digitization and archives today assumes a concept of the archive comparable to the one from the nineteenth century. This concept can no longer serve us; we need to redefine the archive according to its technical condition and the possibilities opened up by that condition. In particular, and as shown in the above quote from the Library of Congress website, we have to recognize that everyone must be their "own digital archivist." But what is an archivist? And why *must* we become our own archivist?

---

[1] Available at the time of this writing: http://www.digitalpreservation.gov/documents/ebookpdf_march18.pdf.

In "A New Archivist" from his *Foucault*, Gilles Deleuze writes:

> A new archivist has been appointed. But has anyone actually appointed him? Is he not rather acting on his own instructions? . . . He will not concern himself with what previous archivists have treated in a thousand different ways: propositions and phrases. He will ignore both the vertical hierarchy of propositions, which are stacked on top of one another, and the horizontal relationship established between phrases in which each seems to respond to another.

This quote has us dwell on both the nature and the potential of the archive and the archivist. Archives are maintained by rules and practices that are normally hierarchical, as Deleuze describes. Archiving is at the same time preserving, selecting, and forgetting, and is guided by rules and by very limited imaginations. Without rules to make connections possible, objects are dispersed everywhere according to their own forces or natures; over time they settle like dust on furniture, and as time goes on, the dust becomes thicker and thicker. The archive becomes more and more *obvious* but less and less *legible*: we all notice that the number of records and assets are growing while the links between each archived object become weaker and weaker. As a result of this sedimentation of time and memories, we are faced with a growing mass of dark matter: millions of documents and objects are displayed with abstract codes and numbers, while our gaze gets lost and distracted. Everything is "there," but most of it invisible to us. Thus, so much in history becomes invisible.

Consequently, the archive needs new rules and new archivist practices have to be reinvented. Naturally, one could add more rules in order to simply expand the archive and include all objects. But one could also invent a totally new technique, one that transforms at the same time the nature of archives and the relations between archived objects. The new archivist—namely, for Deleuze, Michel Foucault—ignores the old horizontal and vertical rules and invents a new archival technique that turns the archive from a closed site into a site of open inquiries. The above Deleuze quote thus highlights the problematics and possibilities of archives—namely, that archives as preservations of history are subject to rules underscored by power and hence prioritize certain truths, and that the traces left in the archive are also the sources of its subversive potential to reconstruct a cartography of power and truth. The rules that govern the archives as well as the techniques of archiving are the two focal points that allow us to develop a method of reappropriating the works of Foucault in order to approach the contemporary question of the digitized archive. I define archive as the selection and classification of accumulated documents and objects.

This chapter endeavors to address two questions: What happened to the concept of the archive after digital industrialization? And, what kind of archivist is necessary and desirable in this new configuration? The ensuing discussion is divided into four parts. The first questions the notion of the archive after digitization/decentralization, and introduces the concept of the personal archive, as the archive has become a social-political and economic project of the digital economy. The second part takes a broader view of the archive, as a technical milieu for individuals. This milieu is not simply an "environment," as many translators from the French would have it. Instead, I want to follow Georges Canguilhem in his well-known article "Living Being and its Milieu," in which he understands the milieu as the constitution of the subjectivity of the living being. The third part of the discussion returns to the question of objects and care, in order to elaborate on the notion that once archives are considered as the necessary constituent of the milieu, the relation between the individual and its milieu has to be rethought. Finally, the fourth part takes up a proposition from Simondon: fostering a technological culture in order to envisage an archivist culture to come.

The archive after decentralization

My first claim: after digitization, we are witnessing the emergence of personal archives, although this digital, personal archive is still to be defined. The personal digitized archive remains in the shadow of industrial programs: tech companies are taking over the role of archivists and constantly integrating and creating new types of archives, and individuals are deprived of the ability to archive by algorithms that serve marketing strategies. Here, we can identify a politics of archives, though it may not be immediately evident at first glance. The aim of this section is to clarify this contemporary archival situation. We shall start again with Michel Foucault. Archives, for Foucault, are traces of enunciations by which one can reconstruct the game of rules (*le jeu des régles*), which in turn reveals the power structure of social and political conditions.

The will to archive turns archives into sites of power. Besides the dominant narratives set up in the archives, we can also observe power in the relationship between institutions and archives. Each institution has its archives that contain its history and discourses. In order to maintain its status quo, each institution needs to give its archive a proper name. Foucault observed the expansion of museums and libraries in modern times and described them as an effort "to enclose in one place all times, all epochs, all forms, all tastes."[2] An archive is also a symbol of authenticity and authority—a monument of modernity. This project of the moderns confronts the biggest challenge in the digital age. This technological development fostered an internal contradiction in the conception of archives as monuments. Indeed, institutions are now under pressure to open their archives, and digitization amplifies this process. It becomes important for them to develop digital strategies and implement new form of interactions between archives and their audiences or visitors. This is quite evident in public institutions such as galleries, museums, and national theaters.

This transition involves multiple procedures: digitization, indexation, and the development of interfaces and algorithms to facilitate public navigation of the archives. We have mentioned above "dark matter," which refers to the present-but-not-annotated data produced over decades in some institutions. The public has no means and likely, therefore, little interest in navigating this dark matter. For example, let us consider an audio-visual archive of hundreds of thousands of hours: how can an online visitor find a five-minute segment that interests him or her from hundreds of thousands of hours of videos? The traditional method—an archivist sitting in front of the computer and annotating every scene by hand—is too time consuming.[3] And how many people have to be employed in order to open up an archive with decades worth of accumulated videos? In my past work with the archives of national galleries, I noticed that the focus after Web 2.0 has always been to develop collaborative annotation among users.

The will to archive as monument, and the desire to move toward public collaboration, is sometimes paradoxical, and is best represented by the tension between open and closed, public and private. Institutions continue to keep their archives in a closed environment (including the Michel Foucault Archive!) in

---

[2] The idea of accumulating everything, of establishing a sort of general archive, the will to enclose in one place all times, all epochs, all forms, all tastes, the idea of constituting a place of all times that is itself outside of time and inaccessible to its ravages, the project of organizing in this way a sort of perpetual and indefinite accumulation of time in an immobile place, this whole idea belongs to our modernity. Michel Foucault (1967) "Of Other Spaces," *Diacritics* 16 (Spring 1986), 22.

[3] See, for instance, A. Lenkiewicz et al. 2012, "Linguistic Concepts Described with Media Query Language for Automated Annotation," www.dh2012.uni-hamburg.de/conference/programme/abstracts/linguistic-concepts-described-with-media-query-language-for-automated-annotation/.

order to maintain and consolidate their status. From their perspective, public engagement also means loosening control over rules and regulations—over the archive's treatment. A very basic response that digital archivists are often confronted with by their superiors is: "Fine, let's do collaborative annotation, but what if the user writes 'xxx is shit' or some other unpleasant comments?" The simplest way is to keep the archive as an intact, central monument: as read only. This contradiction internal to the modern concept of archive prevents any radical development of digital archives from happening. Even though today some of these institutions implement "open policies," these are more or less always strategies of crowd sourcing under the name of the humanities or digital humanities in order to reinforce centralization. Public participation is still restricted to a minimum level, akin the relation between tourists and monuments.

We can understand that this tension has been largely provoked by the advancement of Internet technologies, which are more or less premised on certain conception of decentralization (Galloway 2004). Aside from digitization, we also have to ask: what is an archive after decentralization? On the one hand, decentralization puts the concept of the archive into tension, as we have seen above. On the other hand, every user is producing and collecting more and more data, which makes almost every computer device itself a small independent archive. Between the institutional and the individual, there is Google: Google Books and Google Museums are competing with centralized archives, but in a more "democratic" manner; Google Drives integrate small, individual archives into Google's huge memory. These are ultimately efforts to reappropriate the humanities through digitization and crowd sourcing. Google does not only provide services with higher quality and higher speed, but also goes beyond the traditional relation between archives and the human subject. We could possibly see this as the latest phase in the meltdown of the modern concept of archives and a new way of appropriating digital assets (e.g., data). This new relation between the data center and users created by Google has already eclipsed the previous concept of archives and is characteristic of an industrial paradigm, which we see in similar services, such as Dropbox. Google does not use the concept of the archive or personal archive, but rather data and personalization. It is also from this new vocabulary that we can start outlining a political program of personal archives. The key here is the conceptualization of personal archives, which moves away from the modern conception of archives as monuments at the same time as it acts as a counterforce to the industrialization of memories. It forces us into not only a technical consideration about how to mitigate controls from the service providers or to fight for privacy, but also to rethink our relation with archives and to create an archivist culture to come.

For some readers, it is not evident why this industrialization of memories, pursued most aggressively by Google, is problematic, since many of its users have profited from digitization and indeed find it easier to store their personal data. But let us consider the ongoing Snowden affair, which has raised a new concern on this issue: our data is used for commercial and security purposes. A new strategy has to be reinvented to confront the current issues. The personal archive is one of these strategies. However, it is not just a strategy, as it also reveals a fundamental question that concerns the relation between the human and the technological. I follow Georges Canguilhem in approaching this as a question of the *milieu*.

Archive and milieu

French philosopher Bernard Stiegler has for decades described and criticized the industrialization of technical life. His thought is indebted to the concept of the form of technical life (*la forme de vie technique*), which was first coined by Georges Canguilhem (Stiegler 2011). In the chapter "Machine et Organisme" of *La Connaissance de la vie*, Canguilhem proposes what he calls an organology—a philosophical study to research the relation between organism and machines. Canguilhem went back to the assimilation between machines and organisms in the thought of Descartes and showed that such a position fundamentally involves a reduction of human and nature to automatization. Instead, Canguilhem follows Kant and others in claiming that organisms cannot be reduced to machines and that art cannot be reduced to science. He concludes that a new relation between organisms and machines has to be rearticulated, and that instead of posing the assimilation between the mechanistic and the organic, we should consider the inscription of the mechanic in the organic (Canguilhem 1952, 159). After Canguilhem, Stiegler developed his own concept of the general organology, which transverses human beings and technics through the question of memories by considering technics as *an exteriorization of memories*. Stiegler hence proposes a new industrial program of memories that allows at the same time the preservation of life, and the individuation of human beings. Individuation is an old philosophical question, and can be summarized in the following way: Why does this person named Socrates belong to the human species and why is he different from this person called Plato? Individualization, hence, is also the process of singularization of being, which retains the intelligible in the sensible, the universal in the particular, without the latters subsuming the formers. If we approach the question of individuation from the perspective of memory, it concerns both the *exteriorization* of memories, and the *interiorization* of the *exteriorized* in the present, as the condition under which being can individuate itself.

I want to take up in this section the notion of the preservation of life through archiving by revisiting Canguilhem's thesis, since I think Canguilhem probably gives us a broader perspective to look at the political question than we now have, which comprises at the same time memory (as argued by Stiegler) and milieu (which refers to a certain notion of ecology). Right after the chapter on "Machine and Organism," Canguilhem continues with a chapter called "The Living and Its Milieu." I take this arrangement as an attempt to articulate the reciprocal relation between living beings and the artificial world. I would like to first elaborate on Canguilhem's concept of the milieu before developing a critical assessment of the milieu in relation to archives. According to Canguilhem, it was Newton who moved the question of milieu from mechanics to biology. For Newton, the milieu consists of ether, which is the medium of transmission: "Ether helped him not only resolve the problem of illumination, but also explains the physiological phenomenon of vision and even explains the physio-logical effects of luminous sensation, in other words, explains muscular reactions" (Canguilhem 2001, 8). It is evident that today we are dealing with a digital milieu that did not exist before; we can probably say that data or information has replaced ether, and constitutes a milieu that is more and more pervasive, interactive, intelligent, and also dangerous. The danger comes not only from that fact that the digital environment is dominated by several giant industrial players, but also because what is offered by these companies is commonly understood as neutral tools or services rather than a milieu that shapes individuals.

In the nineteenth century, we find many debates and theories around the question of the milieu, from Auguste Comte, Jean-Baptiste de Lamarck, Charles Darwin, and Alexander von Humboldt, among others. In these debates, we see that the relation between the living and its milieu becomes more and more intimate, while at the same time, the explanation of milieu becomes a scientific tool combining anthropology, biology, statistics, laboratory experiments, and philosophy in order to understand evolution and human behaviors. We can probably say that the primary understanding of milieu is the "atmosphere" surrounding the living being. For Lamarck, milieu implies a specifically fluid surrounding, such as light, water, and air. At the center of Lamarck's theory of the milieu is adaptation, meaning that when the milieu changes, we adapt ourselves in order not to let it go, as if it had not changed at all. The adaptation of the living being to its milieu is admirable, but also problematic, particularly when we stick to a digital milieu constituted by Google, Twitter, and Facebook, and we adapt ourselves to their policies, their interface changes, their modification of APIs, and their abuse of our personal data. The theme of this book, *Compromised Data*, resonates here, though the question is whether we compromise data or we are compromised by data.

It was Darwin who first criticized these naturalist approaches in his introduction to the *Origin of Species*, when he declared: "Naturalists are always referring to external conditions like climate and food as the only possible cause of variations; they are only right in a very narrow sense." Darwin offered two other understandings of milieu: one is a social milieu of competition or struggle for survival and the other is the geographical milieu of natural selection. Darwin broadened the relation of the living and its milieu from external environment to social aspects, that is to say, to the relation among organisms. In my view, Canguilhem did not further develop this aspect of Darwin in his research on the milieu. Instead, as we will see later, it was his student Gilbert Simondon who delved into the question of the socio-technical milieu. Canguilhem concluded his history of the milieu with the beginning of the twentieth century and the work of the biologist Jakob von Uexküll.

In the early twentieth century, Uexküll published several books on the question of the *Umwelt* (the surrounding world), notably a first volume of *Umwelt und Innenwelt der Tiere* in 1909, and a second volume in 1921, which inspired Heidegger's take on the concept of the world and his articulation of the *Umgang* (going around the surrounding world). In the well-known example given by Uexküll, a tick, an insect without eyes, is resting on a branch, detecting signals in order to fall on to the body of a passing animal. Now, let us imagine a cow passing by: the cow creates a setting defined by different parameters, especially the odor of rancid butter that emanates from its cutaneous glands, which triggers the tick to "fall." If the tick is lucky, it can stick itself to the skin of the animal and suck its blood. Otherwise, it will have to slowly climb back to the tree and wait for another passerby. Above, I used the word "setting" instead of milieu since Uexküll uses three words *Umwelt*, *Umgebung*, and *Welt* to describe three different orders of external environment and stimulations: the interiorized world, the relevant world to the animal, and the given world to the animal. Canguilhem declares: "Uexküll distinguishes between them with great care. *Umwelt* designates the behavioural milieu that is proper to a given organism; *Umgebung* is the simple geographical environment; and Welt is the scientific universe. For the living, the specific behavioural milieu (*Umwelt*) is a set of stimuli that have the value and significance of signals." Based on this explanation, we can see in fact that *Umwelt* is no longer a milieu as previously understood. Rather, Uexküll's notion of the *Umwelt* is more in the direction of context. A context is a selection of significations for the subject.

For now, let us stick to the notion of adaptation regarding the milieu. The digital milieu is our actual milieu: it is constituted through archives and allows individuals to be oriented according to specific rules. This moves the political question of archive from the archaeology of knowledge to a new configuration, which I posed above as the question of the milieu. We should follow here Stiegler's critique of the industrialization of memories, which is also concerned with the question of the industrialization of the milieu. The industrialization of the milieu involves memory as well as the modulation of the sensibility to the world. That is to say, our way of *interiorization* of the world becomes effectively controlled, not only by the limitations imposed on access to memories, but also by the internal dynamics of "recollection" or simply "recall." In this regard, we will be able to depart in the following section from the milieu to the reconceptualization of the personal archives as a response to intensive industrialization. The ubiquity of information in digital, calculable forms has created a new situation of work and exploitation, where we enter an endless process of data production, and where we also get lost in an endless black hole of data navigation. The Internet is a huge archive of data and at the same time an enormous black hole that gathers all productivities. Google is the best exemplification of this dual function: on the one hand, we are contributing data by using the Google tools, emails, blogs, Google+, Hangout, and so on; on the other hand, Google gives us search and data management tools to survive in this milieu. Law professor Yochai Benkler has put it well: "Google harnessed the distributed judgments of many users, with each judgment created as a by-product of making his or her own site useful, to produce a highly valuable relevance and accreditation algorithm" (Benkler 2002, 13).

In this digital milieu, we can probably say that users are deprived of their abilities to archive their objects. We have been archivists from the moment we start owning things, toys, books, postcards, letters: we have our own way of organizing and cataloging our belongings. But it is only by now that we are confronting a new situation where we are neither able to archive digitized object, nor able possess or index them by ourselves. There are different levels of inabilities here: Web services become more and more distributed, while data portability is still a problem; cloud computing is moving things from one's hard disk to someone else's server; indexation tools and personal libraries software are still underdeveloped, and so on. It is exactly this inability of archiving, fostered by the technological condition, that opens up a new battlefield for search engines, social networks, cloud computing, and so on. Furthermore, Google's archives differ from that of Foucault's in that power is operating directly through the control of archives at personal levels. That is to say, the archives become a mechanism of direct control over individuals, instead of conveying traces or evidence of power (Foucault 1968, 2001). Now, we have to face a new game of rules that operates more and more on automatic and algorithmic processes. Metadata produced by users become materials of *induction*, to generate patterns for prediction, rules, protocols of control.

It is at this point that we can refer back to Uexküll's notion of the *Umwelt*, and I want to show, in departure from Canguilhem, that the *Umwelt* has more to do with context than milieu. The industrialization of the milieu also leads to an automatization of contexts. That is, the robots and the intelligent agents from Google and Amazon, for example, are able to collect our contextual information and create new contexts for us. They set up the conditions through which, for instance, a user will click on an advertisement, or they sift through information to create incentives for users to buy things online. This is quite evident in their recommendation systems, but it is not simply a question of advertisement. Rather, they become embedded within the evolution of the milieu and reverse the role of the organism as the selector of its *Umwelt*: now algorithms plus data become an *Umwelt provider*. Under this technological condition, it seems quite clear to me that in order to respond to this political and economical dimensions of the Web, we have to politicize the question of archives. Through rereading the relation between the living and its milieu in our contemporary technological condition, I propose that we should all become archivists, and that we should develop practices and independent tools that allow us to take care of our objects. It is exactly the inability to archive, sustained by the current technological condition, that opens up a new struggle between the being and its milieu. In the remaining sections, I reflect on the following questions: What are we archiving and for what do we archive? What does it mean to be an archivist?

Objects and care

To return to the personal archives, I want to move from the milieu back to objects. In an interview with an archivist from a Scandinavian national archive, I asked: "Tell me, what do you do as an archivist, or what do you think you are doing?" The archivist replied: "I need to make it clear; I am an archivist. I don't do indexation; I create contexts." His reply goes a step further than the conventional understanding of archiving as indexing. I understand the question of context as a fundamental difference between storage and archive. Here we see another notion of the context, which is closer to Uexküll's *Umwelt*, but it is not an adaptation of oneself to the milieu but rather an adoption of the milieu as one's own possibility. A context gives us orientations, and reconstitutes our memories, something not afforded merely by storage. Dropbox, Google Drive, and so on are repositories, or places where we can easily ·drop our objects, but they do not give us any orientation. It is also the same with our desktop computers. Indeed, how often do we download the same file (especially academic articles) because it occurs to us much easier to download it again and again than to locate it on our computers or in the cloud? Before we go one step further, however, let us ask: what constitutes digitized objects and why do we have to reconceptualize them? In order to grasp the question of the digital object, we need to look at the particular evolution of the Web environment, namely the decisive movement from Ted Nelson's vision of the Web to Tim Berners-Lee's World Wide Web.

Ted Nelson's vision of the Web was very much inspired by literature, and was concerned with indexation as a process through which one can jump from one link to another. For Nelson, the ultimate goal of the Web was to create a micropayment system for authors. The proposal of HTML during the late 80s—and later the semantic Web in 2001 by Tim Berners-Lee—is one that no longer deals with the hyperlink economy; rather, it deals with a new economy of objects. To put it in simple terms, the semantic Web proposes to use ontologies to formalize data in machine-readable formats. It would be another article to discuss the meaning of the word "semantic" in the semantic Web proposed by

Berners-Lee, but we can claim that at least this formalization gives objects not only identities but also mobilities. It is only in such vision of Tim Berners-Lee that we see the continuation of the care of librarians with digital objects and the emergence of a new type of object-hood defined by structuring metadata and a new practice of care to come (HTML → XML → Web Ontologies).[4]

One of the examples that best demonstrates this is the enormous impact brought by human-machine-readable Web ontologies to library science. In library science, early cataloging schemes like MARC (Machine-Readable Cataloguing) and AACR (Anglo-American Cataloguing Rules) grounded a lengthy effort to address the question of annotation. However, since digitization and the Internet, these schemes have become obsolete and are being replaced by other ontologies, such as XML based DC (Dublin Core) (Howarth 2005). The reason for this is twofold: first, MARC and AACR are specific protocols that cannot be used outside of their limited field, implying that they cannot effectively be integrated into the digital milieu alongside other machines. The second reason, which is more important, is that they cannot be read by humans; they therefore are not able to participate in the universal communication of the global mind. In other words, a book is not treated as an object as such, but rather mere symbolic data. The following example of MARC provides the informational data of a given book and should speak for itself:

"MARC must die" is a familiar slogan that has been commonly expressed among library technicians since the early 2000s (one can also find a specific website created by digital librarians dedicated to this cause: http://marc-must-die.info). This has also ushered in a crisis in the creation of digital objects. Since librarians and technicians working with digital objects must manage a great magnitude of symbols that hardly provide them with any concrete or understandable information, digital librarians are thus condemned to be the

245 10 Rhkjsow fjkslw bf ksjk jsiousol/$c w Hfuyse can Lqzx
250 2c pj.
260 0 Klana: $b Fry Psgh, $c 2001.
300 232p.; $c 28 cm.

Figure 11.1 Information for a book in MARC format.

---

[4] By saying this, I do not mean that the semantic Web is a web of care; on the contrary this has to be questioned. What I wanted to suggest here is that its indexing practice and conceptualization of objects open new ways to understand care. This proposition on Berners-Lee is in debt to a conversation with Professor Howard Caygill and Professor Bernard Stiegler in 2009.

assistants to machines. This has, as a result, revealed one of the most notable phenomena of alienation within the digital milieu. The vision of the semantic Web as a means of generating new forms of objects that are both meaningful to humans and machines, gained a lot of appreciation and interest in various communities. The above MARC information can be expressed in terms of human readable schemes, formatted in XML, simply as:

```
<book>
    <title></title>
    <author></author>

    ...
</book>⁵
```

Invoking this difference between link and objects (conceptualized through the semantic Web) is not to simply applaud the efforts of Tim Berners-Lee to organize and standardize the World Wide Web, but rather to give us a concrete example to understand the relations between digital objects, archives, and archivists in the current technological condition. This shift from abstract/incomprehensible objects to concrete/meaningful objects is a technical invention that allows digital objects to become not only a carrier of information, but also mitigate alienation caused by machines. That is to say, with certain designs the technical object itself can act as an interface that connects human beings and machines together in a "meaningful" way (instead of only typing in abstract symbols like MARC). Simondon calls this technical configuration *transindividuality*. In *Du Mode d'Existence des objets technique*, Simondon writes:

> [The] technical object taken according to its essence, that is to say technical objects as invented, thought and designated, assumed by a human subject, becomes the support and the symbol of this relation that we would like to call transindividual. The technical object can be read as carrier of defined information; if it is only used, employed, and by consequence enslaved, it cannot carry any information, no more than a book which is used as a wedge or a pedestal. (2012, 247)

Through this technical possibility brought by digital objects, we can go back to the question of care that is at center of the relationship between librarians and books, hence also archivists and archives. Today, in order to take care, one must think of the archive as the exteriorization of our memories, gestures,

---

⁵ The more detailed technologies like RDF (resource definition framework) will not be explained here to avoid taking this discussion in another direction.

speeches, and movements. Search engines, social networks, and what one can call "info-capitalism," operate with the goal of transforming care into something efficient and computable. By the end, we are no longer able to organize these digital traces, but leave them on the cloud to be taken care of by others. I take the word *care* very much from Martin Heidegger's *Sorge*. Care is the temporal structure by which we can understand our existence. This theme lies at the heart of Heidegger's *Sein und Zeit*. Care is not only, as we say in our daily lives, "taking care of something," but also temporal structures that create a consistent milieu for ourselves, for our orientation. Heidegger further developed the concept *Besorgen* by describing a concern-less or carefree mode of being with tools, like using a hammer without paying much attention to it; by contrast, *Fürsorgen* describes two positive modes of care.[6] The political implication of *Besorgen* is that today our everyday way of dealing with archives—searching on Google, updating Facebook, or other activities of crowd sourcing—are naturalized as habit, and become something unquestioned, nearly unquestionable. We even tend to detach the Web from archive, ignoring that, at its origin, the Internet is an archive to keep track of meeting minutes and documents.

Fürsorgen is, by contrast, bound up in the concern for one's being, in an affirming worry. It is both passive, in affections and emotions, and active, in anticipations and preparation for the future. What is crucial in *Fürsorgen* is the act of "looking back." Foucault's later interest in care similarly moves toward an understanding of power as rooted in the self-development of care rather than in discourse. When Foucault wrote about the care of the self (*le souci de soi*), he meant a practice of care, of how one occupies oneself, that is comparable to Heidegger's *Nachsicht* (forbearance) and *Rücksicht* (considerateness), which include both worries and affirmations.[7] Foucault uses the example of the figure of Socrates, who kept on asking young people on the street "are you occupying yourself?" right up until his death. We can also say such care is the re-interiorization of the externalized memory, like a technologically modified version of Uexküll's *Umwelt*. This re-interiorization is at the same time temporal and spatial. This practice of care is like librarians who take care of books—wiping away the dust on the cover, putting them in the right place, relating books to different themes. By taking care of these objects, the librarians

---

6   See §26 "Das Mitdasein der Anderen und das alltägliche Mitsein," in Martin Heidegger (2006) *Sein und Zeit* Tübingen: Max Niemeyer Verlag.
7   I interpret *Rüch-* as spatial relation and *Nach-* in terms of temporal terms. Taking care has both temporal and spatial dimensions in the action of looking back.

create a new circuit between objects and themselves. Of course, not all librarians are like this, but this librarian metaphor emphasizes links between objects and archives.[8] In contrast, the deprivation of care is one that systematically destroys these care structures by alienating the relation between objects and individuals. For example, users are seen merely as producers of data and contributors to different sorts of crowd sourcing.

An archivist culture to come

What an archivist needs is not only his or her love of objects, but also skills or technics of care. Care, like power, is not a substance, but relations that are modified according to material conditions. The technics of care and the technologies of care can coincide in the context of archives. While this technological culture of archiving is not yet there, we must bring it to the table as a possibility, that is, call for everyone to become an archivist, as the Library of Congress has proposed. I want to associate this question with the thought of Simondon, not only because Simondon proposed to take care of technical objects (digital objects, in our case), but also Simondon envisaged a technological culture as a possible solution specifically to the problem of alienation as a result of industrialization, and to the opposition between culture and technology in general. The imagination of a technological culture was foregrounded by the encyclopedism of the Enlightenment, especially in the Encyclopaedia of Diderot and d'Alembert. Simondon saw the emergence of encyclopedias as the first time in history that technics such as glass and porcelain making and weaving were presented to the public. Let us recall that one of the goals of Diderot and d'Alembert's encyclopedia was to publish all the secrets of manufacturing, and one of the aims behind this was to contest the priority of liberal over mechanical arts in the medieval tradition.[9] In the

---

[8]   These books are what Bernard Stiegler rediscovered in the work of Donald Winnicott on transitional objects. The first transitional object is the thumb; babies suck their thumbs in order to compensate for the disappearance of their mothers. Please see, Bernard Stiegler (2011) *Ce qui fait que la vie vaut la peine d'être vécue: De la pharmacologie*, Paris, Flammarion.

[9]   "In what physical or metaphysical system do we find more intelligence, discernment, and consistency than in the machines for drawing gold or making stockings, and in the frames of the braid-makers, the gauze-makers, the drapers, or the silk workers? What mathematical demonstration is more complex than the mechanism of certain clocks or the different operators to which we submit the fibre of hemp or the chrysalis of the silkworm before obtaining a thread with which we can weave? . . . I could never enumerate all the marvels that amaze anyone who looks at factories, unless his eyes are closed by prejudice or stupidity." See Denis Diderot (2000) ART/Encyclopaedia, in Charles Harrison and Paul Wood, eds., *Art in Theory, 1648–1815: An Anthology of Changing Ideas*, Vol. 1, Oxford: Blackwell, 585.

17 folio letter-press volumes of the encyclopedia, about 2,900 plates in 11 folio volumes were devoted to technology. In the vision of this project, technological knowledge was supposed to be made transparent to the citizens; mechanical arts attained a status comparable to that of liberal arts.

Industrialization soon cast a shadow to this Enlightenment vision of the technological culture. One confronted a paradox of technological progress: the more advance technologies become, the further we distance ourselves from them. This paradox has two problematics associated with it. First, machines become abstract knowledge; what is presented to workers is an interface of control, and *know-how* is reduced to button pressing. Know-how does not necessarily entail care, but it is the pre-condition of care. Secondly, the mechanization of all artisan skills creates a deskilling among workers since, according to Simondon, automatized technical ensembles replace the human as the technical individual. Industrialization amplifies and speeds up this process. On the one hand, the concretization of technical objects as technical individuals reinforces abstractions of labor and knowledge: a button or a control panel hides away large amount of practical knowledge and social relations. On the other hand, the exchange between labor and capital brings labor in an endless circle of capital reproduction. This is what Simondon understands as proletarianization and alienation through his reading of Marx. I am not suggesting here that one should avoid abstraction and reduction. Abstractions and reductions are necessary in many circumstances, but the question is rather: what kind of reductions and abstractions are desirable? In my view, either the ones that favor co-individuation or ones that produce disindividuation. For example, let us consider two ways of driving cars: (1) one can drive a car by knowing its mechanics and limits; and (2) one can drive by only pressing buttons and exposing the car to its automated limits.[10] In these cases we are dealing with different kinds of abstraction, and different abstractions lead to different relations between the driver and the car (e.g., a care relation). Today, Google and Facebook are producing the later example of use; users are used to press buttons, to satisfy themselves with speed and convenience, without really understanding the problematics behind interfaces and its crowd-sourcing algorithms.

Where is the current industrialization of archive leading? We cannot fully explore this future, but according to our own experience, it is quite evident

---

[10] Example given by Bernard Stiegler (2004) *Philosopher par accident: entretiens avec Élie During*, Paris: Galilée, 43.

that one of the goals is automation: auto-indexing, auto-recommendation, auto-recording, etc. Simondon argues against automation; for him, automation is the lowest level of perfection of technical objects. Simondon proposes to take into account the "margin of indetermination" in the invention of machines. It means the machine of higher perfection (measured by the degree of its being complementary to human beings) should not be perfectly automatic, but needs to integrate the human being into the technical ensemble as one who operates it, as one who lives with it. Human beings cannot be understood simply as users; instead, human beings must restore their position as technical individuals. According to Simondon's analysis, "human individuality finds itself more and more disengaged from the technical function through the construction of technical individual—but this creates actually a malaise, because the human is always searching to be a technical individual, and no longer has a stable place next to the machine: he becomes servant of machine or organizers of technical ensemble" (Simondon 2012, 101). The question is no longer about the sabotage of machines and factories, but rather about how to invent a new understanding of technical knowledge that reconstitutes the machine culture now driven by capital and marketing. This is also our motivation in clarifying the concept of the personal archive as it relates to the industrialization of the milieu.

Creating personal archives is, in my opinion, the creation of an associated milieu. An associated milieu, according to Simondon, is central to the understanding of technical individuals. This concept of the associated milieu can best be explained using Simondon's example of the Guimbal turbine (named after French engineer Jean-Marie Claude Guimbal). The Guimbal turbine solves the effect of the Joule's rule (i.e., overheating) by putting the engine in the river. The flow of the river at the same time sets the engine into motion, and carries away the heat generated by it. In other words, the engine has adopted a river as the energy input (the flow) as well as the cooling agent. This adoption of the external milieu as part of its function, instead of adaptation as we have seen before, is the creation of the associated milieu. The associated milieu also stabilizes the technical individual through a reciprocal causality, and if we understand the associated milieu as a concept applied to the living being, then we can see clearly that there is a new relation between machine and organism described by Canguilhem and further elaborated by Bernard Stiegler.

I would like to invoke here what Simondon calls a technological humanism, which is at the center of his *Du Mode d'Existence des objets techniques.*

Technological humanism is a proposal to reintegrate technics into culture, in order to overcome the misunderstanding of technics as that which "aims at the most serious aspect of alienation that a civilization behaves or produces," so that "each epoch should discover its humanism, orienting it toward the principle danger of alienation."[11] Simondon observes that work is only a phase of technicity; but technicity is not part of work.[12] In our context, the problem of crowd sourcing as work is that the users do not know what they are contributing to while they work virtually through each search and status update. In this relationship between technicity and work lies also the possibility of overcoming the limitation of work by retrieving the potential of technicity. I hope it is clearer now—after our above explorations of the notions of personal archives and the milieu, and associated milieu—why it is necessary to move the question of the personal archive to a new level of discourse. If we ask how Simondon's vision addresses our relationship to personal archives, our answer has to consist of three parts:

1. The creation of personal archive tools to allow the individuals to effectively archive their objects. In the preceding section, we posed this question: how often do we download the same file (especially academic article) several times, because it just seems easier to download it again than to locate it on our computers or in the cloud? There is hardly any open-source software serving this purpose.

2. The development of archiving skills and literacy. Archiving practices are always associated with institutions. In 2013, the US Library of Congress published a leaflet, titled "Perspective of Personal Digital Archiving."[13] This is a positive sign, showing that governments have realized the necessity of encouraging citizens to develop archiving practices. It states that while it is important for organizations to archive, now "the same is true for individuals and families who want to pass on their personal digital memories. One of the still unfolding impacts of the computer age is that everyone now must be their own digital archivist." But what really are archiving practices? Archive practices are skills, which require practices and reflections, and not simply pressing one or two buttons and giving the responsibility away to robots.

---

[11] Ibid., quoted by Xavier Guchet (2011), *Pour un Humanisme Technologique – Culture, Technique et Société dans la philosophie de Gilbert Simondon*, Paris: PUF, 110.

[12] Jean Marie Vaysse (2006), "Heidegger et Simondon: Technique et Individuation," in J. M. Vaysse, ed. *Technique, Monde, Individuation: Heidegger, Simondon, Deleuze,* Hildesheim: Georg OLms Verlag.

[13] Available at: http://www.digitalpreservation.gov/documents/ebookpdf_march18.pdf.

3. New forms of collaboration, including exchange of practices and exchange of content. The development of the personal archive is also a critique of the "share culture," encapsulated by the Facebook's "share" button. Emphasizing the personal archive is a proposal to return agency to human individuals, but not stopping there. Instead, it proposes a return in order to develop a new form of collectivity. We can recall that the P2P architecture was once a utopian idea for data exchange. But the personal archive goes further, and proposes to reflect on different modes of sharing and connectivities. We need to be asking if offline sharing is still possible, and if it can give us benefits that we cannot enjoy online.

All three of these perspectives refer to the concept of the associated milieu that we have seen above, wherein the milieu (the personal archives) becomes one of the functions of individualization (technical individual), e.g. an organized exteriorized memory that can be effectively re-interiorized. The associated milieu also protects the individual from being exposed to too much information or limited by too little information. More importantly, it reduces the risk of automation brought about by industrial programs. This is the agenda that this chapter has been pushing. It is not possible to exhaust this subject in a short piece such as this, but I hope this will initiate discussions on the archivist culture to come.

Conclusion

Under these theoretical interpretations, this chapter calls for a new archivist culture. The centralized institutional archive, as a monument, has met its limit in our time; technological companies such as Google are taking over the role of archivists and pushing this trend to a global scale; individual users are losing their control of personal digital objects due to lack of infrastructure and technological development. This chapter tried to reconceptualize archives and archivists after digitization and decentralization, and proposed to reappropriate archives and archivist practices. It reflected on the question of industrialization of archives vis-à-vis the question of care, and the development of archival tools, which have led to widespread deskilling. The current discussions on searching, open-access, archives, preservation of information, and digital objects often hide away the politics of individuals (both human and technical) under the disguise of "users" and "tools." Users in technological capitalism are what consumers are in consumerist capitalism. Against this, we should demand the reappropriation of knowledge and skills for participants, in order to reintroduce a culture of care and an archivist culture.

This involves firstly an analysis of the relation between human beings and the industrialized digital milieu. At the base of such analysis, we find a materialist ecology, and a political agenda for such an ecology, which aims to transform current living conditions with a new understanding of the relation between organisms and machines. The call for an archivist culture is a proposal to regain the knowledge and skills of living with digital objects. At this level, we need both technics and technologies to "take care" of archives and the self. Such a humanism integrates rather than expels technologies from our life. This humanism is not like the current post-human discourse, which criticizes the human subject as the center of power and desire (which is closely related to colonialism), and the human as the center of the world (Braidotti 2013). Instead this technological humanism saw already that the human has been decentered since the industrial revolution. It returns to the "humanism," not because it wants save the old concept of the human, but rather to relocate the concept of the human. It rallies around the question of care, since care is a reciprocal causality, meaning that one can take care of the self by taking care of others (the old lesson proposed by Socrates to Alcibiades). Here, technical objects and other species are included in this context of care. Within such reciprocity, there is no longer an intentional movement from the subject to the object, but rather a relation within which both complete one another. This completion is here put forward more as a matter of care, and less as a matter of interaction. This approach toward technological development, here focused on the personal archive, aims to contribute to a political economy of data at large.

References

Benkler, Yochai. 2002. "Coase's Penguin, or, Linux and the Nature of the Firm." *Yale Law Journal* 112(3): 369–446.

Braidotti, Rosi. 2013. *The Inhuman*. London: Polity Press.

Canguilhem, Georges. 1952. *La Connaissance de la vie*. Paris: Librairie Hachette.

Canguilhem, Georges. 2001. "The Living and Its Milieu." *Grey Room* 3(Spring): 6–31.

Diderot, Denis. 2000. "ART/Encyclopaedia." In Charles Harrison and Paul Wood, eds. *Art in Theory, 1648-1815: An Anthology of Changing Ideas*, Vol. 1. Oxford: Blackwell, 581–86.

Foucault, Michel. 1967. "Of Other Spaces." *Diacritics* 16(Spring 1986): 22–27.

Foucault, Michel. 1968 (2001). "Sur l'archéologie des sciences. Réponse au Cercle d'épistémologie." *Cahiers pour l'analyse* 9(Summer 1968), reprint in 2001. *Dits et Ecrits, tome 1: 1954-1975*. Paris: Gallimard.

Galloway, Alex. 2004. *Protocol – Control After Decentralization*. Cambridge, MA: MIT Press.

Guchet, Xavier. 2011. *Pour un Humanisme Technologique – Culture, Technique et Société dans la philosophie de Gilbert Simondon*. Paris: PUF.

Heidegger, Martin. 2006. *Sein und Zeit*. Tübingen: Max Niemeyer Verlag.

Howarth, Lynne C. 2005. "Metadata and Bibliographic Control: Soul-Mates or Two Solitudes." In Richard P. Smiraglia, ed. *Metadata: A Cataloger's Primer*. Binghamton: The Haworth Information Press, 37–56.

Lenkiewicz, A., M. Lis, and P. Lenkiewicz. 2012. *Linguistic Concepts Described with Media Query Language for Automated Annotation*. Accessed February 27, 2014. www.dh2012.uni-hamburg.de/conference/programme/abstracts/linguistic-concepts-described-with-media-query-language-for-automated-annotation/.

Simondon, Gilbert. 2012. *Du Mode d'Existence des objects techniques*. Paris: Aubier.

Stiegler, Bernard. 2004. *Philosopher par accident: Entretien avec Elie During*. Paris: Galilée.

Stiegler, Bernard. 2011. *Ce qui fait que la vie vaut la peine d'être vécue: De la pharmacologie*. Paris: Flammarion.

Vaysse, Jean-Marie. 2006. "Heidegger et Simondon: Technique et Individuation." In Jean-Marie Vaysse, ed. *Technique, Monde, Individuation: Heidegger, Simondon, Deleuze*. Hildesheim: Georg Olms Verlag, 5–16.

12

The Haunted Life of Data

Lisa Blackman

Introduction: A case for small data

In recent years, the politics of data, its social and cultural life, and the new methods that cultural theorists may need in order to analyze these, have become subjects of intense interdisciplinary debate across the humanities and social sciences (Ruppert, Law, and Savage 2013; Manovich 2013; Gitelman 2013). The politics of data open up the question of exactly what counts as data, especially in the context of the multiple media transactions that register our presences, both in work and play. These transactions leave traces, which potentially accrue "afterlives" (Fuller 2009). As David Beer and Roger Burrows (2013) suggest, data acquires its own social life, or lives, becoming lively in ways that are difficult to see, comprehend, and analyze solely using qualitative methods of inquiry. Data can be extracted, mapped, aggregated, condensed, measured, and translated, acquiring autonomies and agencies that extend and travel beyond the original event or transaction. Dystopian arguments present the increasing application of metrics to life as the final stage in technology acquiring its own agencies and taking command. Reminiscent of nineteenth- and early twentieth-century dystopian anxieties, machines and, in this context, machine learning are seen now as governing humans in ways that are largely imperceptible, incomprehensible, and thus unpredictable. The so-called "back-end" of social media, for example, provides data that is conjoined with automated practices in complex ways. These recursive relations thus defy calls for transparency and raise ethical questions about data ownership. As many have argued, data repositories potentially create surplus value—revenue and profit for businesses, governments, science, and related actors. Particular data banks and archives are mined, often using proprietary forms of software, which can aggregate vast amounts of data in order to shape and anticipate the future; or this is at least the dream of those invested in a data-driven economy.

These data dreams and anxieties have converged around a new object of interdisciplinary inquiry, big data. This object attracts many scholars and supports a variety of claims, both positivist and post-positivist. The concept of big data also guides new digital methods and practices, including data visualization often based on predictive analytics, hyperlinks, or the frequency or variation of semantic content, such as co-word variation. One of the problems with these methods is that they remediate limited forms of semantic and network analysis and are often designed to produce aggregate correlation. They iron out dynamism, movement, and historical connections that are often significant aspects of data's social life (Beer 2013). When big data becomes the primary object, these aspects are often overlooked, especially when scholars mingle vastly different approaches to epistemology and the ontology of knowledge claims. One of the axioms governing these debates is that so-called big data require new forms of processing, new approaches and methods that challenge the well-rehearsed qualitative/quantitative divide (Savage 2013). This axiom is supported by funding councils, journal special issues, capital investment, and software platforms, methods, and practices. Some argue that this will potentially result in the "end of theory" (Anderson 2008). Although quantitative techniques have always been the main stay of more positivist methods, they are increasingly proffered as the solution to a range of problems that have been more central to the humanities: questions of power, agency, subjectivity, technology, and embodiment, for example. Many researchers remain suspicious of such pronouncements, while at the same time recognizing that the *doing* of culture has changed (Beer 2013, 12: author's emphasis) and that methodological innovation in the humanities is indeed necessary.

This chapter will focus on a case study of what might be called "small data." I follow danah boyd and Kate Crawford's (2012) provocations about the mythology of big data and the assumption that "other forms of analysis are too easily sidelined" (666). The case study presented here is meant to exemplify why "in some cases, small is best" (ibid., 670). It will allow the reader to grasp the micro-dynamics of data generation, and see how data traces can disclose patterns of activity missed if one is guided solely by metrics and computational forms of analysis based on predictive analytics. As boyd and Crawford argue, "all researchers are interpreters of data" (ibid., 667) and big data is not necessarily better data. boyd and Crawford's interventions are made in relation to data generated in social media contexts. This will also be the focus of this chapter. But rather than allow the software platforms or API to generate the data set, the analysis will be guided by a "hauntological" mode of inquiry, which follows the trail or traces of a certain event—what I am calling the "John Bargh priming controversy"—and the different entangled temporalities that it enacts. This event relates to an area of cognitive science known as priming, and the controversy it sparked gained significant traction across social media. It has a historical lineage to psychic modes of experimentation which are part of psychology's often disavowed past, and offers challenges to liberal conceptions of selfhood based on rationality, will, and cognition.

The different temporalities of what we might call "Internet time" carried by the Bargh controversy are disrupted by temporalities which interfere, refract, disrupt, disperse, and cut together—which knot, splice, fracture and create discontinuities. These discontinuous times point toward multiple pasts in the present and futures-yet-to-come. This temporal complexity will be explored in the context of "uncivil discourse" (Ashley et al. 2013) fostered by the controversy as it unfolded online; that is primarily through the communication of sentiment, feeling and emotion, including anger, hostility, defense, pride, and the subsequent management of reputation. However, rather than remain at the level of "uncivil discourse" and sentiment analysis, I will show how this controversy also revitalizes earlier historical controversies, which remain far from settled. These different temporalities appear as traces within the controversy, which set in motion and are carried by data that would otherwise be obscured and omitted by aggregate forms of analysis. As Karen Barad (2010) has argued, hauntological methods—associated primarily with the deconstructive writings of Jacques Derrida (1994)—allow one to think with dis/continuity, dis/orientation, and dis/jointedness. She argues that hauntologies work with erasures and the ghostly entanglements that make such erasures visible. Tracking these ghostly traces however takes work, a work that I argue is displaced if one is guided by particular data-logics and digital methods, such as co-word variation and predictive analytics. This work of interpretation implicates the researcher in what I have called, in other contexts and following the work of Grace Cho (2008), an ethics of entanglement (Blackman 2012).

What counts as data when following the Bargh controversy, which I will explore shortly, becomes a pertinent question. To call it a social media controversy would perhaps be inadequate; it would miss the recursive relationships between broadcast and social media that characterized how and why the controversy gained traction. Furthermore, as many scholars have argued, such a distinction is rather arbitrary given the remediation that characterizes media environments (Bolter and Grusin 2000). However, the controversy was enacted across various social media platforms, including blogs, microblogs such as Twitter, Google+, Facebook, and caught the attention of broadcast media, including newspapers and television news. It also involved online science trade magazines and open-access science journals. The controversy was fueled perhaps inadvertently by the actions of particular individuals: the investigative prowess of a particular science journalist, the irate protestations of a cognitive scientist, and the defensive position of a variety of skeptics. However, their part in the controversy is not reducible to their actions or agency; in this sense each could be considered one of the actors within an assemblage of relations. Furthermore, as complex data scenarios make visible, recursive relations within assemblages of data are difficult to see. Still, the human actors did become intermediaries within a controversy that brings the past into the present and also gestures toward alternate realities, lost futures, or futures-yet-to-come. These lost futures and futures-yet-to-come are carried by the comparison of John Bargh to a Mr. Wilhelm von Osten, the trainer and owner of a horse called Clever Hans in the early twentieth century, who astounded audiences with his remarkable feats and talents (Despret 2004). Why this comparison might upset Bargh and what it discloses about the contemporary field of priming and automaticity research within psychology and cognitive science becomes the subject of the controversy. The significance of this comparison is to be found in digital traces, which throughout the controversy become the object of redaction, removal, erasure, and attempts by many users and interested parties to keep this association *alive*.

The controversy and the data generated is analyzed as an example of "digital hauntology," particularly if we accept that haunting is a form of mediation, a history of the present, which "requires stretching toward the horizon of what cannot be seen with ordinary clarity yet" (Gordon 2008, 195). It involves phenomena within the psychological, cognitive, and brain sciences that are considered oddities, puzzles, and anomalies if one starts from the position that subjectivity is singular, bounded, and circumscribed by the exercise of human reason and self-control. Although the controversy might appear to be of interest only to psychologists or scientists, it carries other controversies that are of interest to arts and humanities scholars. These include: the politics and ethics of open-access publishing; the nature of communication within digital environments and across social media platforms; the politics of science communication and the public communication of science; the question of agency within digital environments; the status of digital archives; the problem with infographics; and the nature of the relationship between narrative and data.

My aim in this chapter is to reanimate the data trails that are obscured or omitted in the narrative framings of this controversy. The meaning and significance of the event, which has been constituted within particular apparatuses of knowledge production and interpretation, is based on giving a "single authoritative representation of the social" usually bound up with linear conceptions of time (Ruppert, Law, and Savage 2013, 39).[1] These forms of "bundled time" (ibid.) obscure, close down, and cover over the spread and circulation of data across different sites, sources, and temporalities afforded by digital devices. These enable new forms of traceability and knowing which allow contagion, flow, and nonlinear temporalities to be followed, tracked, and made more visible. The potential traceability and different temporalities of the digital information that is submerged or displaced by particular practices of knowing—human and nonhuman—is the subject of this chapter. As such, this intervention is strategically designed to show what exceeds data metrics when digital methods are linked predominantly to volume and scale (big data) and opens up a genealogical method which can mine, work with, and attend to the specificities of particular data sets and digital archives. These types of data remain as a persistent and ghostly presence, and can be followed, listened to, and brought to life. This is a political project, one that I hope will be of wider interest to all cultural theorists seeking a rapprochement with the sciences. The data disclose or reveal what exceeds positivism and present the potential dynamism of science—the possibility for science to listen to its own pasts in the present and shape futures-yet-to-come.

The Bargh controversy

John Bargh is a prominent cognitive scientist who received the American Psychological Association's 2014 Award for Distinguished Scientific Contributions.

---

[1] It is interesting to note that although "bundled time" is aligned by the authors primarily with qualitative (non-digital) methods, such as narrative analysis, the remediation of such tendencies—for example, the desire to provide an account or tell a story of an event bound up with particular story-telling devices—is being remediated within particular social media applications. Indeed, the desire for narrative sequencing and the capacity to "tell a story" about an event is remediated within a particular software analytics, known as *Storify*. This tool allows a user to represent a series of Twitter conversations and to create stories using social media. For an interesting account of the controversy see: http://cedarsdigest.wordpress.com/2012/03/21/put-your-head-up-to-the-meta-a-peer-reviews-post-post-publication-peer-review-a-bargh-full-of-links.

He was also made the James Angell Professor in Psychology at Yale University in January of that year. Two years earlier, in 2012, he became the subject of a controversy after he unleashed what was described on Twitter as a tantrum and "scathing personal attack." These purported attacks, posted on his blog *The Natural Unconscious* under the titles "Angry Birds" and "Nothing in Their Heads" were directed at a young Belgian post-doc researcher, Stephane Doyen, and his team who had failed to replicate Bargh's 1996 study of priming. Priming studies use a range of different techniques and experimental apparatuses to attempt to influence behavior, thought, and action in ways not consciously registered (Wetherell 2012). This area of cognitive science and psychology is already controversial with various claims being made, including those made in Bargh's 1996 study, which concluded that participants could be made to walk more slowly to an elevator after being shown words associated with aging. These words were presented in the form of a scrambled language task and were taken to have primed the experimental subjects in ways that they were not consciously aware of. Bargh's blog posts were also directed at the award-winning science writer Ed Yong who had commented upon Doyen's study and its failure to replicate Bargh's study in an entry on his blog *Not Exactly Rocket Science,* published in *Discover.*[2] This post compared Bargh to Mr. von Osten the owner of Clever Hans, who was considered to be an unwitting participant in the performance of Clever Han's prodigious feats and talents. Why this comparison might have upset Bargh is central to the unfolding controversy and opens up questions about experimenter subjectivity, which, in psychology, is considered to be circumscribed by detachment, relationality and to play a more executive role. The failed replication study and Yong's blog post motivated Bargh to rail against the experimental conditions of the Doyen study, the business model of the open-access journal *PLoS ONE,* and the practices of science journalists such as Ed Yong.

The responses in the comments section to the blog framed Bargh's rebuttal as a rant, as defensive, inaccurate, and exemplary of some of the problems that accompany science debate in the era of post-publication peer review (PRRR). PPPR refers to the afterlives of journal articles as they circulate within and across social media with the potential to extend review by contributing to comments sections of blogs and websites, for example. Although it is recognized that PPPR can extend the article's afterlife allowing a bigger readership and more publicity, for many, including Bargh, this comes at the expense of the

---

[2]   "Primed by Expectations: Why a Classic Psychology Experiment Isn't What it Seemed," January 18, 2012.

integrity of science. Bargh's response, which appears to be an attempt to close down discussion, courted further controversy and placed Bargh at the center. His posts gained traction across social media and were amplified by the comments posted on numerous other blogs, on comments sections of the blogs, and discussion forums that picked up on the controversy. As you can see from the visualization below, the traction across social media, including Facebook, Google+ posts, and Twitter is rather small when compared to the volume, scale, and quantity of big data sets. However, by following these data I hope to show why studying small data is important for cultural researchers and what this can reveal about the social life and politics of data and where data becomes compromised.

I will reconstruct the data trails related to what has come to be known as the "priming controversy" by initially presenting the reader with four URLs (see Figure 12.1). Three of the URLs relate to the blog posts by Bargh published in *Psychology Today*. The other relates to the initial blog post written by the science journalist, Ed Yong, published in *Discover* magazine. As you will see from the below visualization, all four posts received minor traction across social media. For reasons that will become clearer, the first two URLs relating to two of John Bargh's blog posts are now "offline," that is, they have been removed from the scene but the traces of the original event remain. The interested reader can find hyperlinks to Bargh's post, commentaries on the post, and responses to the responses, but the actual posts are now elusive. One is taken to *Psychology Today*

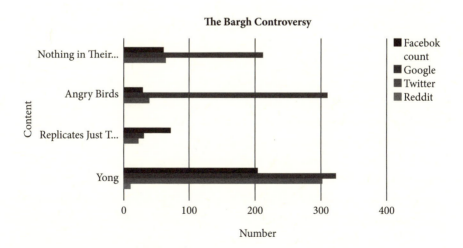

Figure 12.1 The Bargh controversy.

and met with the automated response, "Page Not Found." The subsequent erasure of these posts has been met with humor, puzzlement, and parody and the erasures have been substituted by various images. As a result of potential copyright issues I am unable to reproduce a particular meme, which included an image of Bargh overwritten with the caption, "Didn't Replicate My Study? Must be Self-Published Crap." These images draw attention to the micro-dynamics of scientific debate and the legacy of what were considered Bargh's hostile blog comments.

However, the tenacious reader will be able to find the posts circulated within small Twitter communities. Ed Yong, the science writer, has posted "Angry Birds" (Bargh's first blog post) in a Google cache link available for download as of the time of writing. I generated a visualization of my successful attempts, using Topsy.com, an open-access Twitter analytic (recently bought by Apple), to find links to the deleted posts. Due to copyright regulations I have been unable to reproduce the screenshot and link for the reader. Topsy.com was used to recover tweets from Ed Yong, the science writer, who says that he has a copy of "Angry Birds" and wonders why Bargh has deleted the blog posts. Ed Yong, in a subsequent tweet (eight months ago at the time of writing), has also recovered the erased post "Nothing in Their Heads" (Bargh's follow-up blog post), which can be followed via the link: web.archive.org/web/20120307100648/http://www.psychologytoday.com/blog/the-natural-unconscious/201203/nothing-in-their-heads. Again due to copyright regulations I am unable to provide a screenshot showing the link for the reader, but if an interested reader follows the link above they should be able to recover the post for themselves.

The recovered post was accessed via an Internet archive Wayback Machine, made available to the interested reader by Ed Yong. So that the reader can understand some of the motivations that may have led Bargh to remove the original blog posts, I will stage and reanimate some of the controversy as it unfolded, leading to the erasure of the posts. This erasure has left a series of digital trails and traces that reveal the original event's absent-presence and its hauntological potential, on which I will elaborate below. I will also draw on the recovered blog entries to both reconstruct the micro-dynamics of the controversy and to *perform* the hauntological potential of the data. This will involve taking the reader back to the early twentieth century and to a psychological archive related to priming which contemporary psychology has largely written out of its historiography (Valentine 2012). I will argue that it is primarily the splicing of two rather different temporalities within this controversy that reveals its wider significance and afterlives (Fuller 2009). This hauntological method allows the committed researcher to explore how data can be compromised by the entanglement of what Karen Barad (2010) terms different "spacetime configurings," as well as being compromised by software platforms, processes and practices, and the intentions and motivations of human actors. All of these entanglements are carried by the data—and the data ghosts or absences—that perform the controversy. All of these modalities of becoming-compromised exceed what can be represented by data visualizations that are based on metrics, frequency, and co-word variation. The haunted life of data works against predictive analytics and discloses what can be done when software tools are integrated into more complex qualitative forms of cultural analysis. And, again, this is better illustrated in the context of small data.

Hans the horse: Scene 1—Refraction

Ed Yong begins his blog post "Primed by Expectations" by referring to the figure of Clever Hans, a horse at the turn of the twentieth century who was able to tell the time and solve complex multiplication puzzles by stamping his hooves. Hans' prodigious talents were later linked to his capacity to be moved by minimal unconscious movements unwittingly expressed by his trainer, von Osten (Pfungst 1911), or to what later became known within psychology as the "experimenters expectations." As Yong suggests, the legend of Clever Hans has largely been forgotten although it has caught the attention of many contemporary cultural theorists interested in embodiment and affect (Blackman 2012; Despret 2004). Yong ends this evocative or perhaps provocative opening

Figure 12.2 Hans the horse (Wikimedia Commons).

with the words: "But history, as we know has a habit of repeating itself." The revitalization of the Hans controversy is warranted, Yong suggests, by Doyen's recent failure to replicate Bargh's aging study (1996). This is one of the most heavily cited classic psychology experiments on priming. Doyen et al.'s (2012) failure was published in an open-access journal *PLoS ONE*. This was after Doyen was unable to publish it within proprietary social psychological journals, which have a history of not publishing "null results" or non-replication studies. However, Yong does not make this point in this particular post. Rather, he uses Doyen's failure to raise the issue of how we might understand priming effects, and the role experimenter expectation might play in producing these effects and affects (by provocatively comparing Bargh to von Osten). As a respected science journalist,[3] Yong carefully considers the range of arguments and parameters of the debates and opens up the problem of replication for an interested scientific community for debate, discussion, and consideration.

The post has twenty-five comments, which range from supportive to more hostile and defensive in relation to this comparison. Out of the twenty-five, the first seven comments are supportive and welcome the debate. There is then a post by Joe that shifts the terrain, which I have coded as "mildly hostile." It corrects facts and does some work of undermining Ed Yong's credibility. This is followed by a post from Ed Yong, which clarifies some of the information and openly responds to the comments. Joe responds with an escalation of hostilities and by mildly insulting Yong. The next post by another reader accuses Joe of being "unnecessarily derisive" and defends Yong's reputation as a science journalist. This reader also does welcome Joe's contribution to the debate and follows up some of the issues by comparing the different experimental setups and parameters of the original Bargh study and the Doyen failed replication. Joe responds to this by insulting the person who left this post and Yong, again. He brings up Clever Hans and states that Yong is wrong to make this comparison. As Joe argues, "saying history has a habit of repeating itself is wrong." He claims that he does not mean to be unnecessarily derisive but Ed Yong is "WRONG." The person Joe is responding to deflates hostilities by welcoming his thoughtful comments and apologizes for his reading of Joe's posts, which he mistakes for "road rage" and says that he will ponder the arguments between football matches at the weekend. It is not clear whether this comment is sincere or sarcastic.

---

[3]   Ed Yong has received numerous awards and honours for his science writing. This includes Winner: NUJ Stephen White Award for best communication of science in a non-science context, Association of British Science Writer Awards, 2012.

The next three posts by different readers respond to Joe, asking him for further evidence (that Bargh's study has been replicated by labs across the world), accusing him of being mean-spirited and undignified in his responses, and posting a link to http://psychefiledrawer.org, an online repository where researchers can post failed replication studies for discussion. The archive is based on what Robert Rosenthal, who coined the term "experimenter effect" within psychology, terms the "file drawer problem." This relates to the publishing bias toward positive results purportedly by many proprietary journals that only publish those experiments that replicate "classic" studies. Interestingly, when I followed this link on June 23, 2014, a non-replication of Bargh's 1996 study was the single most viewed experiment (with 15,105 views). The second most viewed was 7,718 by comparison. The next comment on March 7, 2012 posts a link to John Bargh's response to Doyen and Yong.[4] If readers follow the link they will be taken to *Psychology Today* and the automated response, "Page Not Found." Ed Yong responds with a link to a response he has made to Bargh's post.[5] The remaining five posts (which include an acknowledgment of the issues by Yong) include an exchange between one reader and Yong, which corrects some facts and suggests that Yong responds to Bargh in the comments section below Bargh's post on *Psychology Today*, which has since erased the post and comments.

My account of this series of exchanges by a small readership might be considered a good example of how scientific debate is transforming within digital environments. As Ashley et al. (2013) have shown, such discussions are not always rational and can become defensive, sometimes offensive and easily polarized. They can threaten what Papacharissi (2004) has termed the foundation of so-called democratic discussion inherited from classical liberal notion of the public sphere; that debate should be deliberative and not imbued with emotion and affect. As Ashley et al. argue, online debate increasingly leads to what they term a "nasty effect" and threatens the public communication of science and public acceptance of science as primarily being based on truth, fact, and objectivity. The anxieties related to this by scientists are captured by the problems increasingly associated with social media and open-access journals and forums. These anxieties surround the concept of PPPR, where many scientists argue that comments are available to the public as forms of scientific communication. These contribute to the public dissemination of

---

[4] http://www.psychologytoday.com/blog/the-natural-unconscious/201203/nothing-in-their-heads.
[5] http://blogs.discovermagazine.com/notrocketscience/2012/03/10/failed-replication-bargh-psychology-study-doyen.

scientific knowledge and therefore are potentially damaging because of the unprofessional and often nasty tone of comments. The tone of discussion, as we have seen, is not governed exclusively by the norms and conventions of scientific debate and dialogue. Exchange often exceeds the norms of positivist scientific convention and remediates what might previously have been expressed via "closed doors," including private conversations, in closed conference debates and in private hesitancies expressed between relevant actors and agencies.

The Bargh controversy illustrates the assumption made by many media theorists studying social media that such forms of communication are *affective*, spreading emotion and feeling, rather than primarily being informational. This perceived problem and how it negatively impacts on scientific debate, exchange, and the public perception of science was summed up recently by *Popular Science* editor,[6] Suzanne Le Barre and her remarks following the decision to close the comment section of the website. She concludes that "comments are bad for science," reasoning that

> commentators shape public opinion; public opinion shapes public policy; public policy shapes how and whether and what research gets funded—you start to see why we feel compelled to hit the "off" switch. A politically motivated, decades-long war on expertise has eroded the popular consensus on a wide variety of scientifically validated topics.

My restaging of this scene is designed to give a sense of how personal dynamics are entangled with and spliced through different historical temporalities or "spacetime configurings" (Barad 2010). The present scene is shaped by the publishing of a non-replication study and the ad hominem exchange of sentiment and emotion that followed. However, the revitalization of Clever Hans by Ed Yong frames the controversy as also or even primarily being hauntological in nature. That is, the way in which personal sentiments and dynamics governing PPPR revitalize, refract, and bring back some of the lost futures of science, and particularly what Yong calls "the Legend of Clever Hans," a legend that many psychologists will not have heard of, which takes psychology back to its intimate connection to psychic research and experimental practices (Blackman 2012). Ed Yong is intrigued by the way that psychology has actively suppressed and

---

[6] Popular Science is a website that exists to promote scientific innovation and to report on current trends and discoveries in the area of science and technology studies. See: http://www.popsci.com/science/article/2013-09/why-were-shutting-our-comments?

forgotten Hans and how Doyen's restaging arguably takes us back to unresolved issues surrounding how a horse can be moved by a human (and vice versa). What questions and issues this might open up and present to studies of priming in terms of the nature of conscious and unconscious communication is one that Yong suggests is important, even if and although it is disavowed by Bargh's posts. Yong suggests that this is the more controversial aspect of Doyen's study carried by Bargh's comments and the subsequent commentary and discussion. This joining together of a lost historical controversy with a current online social media controversy shows how a single event is more-than-one, and in the rest of the chapter we will go on to explore its more-than-one nature and how it diffracts these different temporalities.

Bargh's retort: Scene 2—Resurrection and the work of interference

Prior to Bargh's "Nothing in Their Heads" post, he had not posted anything on his blog *The Natural Unconscious* for two years. He starts the blog by using the language of resurrection and preempting why he felt it necessary to use his authoritative position to debunk the Doyen study. His rebuke, he informs the reader, is directed at the business model of the open-access journal *PLoS ONE*, (which published the Doyen study), and at what he calls "superficial science journalism." These are both threatening the integrity of science, he insists. *PLoS ONE*, he argues, uses a "pay-as-you-go" model of publishing, which does not demand rigorous standards of peer review or editorial direction. Bargh equates this to self-publication; it lets studies through which should not be published, he argues. Bargh then uses his own blog to engage in PPPR and to offer the expert review and editorial scrutiny, which he insists the article did not receive. He then argues that the self-published nature of the study and its misleading conclusions were exacerbated by the fact that it was commented upon by Yong's commentary on his blog *It's Not Exactly Rocket Science* and specifically the post "Primed by Expectations," which, as mentioned earlier, had some traction across social media. Bargh argues that he was not involved in peer review for this article and that, as the leading researcher in this area (with the most highly cited study) his input was needed to assess the significance of the Doyen non-replication study. Unsolicited, Bargh goes on to do this by critiquing the experimental conditions and set-up of the Doyen study and arguing that Doyen's study was a "bad replication study." He ends the post by drawing a link between "self-published studies" and online media sources, which are the actual problem in Bargh's view. They mislead, distort, interfere, and only work to skew debate in ways that are damaging to scientific integrity. Bargh's post is written with the confidence of a Yale scientist who has "set the record straight."

There are forty-five comments on this post, also accessible via the Web archive link posted by Ed Yong.[7] These posts perhaps disclose what is at stake in PRRR and how social media is transforming scientific debate. Eleven of the posts respond to what are framed as Bargh's mischaracterizations of the business model and editorial practices of the open-access journal *PLoS ONE*. They accuse Bargh of being defensive, of engaging in a rant, of being a bully, and of abusing his own authority and power as a "star academic" (particularly for having a platform on *Psychology Today*, which is considered by some of the commentators to be a "glam mag" with its own agenda). Bargh is also considered incredibly influential in his position as one of the reviewing editors on the board of *Science Magazine*,[8] for example. Bargh's response is also deemed to be "littered with inaccuracies and misrepresentations of his (own) work." At least eleven of the comment posts are directed at Bargh's characterization of the business model of *PLoS ONE* and include responses by *PLoS ONE* editor Peter Binfield. He accuses Bargh of factual errors, including that the journal is commercial (it is not-for-profit) and that it does not engage rigorous peer review and editorial direction. Bargh is directed toward the comments section of the Doyen article and encouraged to make his rebuttal there. The subsequent posts become more heated and make potentially slanderous comments about Bargh, engaging in what could be considered a defamation of character. There is a discussion of cyber-bullying and the aggressive practices of anonymous bloggers, as well as insinuations that Bargh's influence on what gets published is threatened by open-access publishers. Further there are suggestions that open-access not-for-profit publishers could adopt a more "open" review and editorial policy. The key issue framing this debate is anonymity, both in terms of what anonymous peer review encourages (aggressive and negative reviews, for example) and also how anonymous PPPR (i.e., anonymous blog posting) affords the opportunity

---

7   web.archive.org/web/20120307100648/http://www.psychologytoday.com/blog/the-natural-unconscious/201203/nothing-in-their-heads.
8   Interestingly, if the reader uses a search engine such as Google to find a link to Bargh's role as a review editor for Science Magazine, one also finds a copy of Bargh's CV ranked number 2 on the page, closely followed in third position by Ed Yong's subsequent blog post, "A Failed Replication draws a Scathing Personal Attack." This will form the subject of Scene 3.

for bullying, slander, and defamation. I do not know why *Psychology Today* took down the blog post and the subsequent comments but clearly as a "data source" the traces disclose the micro-dynamics of scientific debate and how social media are transforming science debate and communication. They might be considered an interesting repository of compromised data.

Letting the horse lie: Scene 3—Resurrecting ghosts and diffractive reading

Wow, this is going to come back to haunt him.
  —Anonymous comment on Bargh's *Nothing in Their Heads* blog post.

Although Bargh's blog posts "Nothing in Their Heads" and "Angry Birds" have been taken down from *Psychology Today*, the posts are hyperlinked in complex ways to a distributed network of comments, responses, counter-responses, and links to actors, agencies, sites, and practices that have become part of the controversy's extended life and afterlives. To that extent, this assemblage of relations is performative, extending the controversy in unforeseen directions, with unanticipated consequences. The data that carry these relations are visible and invisible, material and immaterial, covering the Internet like a spider web of present and ghostly traces. The four URLs in Figure 12.1 act as attractors or mediators for these data traces, attaching themselves and becoming attached to complex networks of actors whose diffused relations are difficult to see and map. It is a network and therefore defies the logic of network analysis, which is based on being able to see and map relations of influence and association between actors. Networks often inadvertently include relations that are present and visible and those that are anonymous and invisible. Anonymity has plagued network analyses based on mathematical analyses, which produce cartographies that include human actors as well as automated agencies. The inclusion of nonhuman agencies, such as bots, can often skew analyses and include ghostly phenomenon such as deleted accounts, reduced to metrics and read as statistical analyses of influence. As Gerlitz and Rieder (2012) have argued, once these problems are recognized—that the quantitative always-already involves qualitative elements—the quantitative/qualitative distinction makes less sense.

  What is behind numbers? As I have tried to show in this chapter, small data provides a useful lens to explore the complex and fascinating data relations that can emerge from even a minor online happening such as the Bargh controversy. As the reader will have become aware, these relations cannot be contained or sampled according to the affordances of software platforms and practices, such as Twitter and Facebook, whose digital devices generate their own data sets. The data I have followed are cross-platform, are distributed and extend across different temporalities, and are set in motion by minor associations (Bargh with von Osten), which reanimate forgotten entities, anomalies, and controversies. These submerged relations exist as outliers to particular regimes of visibility, making it difficult to generalize about the influence, traction, and politics of data without engaging in some form of *interpretation*. As boyd and Crawford (2012) have argued, numbers do not speak for themselves. In this last section, or scene, I will focus on Ed Yong's response to Bargh's posts. My conclusion to this section will be that infographics and data visualizations that use, adapt, and modify digital methods derived from software platforms are constrained or compromised by all of the above issues. In some ways, I follow Bruno Latour's recent invitation to software developers and programmers in his keynote at the prestigious SIGCHI 2013 conference on Human Computer Interaction. In this lecture he challenges the research community to approach big data in ways that foreground the experience of data's connectedness and the relations these connections form through *time*. As I have found with this case study, the tools that might help embed hauntological modes of analysis within digital methods are still to be configured. The question then becomes what is and is not quantifiable within computational terms?

Ed Yong begins his rebuttal to Bargh's "Nothing in Their Heads" post with an image of a pram; toys are being thrown out of it. The post is titled "A Failed Replication Draws a Scathing Personal Attack from a Psychology Professor" posted on March 10, 2012. It is clear that although this is a carefully considered response to Bargh and the commentary around the study, it is also designed to be provocative. The entry is rather unsurprising and instigates a relevant and timely discussion surrounding the problem of replication within psychology and science more generally. This is the authorized narrative that surrounds this controversy— that the priming controversy discloses the problems with replication, which is considered the cornerstone of scientific innovation, discovery, and progress. As we have seen, this is the single authoritative representation of the event given by Bargh and many others. This is also confirmed by the sixty comments posted to Yong's entry, which for the most part are reasonable and useful discussions of the problems with replication and how this might be improved. Yong is generally welcomed for his careful consideration of this issue and his contribution to opening it up for extended discussion via social media and the mechanisms of PPPR. There are a few detractors from the parameters of this discussion which redraw what is seen as an unfounded association between John Bargh and the trainer and owner of Clever Hans, von Osten. One commentator puts it in thus: "Frankly, I don't think the tone of his post was all that surprising given the insinuation in your post that he had fallen prey to Clever Hans." A subsequent user also picks up on this: "So to compare Bargh's findings with the Clever Hans story is insulting and misleading."

These two comments disclose the hauntological potential of the data and act as traces that set in motion a genealogical trail. Although they are not representative of the majority of the commentary surrounding Yong's entry, they point toward another scene haunting the problem of replication. This problem is overlaid and threaded through with the revitalization of an earlier psychological controversy, one that entangles the discussion with submerged narratives, ghostly figures, displaced actors and agencies, and different temporalities. Time is disjointed, dispersed and diffracted through itself, revealed in data traces that are fleeting and act as outliers to the central discussion and focus. In numerical terms, these traces are inconsequential and insignificant. However, they also point toward the ghosts of Clever Hans and von Osten, who courted controversy at the turn of the twentieth century and are reanimates in this present controversy. It would seem that John Bargh is followed by these ghosts and the area of priming within psychology has continually to be policed in order to prevent these historical associations from surfacing. This is confirmed in the first comment made by Bargh in his later and subsequently erased entry, "Angry Birds" (which I recovered using Wayback Machine as discussed earlier) posted in *Psychology Today* on March 23, 2012. His retort begins:

> The discussion sparked by my previous post has now far transcended the remarks I made in the post itself, in defense of our lab in the face of the "Clever Hans" charge. That was a slur on our lab that had to be responded to in order to set the record straight. Insults like that typically make people angry, and so a lot of heat was generated, but too much heat produces smoke, and smoke obscures clear vision. Let's see if we can continue the discussion without anger and hostility clouding the real issues.

The blog goes on to engage with some of the issues that have been raised in relation to the study and to put the record straight, again. The comments for this entry have not been recovered and no subsequent entries by Bargh have been made in *Psychology Today* since this post. As a cultural theorist interested in affect and phenomena that disrupt borders and boundaries between the inside and outside, material and immaterial, past and present, public and private and self and other, have been fascinated by the unfolding of this controversy and what has taken form (see also Blackman 2012). I was led to this controversy by my own research into the phenomenology of will and what has come to be known as the "half second delay" within affect studies (Massumi 2002; Thrift 2007). I knew that the neuroscientific evidence underpinning this statement was controversial and through my own searches I was directed toward this particular social media controversy. Indeed, I became a very small part of it when I gave a talk at the Max Planck Institute in 2012 at an event called "Experimental Entanglements." I argued that social media science controversies provide an important data source for examining what Hans-Jorg Rheinberger (1994) has termed, following Derrida, the historical movement of a trace (its haunting, perhaps)—the tension between persistence and transformation, which he argues is not captured by Kuhn's more totalizing notion of a paradigm and a paradigm shift to understand change and transformation within science. My contribution was tweeted by a participant to the event and now forms part of the corpus of tweets connected to Bargh's "Nothing in Their Heads" blog post. Rheinberger convincingly shows how science controversies, although considered settled at particular times, have the tendency to resurface in new ways and forms. In his recent work (2010) he has extended this insight to consider what he terms the "economy of the scribble," those traces of practices which exceed the parameters of recognized scientific practice.

Although Rheinberger in this instance focuses on what gets left out of studies once they are written up for publication (scribbles on pieces of paper, workings out, ponderings, etc.) I argue that digital archives represent opportunities to explore such economies within distributed, extended networks of actors, agencies, and practices. These exist as traces, which can be followed, mapped, listened to, and reanimated. Some of these traces are deleted or removed, and as I have tried to show, exist as ghostly presences, requiring ingenuity, tenacity, and some knowledge of software and data practices in order to cover and re-perform. They are lively and disclose some of what is carried by the social and cultural life of data. Data traces can be moved and re-moved, redacted as well as remixed, and require the work of articulation, translation, and staging in order to be made visible. This is a different strategy to predictive analytics and is one that mines and focuses upon the potential of compromised data. These traces often become hidden or covered over by representationalism, by narratives and representations that come to stand in for the event. These obscure the more temporal aspects of events, the historicity of time, and the different temporalities that disclose the more-than-one nature of controversies and events. The strategy of panspectric surveillance[9] led and extended by a hauntological mode of inquiry reveals the dynamic nature of archives and their unexcavated potential. It also opens up questions of ethics and ethical entanglements, how our attempts to repurpose and reimagine data are highly situated engagements. The focus here is much more on the performing and re-performing of archives, rather than conserving them as monuments.

Denouement: Setting the record straight

I have presented here a very partial restaging of the Bargh controversy. It forms part of a bigger book-length project, *Haunted Data: Social Media, Queer Science and Archives of the Future*, which follows three social media controversies in the area of anomalous science, including Priming, Feeling the Future, and Hearing the Voice. I am working with digital methods, where useful, and on developing software tools that can remediate the hauntological dimensions of the analysis. This extends the work of what it means to follow a media object within digital environments. As David Beer (2013) has argued digital archives qualify how we approach movement and circulation when we take data as our object; this is also related to what Adrian Mackenzie (2005) has termed the "performativity of circulation." My analysis extends work in the area of mediation within media studies to consider how social media is transforming science within the context

---

9   Panspectric surveillance is a term used to describe forms of regulation, management and control, which actualise new diagrams of power (Palmas 2011). These are seen to be qualitatively different to Foucaudian panoptic forms of surveillance (DeLanda 1991). One version of what Deleuze (1995) termed "abstract machines" is that which brings together new data-mining techniques, the increasing digitalisation of cultures, with new ways of acting upon (human) subjects (including targeting what many refer to as precognitive, or noncognitive registers of experience). Thus, data analytics and strategies of preemption and anticipation that increasingly organize software cultures are being taken up by business and consumer organizations using "sophisticated techniques that anticipate the propensities of customers to act in certain ways" (Palmas 2011, 339). Palmas's (ibid.) very interesting article in respect of this shift or trend calls for a "political economy of propensity" (352), which can contribute to an excess or "something else" to these debates. The project I partially outline in this chapter is an attempt to enact a "something else" in respect of the cultural politics of data, which mines or exploits where data might become compromised. It is a strategy that performs what lies in excess of current regimes of anticipation and preemption.

of what Mark Deuze (2012) terms "media life."[10] As a temporary denouement to this controversy, I will end with John Bargh's Wikipedia page, which illustrates well some of the competing interests and contrary energies enacted within this controversy. This conclusion will illustrate how the distributed nature of this controversy and its extension across both space and time is closed down (again) through John Bargh's Wikipedia page. I will approach this page as a form of representationalism or "bundled time" (Ruppert, Law and Savage 2013), which erases process, movement, and temporality, replacing these with what Sarah Kember and Joanna Zylinska (2012) term *animations*—images, narratives, and forms of knowledge which erase or occlude those traces or forms of haunted data that exceed particular strategies of *knowingness*.

As I have identified throughout this social media hauntology, one of the refrains or performative statements integral to John Bargh's blog posts has been the desire to "set the record straight." In the process these actions have also threatened to damage his reputation, or have certainly created hostile comments from other users that verge on slander and defamation of character. As many social and digital media scholars have argued, digital archives are "archives in motion" (Beer 2013) and present dynamic and mobile processes which are not fixed in time. However, as we have seen, the capacity of data to move on from the original event and accrue "afterlives" (Fuller 2009) also threatens the performative strategies of individual users. As Zizi Papacharissi (2012) has argued, one of the issues facing social media users is precisely how to engage in forms of self-presentation and self-management in light of the complex digital relations that characterize social media practices. Goffman's (1990) work on "impression management" is seen by many social media theorists as useful to explore the kinds of deliberative action that users might engage in order to manage these tensions and construct a coherent self-presentation. These tensions Papacharissi (ibid.) argues, are heightened within online social platforms, which intensify, she suggests, practices of self-monitoring and self-awareness. She argues that networked performances or performative strategies of subjectivity often resemble "micro-celebrity, personal branding, and strategic self-commodification" (1990).

Now to John Bargh's Wikipedia page. Many prominent academics have Wikipedia pages that might be considered forms of personal branding. They

---

[10] Deuze (2012) argues that there is no external to media life as media are now ubiquitous, immersive, and all-pervasive. As he argues, "media are to us as water is to fish" (x).

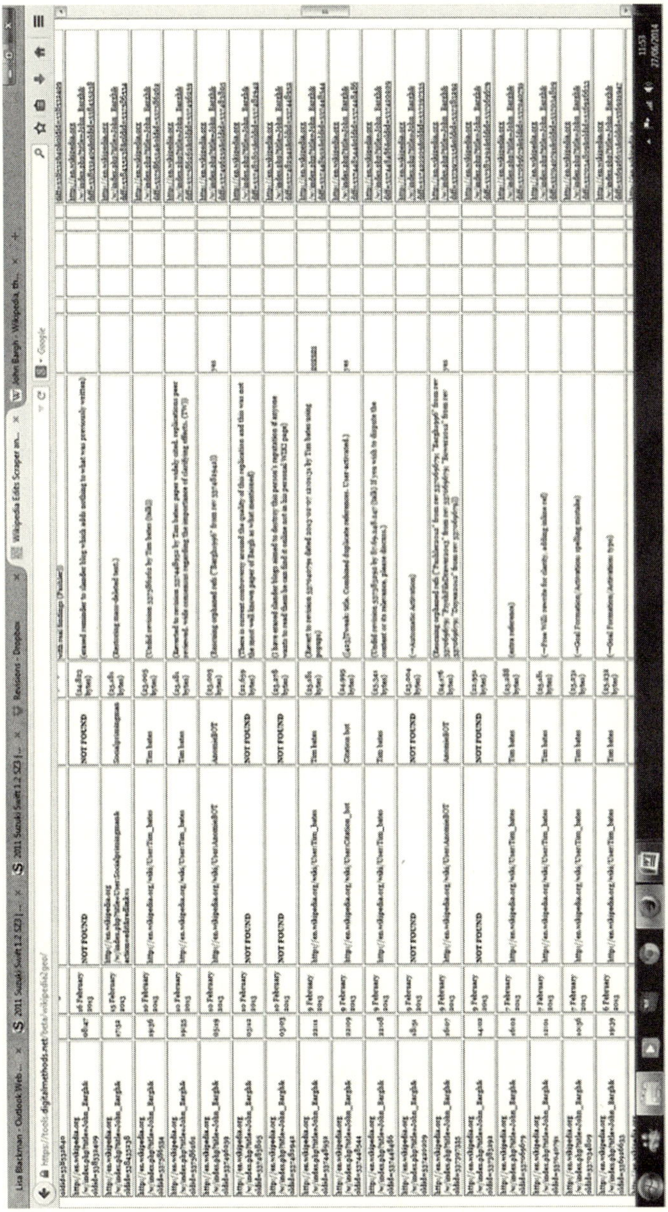

Figure 12.3 Wikipedia Edit Scraper and IP Localizer, https://tools.digitalmethods.net/beta/wikipedia2geo/, courtesy of the Digital Methods Initiative, New Media and Digital Culture, Media Studies, University of Amsterdam.

tell a particular story about the academic's life and career and establish relations of influence, status, and prestige within Google's PageRank algorithm (Rieder 2012). Using a Wikipedia Edits Scraper and IP Localizer,[11] it is possible to see the edited and erased content of this page. This includes attempts by other users to include references to the controversy and what has been erased by the removal of Bargh's blog posts from *Psychology Today*. The edited history discloses the dynamism of this controversy and the work that has to be done in order to remove it from particular regimes of visibility. Although the Wikipedia page "forgets" the erased content, the Wikipedia Edit Scraper is not so forgiving and performs different regimes of remembering and forgetting. An example of this is provided in a screenshot below.

Attempts to "set the record straight" online and to tell a particular story— bound up with specific storytelling devices and narratives—is one that illustrates some of the contrary logics that govern data regeneration, movement, and analysis. The hauntological potential of data and the question of how we reanimate what gets erased from particular practices of remembering and forgetting is a crucial one for cultural theorists committed to exploring the politics of data. Science historiographies are written on the basis of particular narrative conventions often based on stories of linear scientific progress. As Michel Foucault cogently taught us, histories of progress are never simply histories of the unfolding of some purist notion of scientific truth. In this analysis, I have attempted to bring these genealogical insights into dialogue with a hauntology based on what Barad (following Donna Haraway) terms "diffraction as methodology" or rather "reading texts intra-actively through one another" (2010, 243). Within the context of digital and social media, this becomes less about *text* and more about data traces which entangle past, present and future, human and nonhuman, affect and deliberation, and space and time in complex ways. This hauntological method allows the committed researcher to explore how data can be compromised by the entanglement of what Karen Barad (2010) terms different spacetime configurings, as well as being compromised by software platforms, processes, and practices, as well as the intentions and motivations of particular human actors. All of these entanglements are carried by the data and the data ghosts or absences that perform the controversy. In this way, I hope that what might be recognized as a distinctly queer or feminist engagement with what it means "to set the record

[11] https://tools.digitalmethods.net/beta/wikipedia2geo.

straight" can be brought more explicitly into our understanding of where and how data becomes compromised and how we might animate or restage the haunted life of data.

Acknowledgments

I would like to thank Bernhard Rieder who gave proficient instruction in some of the digital methods I use in this hauntology. Also Lucas Freeman for his excellent copy editing.

References

Anderson, Chris. 2008. "The End of Theory: The Data Deluge Makes the Scientific Method Obsolete." *Wired Magazine* 16(7). Accessed June 15, 2014. http://archive. wired.com/science/discoveries/magazine/16-07/pb_theory.

Ashley, A. A., D. Brossard, D. A. Scheufele, M. A. Xenos, and P. Ladwig. 2013. "The 'Nasty Effect:' Online Incivility and Risk Perceptions of Emerging Technologies." *Journal of Computer-Mediated Communication* 19(3): 373–87.

Blackman, Lisa. 2012. *Immaterial Bodies: Affect, Embodiment, Mediation.* London: Sage.

Blackman, Lisa. Forthcoming. "Haunted Data and Social Media Controversies: The Politics of Small Data." *Theory, Culture & Society.*

Barad, Karen. 2010. "Quantum Entanglements and Hauntological Relations of Inheritance: Dis/continuities, SpaceTime Enfoldings, and Justice-to-Come." *Derrida Today* 3(2): 240–68.

Bargh, J., M. Chen, and L. Burrows. 1996. "Automaticity of Social Behaviour: Direct Effects of Trait Construct and Stereotype Activation on Action." *Journal of Personality and Social Psychology* 71(1): 230–44.

Beer, David. 2013. *Popular Culture and New Media: The Politics of Circulation.* New York: Palgrave.

Beer, David and Roger Burrows. 2013. "Popular Culture, Digital Archives and the New Social Life of Data." *Theory, Culture & Society* 30(4): 47–71.

Bolter, Jay and Richard Grusin. 2000. *Remediation: Understanding New Media.* Cambridge, MA: MIT Press.

boyd, danah and Kate Crawford. 2012. "Critical Questions for Big Data." *Information, Communication and Society* 15(5): 662–79.

Cho, Grace. 2008. *Haunting the Korean Diaspora: Shame, Secrecy, Silence and the Forgotten War.* Minneapolis: University of Minnesota Press.

DeLanda, Manuel. 1991. *War in the Age of Intelligent Machines.* New York: Zone Books.

Deleuze, Gilles. 1995. "Postscript on Control Societies." *Negotiations.* Trans. Martin Joughin. New York: Columbia University Press.

Derrida, Jacques. 1994. *Specters of Marx: The State of the Debt, the Work of Mourning and the New International.* Trans. Peggy Kamuf. London: Routledge.

Despret, Vinciane. 2004. "The Body We Care For: Figures of Anthropo-zoo-genesis." *Body & Society* 10(2/3): 111–34.

Deuze, Mark. 2012. *Media Life.* Cambridge, UK: Polity.

Doyen, Stephane, O. Klein, C.-L. Pichon, A. Cleeremans. 2012. "Behavioral Priming: It's all in the Mind, but Whose Mind?" *PLoS ONE* 7(1): e29081.

Fuller, Matthew. 2009. http://www.spc.org/fuller/texts/active-data-and-its-afterlives.

Gerlitz, Caroline and Bernhard Rieder. 2013. "Mining One Percent of Twitter: Collections, Baselines, Sampling." *M/C Journal* 16(2). Accessed June 27, 2014. http://journal.media-culture.org.au/index.php/mcjournal/article/view/620.

Gitelman, Lisa. 2013. *"Raw Data" is an Oxymoron.* Cambridge, MA: MIT Press.

Goffman, Erving. 1990. *The Presentation of Self in Everyday Life.* London: Penguin.

Gordon, Avery. 2008. *Ghostly Matters: Haunting and the Sociological Imagination.* Minneapolis: University of Minnesota Press.

Kember, Sarah and Joanna Zylinska. 2012. *Life After New Media: Mediation as a Vital Process.* Cambridge, MA: MIT Press.

Mackenzie, Adrian. 2005. "The Performativity of Code: Software and Cultures of Circulation." *Theory, Culture & Society* 22(1): 71–92.

Manovich, Lev. 2013. *Software Takes Command: International Texts in Critical Media Aesthetics.* New York: Bloomsbury.

Massumi, Brian. 2002. *Parables for the Virtual: Movement, Affect, Sensation.* Durham, NC: Duke University Press.

Palmas, Kay. 2011. "Predicting What You'll Do Tomorrow: Panspectric Surveillance and the Contemporary Corporation." *Surveillance and Society* 8(3): 338–54.

Papacharissi, Zizi. 2004. "Democracy On-line: Civility, Politeness and the Democratic Potential of On-Line Political Discussion Groups." *New Media & Society* 6(2): 259–84.

Papacharissi, Zizi. 2012. "Without You I'm Nothing: Performances of the Self on Twitter." *International Journal of Communication* 6: 189–206.

Pfungst, Oscar. 1911. *Clever Hans (the Horse of Mr. von Osten): A Contribution to American Animal and Human Psychology.* New York: Henry Holt and Co.

Rheinberger, Hans-Jorg. 1994. "Experimental Systems: Historicality, Narration, and Deconstruction." *Science in Context* 7(1): 65–81.

Rheinberger, Hans-Jorg. 2010. *An Epistemology of the Concrete: Twentieth-Century Histories of Life.* Durham, NC: Duke University Press.

Rieder, Bernhard. 2012. "What is in PageRank? A Historical and Conceptual Investigation of a Recursive Status Index." *Computational Culture: A Journal of Software Studies.* http://computationalculture.net/what_is_in_pagerank.

Ruppert, E., J. Law, and M. Savage. 2013. "Reassembling Social Science Methods: The Challenge of Digital Devices." *Theory, Culture & Society* 30(4): 22–46.

Savage, Mike. 2013. "The Social Life of Methods: A Critical Introduction." *Theory, Culture & Society* 30(4): 3–21.

Thrift, Nigel. 2007. *Non-Representational Theory: Space, Politics, Affect.* New York: Routledge.

Valentine, Elizabeth. 2012. "Special issue on the Relations between Psychical Research and Academic Psychology in Europe, the USA and Japan." Editorial. *History of the Human Sciences* 25(2): 68–84.

Wetherell, Margaret. 2012. *Affect and Emotion: A New Social Science Understanding.* London: Sage.

Index